Culture Control Critique

Critical Perspectives on Theory, Culture and Politics

Critical Perspectives on Theory, Culture and Politics is a new interdisciplinary series developed in partnership with the Centre for Critical and Cultural Theory based in the School of English, Communication and Philosophy at Cardiff University, UK. This interdisciplinary series will focus on innovative research produced at the interface between critical theory and cultural studies. In recent years much work in Cultural Studies has increasingly moved away from directly critical-theoretical concerns. One of the aims of this series is to foster a renewed dialogue between Cultural Studies and Critical and Cultural Theory in its rich, multiple dimensions.

Series editors:
Glenn Jordan, Reader in Cultural Studies and Creative Practice and Director of Butetown History & Arts Centre, University of South Wales
Laurent Milesi, Reader in English, Communication and Philosophy and Chair of the Centre for Critical and Cultural Theory, Cardiff University
Radhika Mohanram, Professor of English and Critical and Cultural Theory, Cardiff University
Chris Norris, Distinguished Research Professor, Cardiff University
Chris Weedon, Chair of the Centre for Critical and Cultural Theory, Director of Postgraduate Studies and Head of the Centre for Critical and Cultural Theory, Cardiff University

Titles in the Series

Culture Control Critique: Allegories of Reading the Present, Frida Beckman
Creole in the Archive: Imagery, Presence and the Location of the Caribbean Figure, Roshini Kempadoo (forthcoming)
Prometheanism: Technology, Digital Culture and Human Obsolescence, Günther Anders and Christopher John Müller, translated by Christopher John Müller (forthcoming)
The Attention Economy: Labour, Time, and Power in Cognitive Capitalism, Claudio Celis (forthcoming)
Postcolonial Nostalgia and the Construction of a South-Asian Diaspora, Anindya Raychaudhuri (forthcoming)
Cultures of the Extreme: From Abu Ghraib to 'Saw' and Beyond, Pramod K. Nayar (forthcoming)
Credo Credit Crisis: Speculations on Faith and Money, edited by Laurent Milesi, Christopher John Müller and Aidan Tynan (forthcoming)
Materialities of Sex in a Time of HIV: The Promise of Vaginal Microbicides, Annette-Carina van der Zaag (forthcoming)
Performative Contradiction and the Romanian Revolution, Jolan Bogdan (forthcoming)
Partitions and their Afterlives: Violence, Memories, Living, edited by Radhika Mohanram and Anindya Raychaudhuri (forthcoming)
Music, Photography, and the Aesthetics of Time, Peter R Sedgwick and Kenneth Gloag, (forthcoming)

Culture Control Critique

Allegories of Reading the Present

Frida Beckman

ROWMAN & LITTLEFIELD

INTERNATIONAL

London • New York

Published by Rowman & Littlefield International, Ltd.
Unit A, Whitacre Mews, 26-34 Stannary Street, London SE11 4AB
www.rowmaninternational.com

Rowman & Littlefield International, Ltd. is an affiliate of Rowman & Littlefield
4501 Forbes Boulevard, Suite 200, Lanham, Maryland 20706, USA
With additional offices in Boulder, New York, Toronto (Canada), and London (UK)
www.rowman.com

British Library Cataloguing in Publication Information Available
A catalogue record for this book is available from the British Library

ISBN: HB 978-1-7834-8800-1
ISBN: PB 978-1-7834-8801-8

Library of Congress Cataloging-in-Publication Data

Names: Beckman, Frida, author.
Title: Culture control critique : allegories of reading the present / Frida Beckman.
Description: London ; New York : Rowman & Littlefield International, 2016. | Includes bibliographi-
    cal references and index.
Identifiers: LCCN 2015047395 (print) | LCCN 2016008546 (ebook) | ISBN 9781783488001 (cloth :
    alk. paper) | ISBN 9781783488018 (pbk. : alk. paper) | ISBN 9781783488025 (electronic)
Subjects: LCSH: Allegories. | English fiction--20th century--History and criticism. | Motion pictures-
    -Political aspects--History and criticism.
Classification: LCC PN56.A5 B43 2016 (print) | LCC PN56.A5 (ebook) | DDC 303.3/3--dc23
LC record available at http://lccn.loc.gov/2015047395

∞™ The paper used in this publication meets the minimum requirements of American
National Standard for Information Sciences Permanence of Paper for Printed Library
Materials, ANSI/NISO Z39.48-1992.

Printed in the United States of America

Contents

Acknowledgements

The research for and writing of this book was funded largely by a generous grant from the Swedish Research Council. The warm welcome from the Department of English, Stockholm University, Sweden, has also contributed greatly in enabling the completion of the manuscript. This book constitutes a part of a larger project of mine on control, which has been stimulated and supported by what was once a secret 'Society for the Study of Biopolitical Futures'. I owe special thanks to Gregg Lambert, who invited me to become an original member of this society. I would also like to thank its members for thought-provoking discussions, important feedback, and, not the least, for general inspiration. I am particularly grateful to Jeff Nealon for his sharp and unflinching comments and advice and also to Brad Evans, Gregory Flaxman, Adam Nocek, and Cary Wolfe for continuous conversations. Various parts of the project have been presented at conferences in Sweden, Europe, and the United States, where I have received important feedback from colleagues. The students in my political allegory class also helped me work through some of the ideas.

Charlie Blake has not only offered generous feedback and continuous discussions, he has also been patient and confident when I haven't been. I don't know how to thank him enough. Two anonymous readers also provided very encouraging and helpful feedback and I have returned repeatedly to some of the formulations in their reports. The series editors supplied speedy and constructive feedback towards the end of the process. I would also like to thank Gene Holland for serving as the matchmaker with the team at Rowman & Littlefield International and, of course, to this team itself, especially Sarah Campbell, Martina O'Sullivan, and Sinéad Murphy.

I will always be grateful for the privilege of having a supportive and loving family. Yvonne Beckman, especially, continues to make my life as a scholar and a mother possible. I am deeply thankful also to and for friends near and far.

The book is dedicated to Julia and Logan, as always.

* The section of chapter 4 that pertains to J. G. Ballard's last four novels was previously published, in a slightly different form, as 'Chronopolitics: Space, Time and Revolution in the Later Novels of J. G. Ballard' in *Symploke* 21 (1–2): 27–89.

Preface

As with Paul de Man's 1979 study *Allegories of Reading: Figural Language in Rousseau, Nietzsche, Rilke, and Proust*, one might say that the present book 'started out as a historical study and ended up as a theory of reading' (de Man 1979, ix). In order to be able to write a historical reflection on Romanticism, de Man set out to read Jean-Jacques Rousseau but found himself struggling with the 'local difficulties of interpretation'. Thus, his initial focus on historical definition came to shift to the issue of reading itself. By bringing out the tensions of reading and analyzing the function of rhetoric, de Man ends up questioning historicism and any totalising, or 'genetic', model that claims to grasp a unity of meaning, be it on the level of the literary work or history. The move away from attention to form to attention to reference, that is, to 'the nonverbal "outside" to which language refers,' and to 'the external politics of literature' that he witnesses in his own period reflects, he argues, a recurrent opposition between intrinsic and extrinsic criticism that relies on 'an inside/outside metaphor that is never being seriously questioned' (de Man 1979, 5). The present study is not of or on de Man, but it has followed a similar trajectory to the one de Man records. It was born from the ambition to say something about our present moment and the specific mechanisms of what has come to be called 'control society', but I soon found myself intrigued by the local complexities that the act of reading and interpreting these texts and mechanisms entails. My ambition of approaching a text through the network of technological, digital, political, social, philosophical, and theoretical configurations of what a text is and what it does ran up against the possibility of saying anything at all—of claiming an interpretative position vis-à-vis the contemporary culture at hand.

The strategies of reading that de Man developed have been accused of resulting in a 'debilitated criticism whose main effect is political paralysis' (Lentricchia 1983, 20). For de Man, Frank Lentricchia argues, radical political action and collectivity are possible only at the expense of the attempted lucidity of self-knowledge (Lentricchia 1983, 41). As a consequence, de Man's attention to form is seen to come at the cost of political efficacy. By letting de Man's concerns with questions of the inside and outside of texts frame the present project and by bringing up the charges of political debilitation against him, I want to underline that what is at stake is exactly the possibility of an engagement with literature and culture that is both formal and political. Where de Man's work questions conceptions of inside and outside through close inspection of Rousseau's eighteenth-century fictional, religious, and political writings, the heart of the matter in the historical context of the present book is the way in which age-old questions of inside and outside and of meaning and interpretation seem to have come to a new crossroads in the face of the all-encompassing tendencies of contemporary culture and politics. The rhetorical tropes that de Man employs to challenge referentiality, representation, and historicity allow him to demonstrate that allegory is at work in all texts in a way that counters the denominational, which, supposedly, differentiates between the nonfictional and the fictional. Here, I approach the relation between allegory and the text from a contemporary perspective, which, unlike that of the Romantic period, eagerly affirms the allegorical as a representational tool. But while de Man could afford the ambitious claim that the result of the shift that he and many of his generation effected could take us to a 'rhetoric of reading reaching beyond the canonical principles of literary history which still serve, in [his] book, as the starting point of their own displacement' (de Man 1979: ix), the present study has more humble ambitions. Rather than aiming for a point beyond any principles, not least those canonically linked to literary history, I seek to test the classic rhetorical device of allegory against some of the cultural and political tendencies of our present historical moment.

The motif of allegory is, as Jacques Derrida points out, one that recurs in de Man's writing 'like the unique and plural touchstone by which all readings and all literary and philosophical corpuses are measured' (Derrida 1989, 36). But allegory is also a concept that has pervaded philosophical, religious, and literary scholarship for as long as representation has been an issue. To delimit a study on allegory to any one of these fields or to de Man's work alone would inevitably be to severely delimit our understanding of its function. Yet, and because of the classic standing of *Allegories of Reading* in literary theory, because it stands there fundamentally proving the impossibility of a purely 'literary' theory, because questions of the political efficacy of literary theory repeatedly refer back to de Man's work, and because he has been positioned as the personification of Theory as well as a central figure for its 'afterlife',[1] I have, as my title suggests, allowed de Man's book to function as a loose framework for the present study. Like his book, the first section of the book (called 'Rhetoric' in his) consists of a set of discussions around figural language in general and allegory in particular. Like him, I thereby hope to construct a set of conditions for the subsequent readings. De Man's second section (called 'Rousseau') centres, as his subtitle suggests, on a reading of Rousseau's work employing the understanding of figural language and allegory laid out in the first section. The second section of the present book does not delimit itself to a single author. My 'problem' is not Rousseau but a kind of contemporary allegory that seems to interfere with the possibility of cultural critique today. Also, my study is not systematic in the same way as is de Man's. I will not be bold enough to excuse its shortcomings by comparing them to his work.[2] This book does, however, attempt a methodology that, to some extent, mirrors de Man's. Like him, I focus on a set of key words that are central to ways of reading in a contemporary context. Where de Man discusses Rousseau and allegory through terms central to his contemporaneity such as freedom, future, man, society, politicality, referentiality, rhetoric of self, time, space, judgement, State, the machine, and irony, I explore contemporary culture and allegory through terms that seem key to our present such as space, time, and vision, and totality, control, and critique. While my first set of terms is central to all organisations of modern society, the second set seems crucial to contemporary cultural and political debates. Where de Man's aim is to bring out a way of reading 'in which rhetoric is a disruptive intertwining of trope and persuasion', I feel challenged to maintain such a way of reading while remaining sensitive to the particular logic of politics and rhetoric today.

NOTES

1. This equation between de Man and Theory has been debated, and any attempt to account for these and other debates regarding his work is beyond the scope of this project. But for a distinctly critical reading of de Man as a charismatic and oppressively influential master of theory, see John Guillory's *Cultural Capital: The Problem of Literary Canon Formation* (Chicago: University of Chicago Press, 1993). For a nuanced set of readings of the de Man that we 'survived' and whose heritage we are faced with, 'for better or for worse', see the collection *Material Events: Paul de Man and the Afterlife of Theory*, edited by Tom Cohen, Barbara Cohen, J. Hillis Miller, and Andrzej Warminski (Minneapolis: University of Minnesota Press, 2001). The quote is from the introduction to the volume, 'A "Materiality without Matter"?' by Tom Cohen, J. Hillis Miller, and Barbara Cohen, xvii.

2. Nor, for that matter, will I enter into the debates about the ethical shortcomings of de Man's activities in other areas, which is not to suggest that they are not important.

Introduction

This book attempts to address the current crisis in critique and situate it in relation to what it sees as a powerful tendency towards political allegory in contemporary Anglo-American culture. This tendency, as will become apparent, can be understood in relation to the totalising tendencies of control society. The study takes off from an observation of the remarkable number of recent more-or-less mainstream novels and films allegorising political structures and systems. In literature, and especially in literature for young adults, the trend is quite marked, with the most popular examples being Suzanne Collins's *The Hunger Games* trilogy (2008–2010) and Veronica Roth's *Divergent* trilogy (2011–2013). In visual culture, an overt engagement with contemporary political issues has become increasingly prevalent, and films that are explicitly political 'are filling theaters and collecting awards' (Haas, Christensen, and Haas 2015, vii). Apart from displaying a political setting also in a more general sense, not the least in TV series such as *The West Wing* (1999–2006), *Homeland* (2011–), and *House of Cards* (2013–) to mention but a few, numerous films have been made in the new millennium that seem to do more than simply evince a popular interest in contemporary politics. Kurt Wimmer's *Equilibrium* (also known as *Cubic*, 2002), Omar Naim's *The Final Cut* (2004), David Niccol's *In Time* (2011), J. C. Chandor's *Margin Call* (2011), Andrew Dominik's *Killing Them Softly* (2012), Neill Blomkamp's *Elysium* (2013), James DeMonaco's *The Purge* (2013) and *The Purge: Anarchy* (2014), Anthony and Joe Russo's *Captain America: The Winter Soldier* (2014), adaptations of Collins's *The Hunger Games* novels (2012–) and Roth's *Divergent* books (2014–) as well as children's films such as Carlos Saldanha and Chris Wedge's *Robots* (2005) and Andrew Stanton's *Wall-E* (2008) constitute central examples of allegories of the current political climate that maintain a critical edge. These are texts and films that build on what Ismail Xavier notes as a tradition of allegorising the fears arising alongside scientific development, modern technology, and increasingly autonomous intelligence systems. They can also be linked to the postmodern phenomenon of 'conspiratorial texts' theorised by Fredric Jameson that feature schematic allegories of high-tech systems and impersonal bureaucracy (Xavier 2004, 339). Building on this 'allegorical turn fostered by the maze-like impression triggered by contemporary society' (Xavier 2004, 339), the literary texts and films that I discuss in the following chapters engage quite directly and consistently with the problems of political control as it has emerged in the past decades.

Let me give you a first example. Andrew Dominik's film *Killing Them Softly* (2012), which is based on the 1974 novel *Cogan's Trade* by George V. Higgins, is set in 2008 rather than the mid-1970s of the original narrative. This shift is performed with the explicit aim of linking the narrative to the contemporary state of world economy and politics. The director explains this motivation as follows: 'as I started adapting it, it was the story of an economic crisis, and it was an economic crisis in an economy that was funded by gambling—and the crisis occurred due to a failure in regulation. It just seemed to have something that you couldn't ignore' (Wright 2012, n.p.). At the centre of the film is a robbery during a game of poker. The same players have already been robbed once before. This earlier robbery, we learn, was set up by the proprietor of the poker ring himself, Markie Trattman (Ray Liotta) with the aim to collect insurance money. This new robbery, however, is staged by a man named Johnny Amato (Vincent Curatola) who is convinced Trattman's past will make him a prime suspect also for this new one. His assumptions proving at least partly correct, a member of the Mafia, Driver (Richard Jenkins), hires hitman Jackie Cogan (Brad Pitt) to kill Trattman, not necessarily because he is guilty, a fact which Cogan increasingly questions, but because gambling has waned since the robbery and locating and eliminating a scapegoat will help get business going again. Cogan does kill Trattman but also Amato and one of the robbers. The final scene of the film takes place in a bar with the presidential election of Barack Obama in 2008 being broadcasted on television. Here, Cogan meets up with Driver to collect his fee, and the film culminates in a long speech by Cogan where both America's past and present are vehemently criticised. After accusing Thomas Jefferson of being but a rich wine snob 'sick of paying taxes to the Brits', Cogan's, and the film's, final lines address the presidential election. 'This guy', he says, referring to Obama, 'wants to tell me we're living in a community. Don't make me laugh. I'm living in America. And in America you're on your own. America is not a country—it's just a business. Now fucking pay me.'[1]

We do not need the director's clarifying comments about the setting to see how the portrayal of the perpetuation of business as a goal that overrides ethical concerns of truth, guilt, and responsibility is not just a commentary on but serves also an allegory of the development of capitalism in the United States in general and the financial crisis of 2008 in particular. The card game, itself a miniature version of the gamble with money at the core of capitalist investment banking, serves to allegorise the mercilessness and hypocrisy of capitalism that the financial crisis brought out with such deadening clarity. Unsurprisingly, the political dimensions of the film did not go unnoticed by its reviewers. The *Guardian*'s Peter Bradshaw called it 'a compelling comment on economic bloodletting in the real world' (Bradshaw 2012, n.p.), and Steven Zeitchik wrote in the *Los Angeles Times* that 'though it was written before the Occupy movement took hold, it is arguably the first post-Occupy film' (Zeitchik 2012, n.p.). Brad Pitt, who also stands as coproducer of the film, strives to capture the contradiction of utilising the system against itself while staging a belief in change vaguely reminiscent of the repurposing strategies of alternative cultural and critical movements of the past: 'There's something noble about making something that says something, that uncovers something, and being able to [*sic*] it within that system where it has to be profitable or the thing doesn't get made. I find that an interesting relationship' (cited in Wright 2012, n.p.).

This 'interesting relationship' is also explicitly highlighted by Anthony Russo, one of the directors of the most recent Captain America films, *Captain America: The Winter Soldier*. Russo explains that he aimed to create 'an exciting narrative for a Hollywood action film while also giving people something deeper and more personally relevant to think about' (Shear 2014, n.p.). In the original 1940s comic books, Captain America emerged as a response to wartime anxieties during the Second World War. In its most recent incarnation, the character and story line seem to respond to the Obama administration and to anxieties connected to drone wars and surveillance. Of special interest here, and I return to this point in chapter 5, is how the directors respond to the particular way in which the Obama administration, unlike governments 'for thousands of years', has not worked to hide its political strategies. As we will see, this is itself a political strategy that, as Michael Rogin suggests, attempts to purposefully 'hide' things in full view. From the perspective of the *Captain America* directors, however, leaving the national agenda on security and drone surveillance in the open has created debate and what they see as a 'creative tension'. 'We tried', as Russo puts it, 'to come up with a fantasy expression or an allegorical expression of where those anxieties and problems can lead' (Shear 2014, n.p.).

Pitt's and Russo's commentary on the purposes and aims of their own work constitute two examples of a wider current tendency to explicitly present mainstream film as political allegory. To underline the persistence of the phenomenon, I will offer a few more examples of this recurring trend. Set almost exclusively in the interiors of a Wall Street investment bank, Chandor's *Margin Call* offers a fictionalised portrayal of the hours leading up to the financial crash in 2007–2008. Having discovered a fatal imbalance in the leveraging towards their mortgage-backed investments and thereby the extreme volatility of the financial situation, the temporal setting of the film covers the hours of crisis meetings of those in charge. It also portrays their ultimate decision to sell off their mortgages before their situation is discovered thereby loading off their losses on others. With its blatant similarities to the bankruptcy of Lehman Brothers in 2008, the film has been described as a 'fascinating complementary portrait of the financial crisis' (Werner 2013, 643). Chandor's film, as Andrea Werner shows, may be said to follow a trend of films portraying 'dramatised treatment of business ethics-related topics'. Further examples include whistle-blowing in Michael Mann's *The Insider* (1999), lobbying in Jason Reitman's *Thank You for Smoking* (2005), and corporate abuse of human rights in the Third World in Fernando Meirelle's *The Constant Gardener* (2005) (Werner 2013, 644). In *Margin Call*, the logic of the investment bank emerges not so much as a logic of evil greed reserved for the bankers but as a logic of the greed that pervades Western contemporaneity. As one of the protagonists states:

> People want to live like this in their cars and big fucking houses they can't even pay for, then you're necessary. The only reason that they all get to continue living like kings is because we got our fingers on the scales in their favor. I take my hand off and then the whole world gets really fucking fair really fucking quickly and nobody actually wants that. They say they do but they don't. They want what we have to give them but they also want to, you know, play innocent and pretend they have no idea where it came from. Well, that's more hypocrisy than I'm willing to swallow, so fuck 'em. Fuck normal people.

The link between the people and the banking system is complex, director Chandor suggests in an interview. 'Our movie may just be the time to sit there and think about it a little bit' (Benardello 2011, n.p.).

Some films also position themselves quite explicitly in a classical tradition of political allegory. Kurt Wimmer's film *Equilibrium* depicts a totalitarian society called Libria, which has achieved ultimate functionality by prohibiting emotions and everything that may inspire them, such as art. The citizens are obliged to take a drug, 'Prozium', that suppresses these unwanted tendencies, and any 'sense offence', that is, failure to take the drug and thus allowing yourself to feel, is punishable by death. Despite this threat, the outskirts of this society, the 'Nether' regions, harbour rebels hiding cultural objects and working towards revolution. Much like the 'firemen' in Ray Bradbury's classical allegory *Fahrenheit 451* (1953) who burn down houses harbouring books, clerics frequently raid these regions, destroying the art, literature, and music hidden there and executing those hiding it. Ultimately, these rebels, along with the film's protagonist, rise up and kill the 'Father' who is in charge and, in destroying the Prozium factories, pave the way for a revolution. Wimmer's film, like the other works discussed here, is a blatant allegory of contemporary Western late-capitalist culture. While science-fictional in some sense, the avoidance of any high-tech futuristic technologies and the employment of a Berlin neofascist architecture work to underline that the film serves as an allegory of the present rather than merely operating on the level of dystopian science fiction. And indeed, like the directors of *Killing Them Softly*, *Captain America: The Winter Soldier*, and *Margin Call*, the director of

Equilibrium openly declares his desire to comment on the present. In response to the strong similarities between his own film and classic political allegories such as Bradbury's novel but also Aldous Huxley's *Brave New World* (1932) and George Orwell's *1984* (1949), Wimmer explains that his film has a different message: '1984 is about socialism; Fahrenheit 451 is about McCarthyism—subjects which I don't think have any resonance today—whereas Equilibrium is about something else: in America right now there's a trend among people or the government to try and control what we feel' (Hughes 2013, n.p.). Implicitly acknowledging the affinity to these earlier texts, Wimmer seeks to redirect their criticism to the new political reality he diagnoses. This new reality is no longer shaped by ideological convictions but by the control of affect. In more theoretical terms, this shift is a move from a politics of conviction to a more general intensification of a biopolitics that centres on monitoring life at its core.

Elysium director Neill Blomkamp follows on this trend when he explains that his 'movie is meant to be an allegory for class warfare—rich and poor.' The division of the rich on the pleasurable planet Elysium and the poor struggling on the depleted planet Earth can be seen either to stand for the gaps between the fortification of gated communities on a national level or between nations and the way immigration works between the Third and the First Worlds (Brooks and Barnes 2013, n.p.). James DeMonaco, director of *The Purge* and *The Purge: Anarchy* (as well as of the forthcoming third film on the theme), which allegorise the division of rich and poor in an American context, situates his films within the framework of 'smuggler's cinema'. This is a term he has picked up from Martin Scorsese that involves making the genre films the market requires while smuggling your own ideas into them (Lambie 2014, n.p.). Tellingly, however, of the way in which political messages of a certain kind have come to be affirmed by mainstream production companies is the fact that DeMonaco did not actually have much trouble smuggling his ideas into Hollywood. Worried about getting his political message through the machinery of mainstream production, the response DeMonaco received was surprisingly positive—'Universal was like, "Absolutely, let's make a movie that works on two levels, as entertainment but also as a film that will make people think"' (Donato 2014, n.p.).

Even if we were not sufficiently unsettled by the idea that a major Hollywood studio is happy to 'make people think', thus readily accommodating for directors with such ambitions, we would still need to ask how helpful the ambition to uncover something is in a system that, by its very definition, works to add in all levels within itself. Stephen Best and Sharon Marcus suggest in their introduction to what they hope to be an emerging practice of 'surface reading' that the immediate accessibility of contemporary visual culture as well as the obviousness of eight years of a Bush regime that 'may have hammered home the point that not all situations require the subtle ingenuity associated with symptomatic reading' point towards a need to attend to 'what is evident, perceptible, apprehensible in texts' (Best and Marcus 2009, 2, 9). After decades of the symptomatic reading associated with psychoanalysis and Marxism, Best and Marcus suggest that the strategy of uncovering latent meaning and hidden structures is not sufficient to account for texts that wear the structures that give rise to them 'on their sleeves'. Rather, what is required today is a correct description of the objects themselves—to 'produce undistorted, complete descriptions' of things (Best and Marcus 2009, 18). On the one hand, proponents of surface reading have a point regarding the tendency towards what at least looks like transparency—and one that we have cause to return to repeatedly throughout this study. On the other hand, this same point also makes surface reading a potentially precarious strategy. As we will see in the coming chapters, many critics have noted how contemporary culture accommodates our need to critique political structures and thus comes to perform our political critique for us. In this light, any sense of resistance such performances may yield is efficiently harnessed in the service of the control society it supposedly critiques.

Control society, the definition and precursors of which I elaborate further in the next chapter, essentially constitutes an intensification and development of the biopower that Michel Foucault theorises as part of disciplinary societies. In the place of the regulatory methods of power that rely on institutions and identities, Gilles Deleuze notes, society increasingly comes to skip such detours and intervenes instead in a more fluid way into all levels of being and agency. If anything, institutions and identities become deterrents in a control society that relies on being able to modulate and stimulate codes, affects, and desires in a more direct and free-floating fashion. And of course, a successful control society controls also our desire for change, the restlessness of time, and any call for revolution. Having also noted the increasing tendency towards political cinema in the present, the authors of the book *Projecting Politics: Political Messages in American Films* suggest that the 'overriding importance of economics to the film industry makes all the more remarkable the twenty-first-century increase in the production of films depicting political processes, exploring the politics of war, and showcasing characters inscribed by their proximity to institutional power' (Haas, Christensen, and Haas 2015, 8). In the light of theories of control society, I wonder if this relation really is that remarkable. In this context, texts and films of the kind analysed here could be seen as what Jean Baudrillard calls the 'conspiracy of art', that is, our essential impossibility of stepping outside contemporary society to critique it. What appears like critique is really an internal function of the system itself and ultimately serves to consolidate and confirm power relations rather than challenge them. Therefore, I would like to inquire further into this relation and into this 'new interest by filmmakers in creating, and by the public in watching, ideologically charged films' (Haas, Christensen, and Haas 2015, 8) by considering the function of this trend in relation to mechanisms of control. In an essay from the mid-1970s, Jameson points towards 'the ideological function of overexposure in commercial culture' as it works to familiarise and thereby deflate the danger of the social conjuncture of the period — student revolts, resistance to authority, drugs, and political militancy. 'To name something', he suggests, 'is to domesticate it, to refer to it repeatedly is to persuade a fearful and beleaguered middle-class public that all of that is part of a known and catalogued world and thus somehow in order' (Jameson 1977, 847). Is this how we should understand the proliferation of political allegories of financial crises and global inequalities of the twenty-first century?

Historically, political allegory has provided the means to convey hidden messages and has been used as a weapon against censorship and authoritarian rule. As such, allegory has specific ties to cultural critique. As a rhetorical device, allegory allows for complex and hidden messages to be conveyed by other means. Indeed, Oxford dictionaries define allegory as 'a story, poem, or picture which can be interpreted to reveal a hidden meaning, typically a moral or political one' (*Oxford Dictionaries*, n.p.). And indeed, at least in a Western context, the most canonical modern allegories are political: Huxley's *Brave New World*, Orwell's *Animal Farm* (1945) and *1984*, and Bradbury's *Fahrenheit 451*. Like these classic texts, the contemporary works I am referring to here are what Gary Johnson calls 'strong allegories' in that they, unlike 'weak allegories', which may be only partly allegorical or only vaguely so, provide a clear and all-encompassing allegorical message. Such strong allegories are not unlike Northrop Frye's conception of 'actual allegories', which build on explicit relations between the work in question and external events or ideas. Strong allegories are narratives 'that not only facilitate the process of abstraction and that limit both the number and range of themes that might be abstracted from the various motifs' but also have themes that include 'what we might call a predicate, or a proposition, relating to the emergent idea' (Johnson 2012, 40). Johnson brings up Orwell's *Animal Farm* as an example pointing not only to the consistency of Orwell's overtly political allegory but also to his explicit purpose of making it so. If the clear allegorical structure of the narrative itself is not enough for the reader to 'get it', the author's professed intentions of constructing a narrative about what he saw as the perversion of socialist ideals in Russia positions the texts in direct relation to political issues. As have seen already in the case of Pitt's, Russo's, Chandor's, Wimmer's, Blomkamp's, and DeMonaco's comments above, and there are more examples to come, the contemporary trend to which they have all contributed is similarly and repeatedly accompanied by avowed authorial political intentions. On the one hand, then, this trend thus follows a more classic pattern of strong political allegory. On the other hand, it is hard to conceive of texts that are so clearly commercial as well as mainstream in terms of political critique without irony. And yet, a prevalent characteristic of these texts is exactly the resistance to irony in the very particular sense of that which inevitably disrupts the coherence and continuity of allegory. Especially in contrast with the J. G. Ballard novels analysed in chapter 4, and that arguably try to resist allegory, the consistency of the popular allegories mentioned so far as well as the ones analysed in chapters 5 and 6 seems important to interrogate.

If 'allegories are the natural mirrors of ideology' as Angus Fletcher suggests in his classic study *Allegory: The Theory of a Symbolic Mode* (Fletcher 1964, 368), then what exactly does this contemporary trend of mainstream political allegories mirror? On the one hand, there may be something encouraging about the fact that political critique has risen to the surface as an important theme in contemporary culture. Reflecting on the dark sides of how neoliberal capitalism has developed as part of control society, there is food for thought and perhaps a raised awareness to be won among a mainstream audience. On the other hand, there is something terribly discouraging about the way in which political critique has been subsumed into the culture industry. Is political resistance really supposed to be entertaining? Having our political critique performed for us while also looking at sexy characters, car chases, and famous film stars may also seem like the ultimate form of cultural control—the complete subsumption of the will to change. Crucially, and despite the expressed objectives of the directors just listed, this is a charge that I do not mean to direct at individual writers and directors. Rather than questioning the intentions or sincerity of individuals, what demands attention is the larger trend on both a thematic and a formal level. In this trend, the political message promoted by the allegorical format seems apparent while the irony is less so. Irony constitutes a central dimension of allegory for both de Man and Walter Benjamin. For them, irony underlines the inevitable disruption of the coherency and correlations that the allegorical nonetheless works to set up. In addition, and as Kevin Newmark remarks, irony is 'historical because it interrupts the reign of a formal causality that would otherwise be machinelike in its imperviousness to anything other than its own predetermined and crushing movement' (Newmark 2012, 11). The relative absence of irony in the strong political allegories analysed here confirms the idea of a 'concordant' mode of interpretation, which, as Johnson suggests, is encouraged by allegories that give the reader a clear path to follow between the narrative and its implied phenomenon (Johnson 2012, 40). As such, these allegories attain a somewhat eerie quality as we are caught in a feedback loop 'in which all of the inputs propel the interpretation in the same direction' (Johnson 2012, 40). A key problem with such subsumption is that it seems to underline the complete disappearance of a position from which the system could be critiqued.

In underlining this disappearance, the contemporary trend of popular political allegory speaks straight to the current crisis in critique. As I noted in the preface, de Man's aim in the 1970s in which he wrote *Allegories of Reading* was to construct a new rhetoric of reading in the face of local difficulties of interpretation. These difficulties of interpretation ended up redirecting him from the idea of a historical study to a deconstructive approach to literary analysis. The decades following his work turned out to be those most intensely preoccupied with deconstruction and Theory. If we were to try to encapsulate the core ambition of Theory as Theory, it may be the ambition to deconstruct the totalising tendencies of logocentrism and a capitalist system based on alignment and streamlining. For Theory, the teasing out of unstable meaning and hidden differences constitutes a way of questioning and resisting the ideas of identity and continuity on which such systems are based. The fate of Theory was much discussed during the last parts of the twentieth century, and we have repeatedly been positioned post- or after, or beyond Theory. And this is not even 'the first time that Theory has been reported dead'. In fact, the editors of one of the many books on posttheory continue: 'This is not the first time that reporting the death of Theory has been reported dead' (McQuillan, Purves, and Thomson 1999, ix). I will refrain from entering into these debates on Theory with a capital T, but relating back specifically to its central aims of questioning identity and continuity, it is important to note its interrelation with the gradual transition and intensification of the mechanisms of power in the past decades. Totalising gestures no longer constitute the main mode of power. Indeed, Jeffrey T. Nealon points out, rather than attempting totalising structures of meaning and production, the very modus operandi of contemporary global capitalism is by means of openness, dispersion, differentiation, and singularisation. Nealon goes so far as to suggest that global finance capital is 'the most intense example of deconstruction' itself (Nealon 2012, 124). Thus deconstruction 'the once proud king of the critical discourses' is being 'eaten alive, co-opted, by the inexorable machine that is capitalism' (Nealon 2012, 123).

So, many critics are asking, what theoretical tools do we have to deal critically with our present moment? 'What has become of critique?' Bruno Latour asks again and again in a 2004 article in *Critical Inquiry*; 'What has become of critique?' 'What has become of critique?' 'What has become of critique?' This word-by-word repetition echoes what Latour identifies as a need to 'retest the linkages', as a good military officer would, between the threats and the equipment to meet them and, if need be, revise the paraphernalia (Latour 2004, 231). So far, he argues, we have failed to perform this test on the linkages between critique and our political reality, and we are therefore stuck with 'a critical spirit [that] has sent us down the wrong path, encouraging us to fight the wrong enemies and, worst of all, to be considered as friends by the wrong sort of allies because of a little mistake in the definition of its main target' (Latour 2004, 231). In 2005, Baudrillard's *Conspiracy of Art* was republished and through its manifestos, interviews, and essays echoes a sense of nihilism. Where Latour urges us to rethink the role and nature of critique, Baudrillard points to the way in which contemporary art has lost its desire to deconstruct representation and 'crack the secret of desire and the secret of the object'. The result is a banal aesthetics of obscene visibility (Baudrillard 2005, 25). The force of resistance is gone as is the critical imperative. Distance and transcendence are replaced by null-and-void excess and indifference. In 2007, Antonio Negri published an article in *SubStance* where he notes that the critique of culture as it has been foregrounded and perpetuated from Theodor W. Adorno and Max Horkheimer and onward has exhausted itself. The innovative elements that such critique once had have now become banal and repetitive, smothered completely by the repetitive production of images under capitalism (Negri 2007, 48).

The crisis in cultural representation and critical theory thus identified from different perspectives in the early years of the new millennium speaks to a general sense of subsumption and immersion of culture and cultural critique discussed throughout a post-Marxist tradition ever since Herbert Marcuse and more recently identified as a central mechanism of control society. The social and political development in the West over the past decades has enabled capitalism to systematically incorporate everything within itself and created a system that, as Baudrillard puts it, 'thrives by persecuting itself' (Baudrillard 2005, 69). The critique that seemed so potent in the youth of deconstruction and social constructivism is seen to have turned into a popularised nihilism, suspicion, and instant revisionism that do little but add 'ruins to the ruins, adding even more smoke to the smoke' (Latour 2004, 228). Information and affect are neutralised by the perfect circle of trash culture making truth either 'imposed or vulgar' and indignation 'no longer possible' (Negri 2007, 48). However, and in 'these most depressing times', as Latour puts it (Latour 2004, 226), our task must be not to give up but to identify ways beyond this theory trouble. Latour does not give up but calls for 'a second empiricism' and 'a return to the realist attitude' as a 'next task for the critically minded' (Latour 2004, 232). Negri does not give up but calls for a new terrain for the critique of culture—one that builds on 'the capacity to remain within, to hollow out language from inside and make the material desire for transformation emerge' (Negri 2007, 50). Even Baudrillard does not fully give up, although his distinctive nihilism does dampen his spirit: 'It is not a question of hope' he underlines, but an 'act of faith', one 'without which I would not do anything myself.' And, he continues, 'I have no illusion, no belief, except in forms' (Baudrillard 2005, 59).

The present book may be seen as another attempt at not giving up. It looks in detail into ways in which control society incorporates opposition and critique within itself. It investigates the unsettling tendency of contemporary culture to perform what seems like cultural critique in the light of how society thrives by persecuting itself in a Baudrillardian vein.

It also explores how space, time, and vision are folded into control society leaving little, if any, room for an outside or at least alternative position from which it can be critiqued. It suggests, with Deleuze, that culture and critique now work by means of the modulations of a society that is no longer in need of enclosures or exclusions but functions rather by continuous infolding. But this book also explores what the 'new terrain' of cultural critique that Negri calls for might look like and where we might be able to find the 'new weapons' that Deleuze believes we need to shoulder. With Michael Hardt and Negri it argues that the 'nihilistic recognition' that there is no outside where we could locate 'political purity and "higher values"' must be 'only a tool, a point of passage towards constructing an alternative project' (Hardt and Negri 2009, vii). With Negri in his recent response to Accelerationism, it wants to acknowledge that 'the future appears to have been cancelled by the imposition of a complete paralysis of the political imaginary' at the same time as it wants to be able to say 'There is still space for subversive knowledge!' (Negri 2014, 365–66).

While Hardt and Negri's aim is more exclusively political in that they strive to articulate 'an ethics of democratic political action within and against Empire' (Hardt and Negri 2009, vi), the current book is more directly aimed at the dynamics between contemporary politics and culture. It explores the new terrains of cultural critique by coupling these concerns regarding the crisis in critique with another contemporary critical endeavour: new formalism. In a 2003 article in *PMLA*'s section 'Theories and Methodologies', W. J. T. Mitchell suggests that 'some new notion of form, and thus a new kind of formalism, lies before us'. Evoking Jameson's insistence on linking 'the "form/content" division in literature to the "superstructure/infrastructure" split in political economy', Mitchell argues that a renewed and politically informed commitment to form has political potential today exactly because idealist-materialist, nature-artifice distinctions are undergoing transformation. In fact, and as he concludes his short piece, he is convinced that 'a commitment to form is also finally a commitment to emancipatory, progressive political practices united with a scrupulous attention to ethical means' (Mitchell 2003, 321–24). While Latour moves from Martin Heidegger to Alan Turing in order to return to a kind of realism that can take seriously the stakes in contemporary culture and to look at the way in which things have become Things again, the current project is informed by an attempt to look at how texts become Text again. This does not, however, take us down the route of textual materialism as 'a mode of analytic objectification that focuses on the physical properties of an embodied text' as Bill Brown summarises the diverse critical strategies included under this heading (Brown 2010, 25). Rather, the critical strategy employed here is one that interrogates the tensions between what cultural texts do and what they mean through one of the most central formalist deceits of representation—allegory. Allegory is the common form of the internalised type of critique discussed above. At the same time, there seems to be a profound and intriguing disjunction between a control society in which the outside seems to have disappeared and the way in which society continues to be allegorised. This way, the tensions of inside/outside that have been identified as central to control society can be discussed in relation both to classic philosophical and religious questions of immanence and transcendence and to literary theoretical engagements with representation and allegory.

The book is divided into two interrelated sections. The first one outlines the conditions for critique in the nexus of three fields: philosophically in terms of immanence and transcendence, politically in terms of control society, and formally in terms of representation and allegory. The first chapter, 'Culture, Control, Critique', addresses the question of critique as it can be related to theories of the intensification of biopolitics in control society. It outlines the modern relation between politics and cultural critique reaching from the Frankfurt School in the 1940s through Foucault, Deleuze, Baudrillard, and Hardt and Negri in the present. It addresses the status of the classic cultural critique performed by the Frankfurt school, especially Adorno and Horkheimer, as well as the arguments that this critique is no longer sufficient to account for contemporary cultural politics. Outlining the essentials of Foucault's theories on biopolitics, it positions these in relation to Deleuze's seminal work on how these theories must be expanded to take on the intensification and modification of disciplinary methods in control society. Finally, the first chapter addresses questions of totality and totalitarianism in relation both to the question of cultural critique and to contemporary modes of control. Because allegory, at least in its Benjaminian conception, harbours an essential relation to the ruin of totality and because control society may be seen as an 'inverted totalitarianism' as Sheldon S. Wolin puts it, these concepts are central to my analysis. The second chapter, 'Formalism, Allegory, Totality', addresses the issue of a return to formalism as a potentially useful political methodology. Outlining some of the central arguments in new formalism pertaining specifically to how a commitment to form may provide a means to discuss cultural and political practice, it begins to discuss ways in which allegory as a formal conceit may be related to mechanisms of control. This chapter also returns and builds on the notion of totality in relation to allegory more specifically.

The second section of the book takes what it hopes at this point to be a grounded analysis of allegory and the conditions of representation and critique developed in the first section to a more detailed analysis of how contemporary configurations of space, time, and vision are allegorised in contemporary culture. Thus, the third chapter, 'Space, Allegory, Control', traces distinctions between inside and outside and the political construction of space in contemporary culture using as its framework the literary works of J. G. Ballard. Offering a longtime engagement with the politics of time and space while, I argue, resisting but gradually giving in to the allegorical impulse, Ballard's oeuvre enables a discussion of how political constructions of space can be linked to an allegorical imperative. Ballard's works, I suggest, speak to new formations of allegory in control society. This is a secularised form of allegory that reemerges in postmodernity and that constitutes not only an abandonment of transcendent meaning but also a reflection of a political system based on the recuperation of all its outsides. As I show, Ballard also helps us see how irony can become a key tool in negotiating such all-encompassing tendencies. While this chapter thus provides a historical context of the discussion of how control and allegory are interlinked from the 1960s to the present, chapter 4, 'Time, Allegory, Control', approaches these developments by comparing Ballard's short story 'Chronopolis' (1960) and Niccol's film *In Time* (2011). Reading these two very different allegories of the temporality of production side by side enables a comparative analysis of the intensification of control informed by Jameson's theorisation of the return to allegory in postmodernity. Here, the allegorical dimension is interrogated in terms of a questioning of how the neat correspondences set up in the film create a mirage of politics that deflects rather than reflects from the logic it seems to critique.

The fifth and final analytical chapter, 'Vision, Allegory, Control', explores key developments in the relation between vision and power in the shift between disciplinary and control society, and looks to contemporary mainstream culture with an eye to its effects on questions of representation. In some ways at the centre of our argument about the 'political spectacle', the deployment of visuality in control society is addressed in relation to the allegorical construction of Collins's trilogy *The Hunger Games*. Building on the argument that postmodern politics hides its logic in full view, the chapter interrogates not what we are allowed to see but how we are allowed to see it. The allegorical, it argues, draws attention to content rather than form, thereby distracting from the function of the cultural artifact itself. The concluding chapter refers back to the discussions and analyses in the earlier chapters while positioning these readings of specific texts in relation to a variety of cultural references. The intention is to situate the project in relation to questions of its periodisation and to discuss the intensifications of control in the period since the 1960s until the present. Returning briefly to William S. Burroughs as a forerunner of control theories, the objective is also to position the analyses of the study in relation to a more distinctly literary tradition of portraying control. The purpose is not so much to summarise as to contextualise and open up the discussion of the conditions of cultural critique in control society in a larger setting. In the light of this setting, the book notes a deceptive anachronisticity at the heart of the contemporary tendency towards allegory and underlines how analysing this tendency requires an increased attention to the politics of form.

NOTE

1. I would like to make a disclaimer here regarding the quotations from films throughout this book. Since I have not had access to the screenplays in question, my quotations are based directly on the audiotrack and may therefore include minor inaccuracies.

ONE

Culture, Control, Critique

History discloses numerous crises in representation and critique. Indeed, the problem of representation is situated at the heart of philosophical as well as religious discourses. It has given birth to various theories and practices relating to, for example, analogy, allegory, and iconography as well as to responses to sublimity and historical traumas. Critique, in the way it is understood here as relating to how to respond theoretically to political, cultural, and social developments, has also always constituted a problem. This problem has been intimately related to the question of representation as the possible space or position from which critique is possible. This question of position has in turn developed alongside conceptions of agency, subjectivity, rights, and the notion of the human itself. The very notion of the human as it derives from Aristotle rests on a distinction between life that just is—*zoe*—and life that is informed by a political community, and thus by a potential and a right to a critical voice—*bios*. As Aristotle puts it: 'It is a characteristic of man that he alone has any sense of good and evil, of just and unjust, and the association of living beings who have this sense makes family and a state' (Aristotle 1920, 29). Thus, the possibility to critically interrogate a state of affairs relies, from the perspective of Classical Greek thinkers, on a politics of inclusion and exclusion, an inside to the polis and an outside. The beginning of biopower in the seventeenth century and its development during the classical period as Michel Foucault delineates it is centrally a repositioning of this distinction between inside and outside in terms of life. Bare life is no longer excluded but is rather included in a politics built on controlling, regulating, and administrating life in all its dimensions. The 'threshold of modernity' as Foucault puts it, and thereby the break with the Greek separation of life into *zoe* and *bios*, 'has been reached when the life of the species is wagered on its own political strategies' (Foucault

1

1990, 143). Passing this threshold, political life ceases to be identified in relation to an outside and becomes, rather, pervasive of all spaces, actions, and bodies. From this point onward, critique cannot be performed without the simultaneous recognition that every position, including the one from which critique is expressed, is always already informed by the processes of administration that have monitored and regulated the very body and mind of this position. This, then, is the birth of a crisis in critique that has come to shape modernity and, in the wake of Foucault's seminal work on biopolitics, postmodernity.

In *Society Must Be Defended*, Foucault outlines the gradual transitions of systems of power from sovereign power and disciplinary power to biopower. Sovereign power is, essentially, a hierarchal and clearly identifiable form of power that makes clear separation between the ruler and the ruled, between ordering and obeying. This power is built around the absolute right to kill—'to take life or let live' (Foucault 2003, 241). Locating the emergence of disciplinary power in the seventeenth and eighteenth centuries, he notes how such power functions by means of the separation, alignment, serialisation, and surveillance of bodies. Bodies are organised in space according to principles of visibility, trained and rationalised in order to increase and ensure maximum productive force (Foucault 2003, 424). Disciplinary society works according to an 'individualising' mode maximising productivity and control by means of the organisation of bodies. Foucault observes that towards the second half of the eighteenth century, a new technology of power is on the increase that does not replace but modifies such disciplinary techniques. This new technology of power, while 'embedding itself in existing disciplinary techniques', exists on a level that is less concerned with individual bodies and more with the human species as a whole. This 'biopolitics of the human race' is engaged with life itself, directly taking as its object the regulation of life in terms of biology and the environment. Instead of primarily monitoring individual bodies, biopower aims to intervene in a more immediate fashion into the various aspects of life—health, reproduction, the regularity of the population. Thus biopower is not concerned with disciplining bodies so much as with regularising life. As Foucault puts it more succinctly: 'The mechanisms introduced by biopolitics include forecasts, statistical estimates, and overall measures. And their purpose is not to modify any given phenomenon as such, or to modify a given individual insofar as he is an individual, but, essentially, to intervene at the level at which these general phenomena are determined, to intervene at the level of their generality.' This way, the goal is establishing equilibrium and maintaining an average (Foucault 2003, 246). Foucault describes disciplinary—and biopower in terms of two series—'the body-organism-discipline-institutions series, and the population-biological processes-regulatory mechanisms State' (Foucault 2003, 250). These two series are not oppositional so much as complementary, as can be seen, for example, in the way in which some elements, like medicine, which can be applied to both, or the norm, which circulates between the two, bring the two series together (Foucault 2003, 252–53). These two series—the disciplinary and the biopolitical—coexist from the eighteenth century onward and in one of his 1976 lectures at Collège de France Foucault notes that they are still on the advance (Foucault 2003, 254).

In a conversation with Antonio Negri in 1990, published as 'Control and Becoming', as well as in a brief but seminal essay titled 'Postscript on the Societies of Control', Gilles Deleuze returns to how Foucault theorises this shift in the distribution of power. Deleuze's theories of control are inspired not only by Foucault but also by Paul Virilio and William S. Burroughs, and they have subsequently inspired major works such as Michael Hardt's and Negri's work on Empire. Centrally, Deleuze looks at how Foucault's theories may be advanced to correspond to more recent developments in such distribution. Briefly, while Foucault's disciplinary societies rely on the spatial distribution of control by means of institutions, molds, and identities, and the biopolitical mode relied on regulatory and statistical strategies, the control society that Deleuze identifies is based on a form of free-floating control by means of modulations and individual codes. Foucault, Deleuze points out, was one of the first to articulate this move away from the disciplinary model (Deleuze 1995, 174). The idea of control society thus does not break off from Foucault's analyses of biopower so much as it constitutes a continuation and elaboration of disciplinary and regulatory technologies that Foucault had already begun to theorise. While the transition between sovereign rule and disciplinary society constitutes a more radical configuration of power that replaces the hierarchy of rule with a more diffused institutionalised politics based on disciplinary methods, the subsequent development of a disciplinary model into a regulatory practice is, as we just saw through Foucault, rather an elaboration of this model. What we via Deleuze thus come to discuss in terms of control society should be seen as a further intensification of these regulatory methods. Because freedom and discipline are fundamentally bound to each other in the liberal society that Foucault analyses, the introduction of additional freedom depends on an increase in control and intervention. 'That is to say, control is no longer just the necessary counterweight to freedom, as in the case of panopticism: it becomes its mainspring' (Foucault 2008, 67).

In this light, the increased 'freedom' that results from a further demise of governing institutions is dependent on a reconfiguration of modes of control. Control society thus comes to be more intimately associated with the state of late capitalism that marks our contemporaneity. This development, Hardt argues, entails that earlier political theory, such as that of Georg Wilhelm Friedrich Hegel and the 'postcivil' theories of Antonio Gramsci and Foucault, no longer suffice to 'grasp the dominant mechanisms or schema of social production and social ordering' in the contemporary West (Hardt 1995, 34). Deleuze's essay on societies of control, Hardt argues, must be seen in this context. It can serve as 'a first attempt to understand the decline of the rule of civil society and the rise of a new form of control' (Hardt 1995, 34). This type of political control is also intimately connected with the increasing speed of communication and information and the ways in which they have put institutions and enclosures into crisis. While the influence of disciplinary society and its institutions certainly has not vanished, power today is not most efficiently exercised by means of discipline and punishment but rather by means of controlling information.

The crisis in critique briefly outlined in my introductory chapter is a response to this type of control and its effects on developments in politics, culture, and representation. In different ways, Bruno Latour, Jean Baudrillard, and Negri all respond to the way in which the nature of the power formations that monitor life has changed. Jeffrey T. Nealon notes that as the logic of global finance capital builds on hybridity and fluidness and as the liberation of desire becomes a government encouragement in the face of the war on terrorism, the genealogy of much postmodern theory stemming from the 1980s is becoming 'increasingly unhelpful' (Nealon 2012, 20). Similarly, Latour is concerned that when we are passing on to students the critical spirit of the poststructuralist period, we are preparing them to fight 'wars that are no longer possible, fighting enemies long gone, conquering territories that no longer exist' (Latour 2004, 225). The once-so-crucial battles of questioning notions of scientific truth, of interrogating received reality, and of probing ideological biases informing supposed matter of facts, Latour argues, have turned not only into *'instant revisionism'* that prevents us from intervening into events. These battles have also turned into a popularised mode of conspiracy that plays right into the hands of the social and political systems they were meant to critique. Like weapons smuggled through a border and ending up in the wrong hands, the 'neutron bomb of deconstruction', 'the missiles of discourse analysis', and 'the virus of critique' now serve to undermine an engagement with empiricism rather than, as was really the point, to renew it. Such renewal, Latour argues, is absolutely crucial to politics (Latour 2004, 230–31). At the same time, what Baudrillard suggests is that the problem for art is that the hyperreality of the image makes critical reflection redundant as it inevitably reflects back on itself. The collusion of art and discourses on art evinces a paranoia of meaninglessness, which entails that 'there is no longer any possible critical judgment, and only an amiable, necessarily genial sharing of nullity' (Baudrillard 2005, 28). Again, the critical spirit has been devoured by the spectacle itself, and as Baudrillard's fictionalised appearance in the modern classic *The Matrix* suggests, his own persona has been sucked up into the very popularised metadiscourse that he attempted to critique. In addition to Latour's and Baudrillard's disenchantment with the power of critical discourse in the present, Negri's call for a new critique and acknowledged redundancy of cultural critique after Theodor W. Adorno and Max Horkheimer too constitutes a response to the neutralisation of information and the perfect circle of trash culture that continually feeds on itself in contemporary society. What Latour, Baudrillard, and Negri are all responding to, in other words, is this shift in the way in which political power is exercised and the crisis in critique that follows.

CULTURAL CRITIQUE FROM THE
FRANKFURT SCHOOL UNTIL TODAY

The identification of the way in which society as well as its individuals have come to be shaped by a political system of total administration was made in the early 1960s by Herbert Marcuse. An active participant of the Frankfurt School in its early period, Marcuse, like Adorno and Horkheimer, recognised the increasing political power of communication and mass culture in the postwar United States. For Marcuse, the new forms of control emerging in this period are new because they rely on an administration and organisation that undo individual will in favour of a total administration of needs and desires. What emerges in the place of a dialectical subject-object relation that, for Marcuse, would accommodate the possibility of radical change is a self-contained, one-dimensional society and a one-dimensional man who cannot easily transcend and thereby critique or transform his own conditions. Under these conditions, individual thought is 'absorbed by mass communication'. As Marcuse puts it, words and images are losing 'the tone which were formerly antagonistic and transcendent to the prevailing order' and they thereby also lose 'their alienating power' (Marcuse 1993, 181). Material as well as intellectual needs are implanted in the individual, and modes of satisfaction are preconditioned (Marcuse 1991 [1964], 6–9). Both cultural critique and culture itself are imbricated in this total administration. Intellectual opposition 'seems to become increasingly impotent' at the same time as art loses the 'alienating force' upon which its political potential depends. Absorbed into the monopolistic system, 'Revolutionary art becomes fashionable and classical. Picasso's *Guernica* is a cherished museum piece' (Marcuse 1993, 181–82). Marcuse also recognises how developments of the rational, productive, and technical administration of society point towards an increasing difficulty for individuals to 'break their servitude and seize their own liberation' (Marcuse 1991 [1964], 9). Marcuse did believe in the possibility of radical change, however, and encouraged radical forms of action, not the least in his later books, as Douglas Kellner notes (Kellner 1991 [1964], xxxvi). And his hopes for the 'Great Refusal', that is, 'the protest against that which is' (Marcuse 1991 [1964], 66) were, as Kellner points out, at least partly and momentarily realised during the student protests in the late 1960s (Kellner 1991 [1964], xxxvi). Yet, Kellner notes, the development of late capitalism in the West has proven Marcuse's theory about total administration only too right (Kellner 1991 [1964], xxxvii).

For Marcuse, one-dimensional society stands in opposition to the freedom of the individual subject. He strongly believes in such a subject and puts his hopes to it for a political alternative to total administration. Even as he theorises the emergence of a one-dimensionality that flattens and swallows all opposition into itself, his Hegelian/Marxian approach nonetheless implies that the seeds of change must be located by means of transcendence or, as Kellner puts it, in 'another realm of ideas, images, and imagination that serves as a potential guide for a social transformation' (Kellner 1991 [1964], xvii). The key to radical change thus to some extent lies outside the one-dimensional realm in which subjects have been caught. Change depends on a reappropriation of the true will, needs, and freedom of the individual subject. Art, 'as an instrument of opposition', depends on 'its power to remain strange, antagonistic, transcendent to normalcy and, at the same time, being the reservoir of man's suppressed needs, faculties and desires, to remain more real than the reality of normalcy' (Marcuse 1993, 182). Marcuse was thus early in his analysis of forms of internalised political control that are more effective today than ever. His theoretical approach relies on a specific kind of post-Marxist dialectical politics that puts its hope to the identification and claiming of realms other than the existing form. Even as the undermining of this other realm lies in the very nature of the kind of control he theorises, the importance of this realm for the possibility for change is absolutely essential. Without it, it becomes impossible to think and without it, it becomes impossible to negate existing conditions and produce something new.

This other realm, conceptually originating from the Hegelian dialectic and constituting, of course, also a central tenet in the nature of political conflicts and struggles as theorised by Karl Marx, has continued to be an essential if contested part of many modes of post-Marxist theories of resistance. The notion of an 'outside' to culture, to ideology, and to capitalism constitutes a point of debate and dispute in various instantiations of post-Marxist and postdialectical theory. Central to this debate is the extent to which a politics of resistance, subversion, and critique can be seen as the labour of alternative cultural expression, a critique performed to some extent from the 'outside'. From post-Marxism to posthumanism to varieties of new materialism and biopolitical reflection, the notion of the 'outside' continues to be a point of contention in contemporary theory, and especially when aligned with or opposed to recent delineations of culture, capitalism, and the complex legacy of critique. At stake are oppositional notions of resistance, subversion, and alternative cultural expression as they weave through a range of artistic and political movements in modernity and postmodernity. Not only in the realm of critical thought but also in the realm of action and cultural critique, the idea that it is possible to establish a position other than the one in which we are controlled has remained crucial. Post-Marxist politics of resistance, subversion, and critique has typically been the labour of alternative cultural expression. The avant-garde, the politics of perversion, the punk, the underground—the arena for critical commentary has been markedly positioned as an 'other' to the society it critiques. This 'other' or 'outside' has been a position purposefully created by those in resistance, but also by society itself as it has delegated critique to its margins through censorship and other less-overt forms of cultural politics. Since Guy Debord, at least, and especially in the early phase of his work, the importance of searching for a position outside 'the society of the spectacle' has been central. While it is a central tenet for Debord and other Situationist activists that the society of the spectacle infiltrates all levels of life, their early work was characterised by a firm conviction that it is possible to contradict and challenge this all-encompassing commodification. Situationist tactics, as Sadie Plant puts it, 'revealed the spectacular nature of capitalist society and could maintain a position in contradiction to it' (Plant 1992, 4).[1] Although it is continually under threat of alienation and complete usurpation of commodified relations, the individual subject is still seen as a site for transcendence and resistance. Since then, however, both the notion of a transcendent subject and the possibility of an outside have become increasingly precarious. The idea of the individual subject on which both Marcuse and many of those involved with Situationist practices rely, not to mention the conception of the true freedom, will, and needs of such a subject, has since been under question both theoretically and by means of the further development of the control mechanisms Marcuse himself identified. The intensification of the forms of control he theorises already in the 1960s suggests that it is time to call off the search for a transcendent subject or even a transcendent realm from which alternative political change can be projected.

Marcuse argues that the one-dimensional result of the new mechanisms of control entails a 'paralysis of criticism' (Marcuse 1991 [1964], xil). The absorption of the subject into the social threatens to collapse the possibility for opposition. He gives as an example how transcending elements in 'higher culture' are desublimated by technological rationality and thereby evacuated of oppositional force. 'Cultural values' are liquidated not through rejection but through wholesale incorporation. Marcuse argues against what some would call the democratisation of culture. This new distribution, he argues, is rather a commodification of literature and art that depletes these works of the alienation, contradictions, and antagonistic contents they previously articulated. Through this new totalitarianism, most contractions come to coexist in a peaceful indifference that invalidates 'the very substance of art' (Marcuse 1991 [1964], 66). Because the power of fiction and art to subvert everyday experience and expose its deceptiveness is dependent, for him, on their capacity for negation, this same power is eliminated as fiction and art become absorbed into the everyday itself (Marcuse 1991 [1964], 67). The totalitarian tendencies of the society he responds to are at odds with the Marxist holism he dreamed of. Like Adorno, Martin Jay notes, Marcuse combined a desire for a normative totality in the future with a pessimistic view on the 'false totality' of their present (Jay 1984, 219).

Totality, as Jay notes in his ambitious overview of the various interpretations of this concept in Marxist theory, has been a much-privileged concept in the discourse of Western culture. For a long time, it has resonated with affirmative notions of coherence, meaningfulness, and community and stood as a contrast to concepts like alienation, fragmentation, and estrangement (Jay 1984, 21). Totality in this conception strives for coherence as a goal in theological, philosophical, and/or political terms and is normative—it is an aspiration, not a fact. Jay's study takes its starting point with the Greeks and attempts to conceptualise man's relation to the whole in terms of the universe (as in Plato) as well as to the State (as in Aristotle) and moves through the wealth of understandings reaching from Jean-Jacques Rousseau to Baruch Spinoza to Hegel, from Friedrich Schiller to David Hume to Immanuel Kant, and on to Marx before arriving at the various and distinctly conflicting conceptions of the concept in a post-Marxist context. The belief in the very capacity to know the whole, Jay notes, can be linked back to Enlightenment ideas that, while themselves more focused on individualism and self-interest, nonetheless implicitly promoted 'longitudinal' conceptions of totality. Such conceptions rely on the belief in the possibility of recovering a coherence and structure of history and insist on the possibility of understanding the world as a whole (Jay 1984, 30). When it comes to Marx and his debt to Hegel, the importance of understanding society as a whole constitutes a key to his politics. Indeed, Jay points out, the diversity of understandings in the post-Marxian tradition does not preclude the general agreement that Marx was a holistic thinker (Jay 1984, 61). Of the many post-Marxist conceptions of totality—reaching from György Lukács to Jürgen Habermas—the conceptions of totality that we can trace through Horkheimer, Marcuse, and Adorno are of particular interest to the present study. Recalling that Negri's call for a new cultural critique outlined earlier is directed directly at the redundancy of those long-standing versions promoted by the Frankfurt school, this seems like a reasonable starting point.

The understanding of totality differs quite radically between these Frankfurt thinkers as well as over time. While Horkheimer's earlier work suggests an optimistic belief in the feasibility of pursuing normative totalities, his later work is characterised by declining optimism. As Jay notes, the events of the 1930s and 1940s seemed to disprove the earlier belief in the possibility of realising the normative totalities of a socialist society built on a true community of fulfilled subjects. Instead, the notion of totality came to be increasingly associated with oppressive integration and one-dimensional homogeneity (Jay 1984, 216). Totality, he points out, became 'little more than a synonym for totalitarianism' (Jay 1984, 219). Horkheimer's faltering belief, which was interspersed with intermittent bursts of hope, can be related to the influence of Adorno. Adorno's belief in normative totalities was, Jay notes, more fragile than any of the other Western Marxists (Jay 1984, 242). Influenced by his increasing lack of belief in the possibility of political change, Adorno understood totality mainly in negative terms and located the breakdown of totality in the crisis of idealism. He investigated efforts to reconstitute totality by existentialists and phenomenological thinkers but could not find enough justification in their thought (Jay 1984, 256). By the time Adorno and Horkheimer wrote *Dialectic of Enlightenment* in the early 1940s, the positive connotations of the notion of totality were virtually gone. At this point, totality was seen as an oppressive tendency and linked to fascism and anti-Semitism. The idea of a universal, coherent, and graspable history expressed as the longitudinal form of totality was specifically rejected (Jay 1984, 262). In the end, Jay notes, 'Critical Theory, and Adorno's work in particular, had irrevocably demolished the foundations of Western Marxism's initial concepts of totality' (Jay 1984, 274).[2] In contrast to Adorno and Horkheimer's increasingly negative view of totality, however, Marcuse continued to insist on a more optimistic view. Although he occasionally gave in to the more pessimistic view of his Frankfurt School colleagues, such as in his *One-Dimensional Man*, he continued to explore ways to go beyond the impasses in which they had gotten caught. Indeed, Jay notes, Marcuse 'continued to look for cracks in the façade of one-dimensional 'totalitarianism' until the end of his life.' He also remained insistent on the importance of totalistic analysis because it 'would conceptualize society as a whole and demand its complete replacement' (Jay 1984, 221).

There is, then, a clear ambivalence regarding the notion of totality in the post-Marxist tradition. Hopes for a Marxist holism compete for dominance with the disillusionment of a totalitarian present. What seems perfectly clear, however, is that the intensification of the mechanisms of control that has taken place since the days of Frankfurt school criticism suggest little possibility for curing the paralysis that it identified. Quite the contrary, the subsumption of culture and cultural critique within its own system has become one of the essential characteristics of control society as it has developed since then. If the counterculture contemporary to Marcuse could still work to position itself as separate from institutions of power, such as in the student revolts, the configuration of such institutions into more distributed modes of control makes such separation increasingly difficult. As Virilio puts it in relation to visuality, for example, control under the conditions of the extensive time of human perception, or 'visual subjectivity', is superseded by control by means of automated vision in which seeing is not limited to a particular physical space and viewpoint. The configuration of power by means of institutions and identities, and thus of an inside and outside, that characterised Foucault's disciplinary society are shattered into an all-encompassing dissemination of power on all levels both within a specific society and in the world. Totalitarianism has become 'globalitarianism', that is, a distribution of power that is no longer linked to specific territories but that 'is everywhere that one can be under control and surveillance' (Virilio 1999, 38).

Because both totality and totalitarianism are concepts of some relevance to our analysis of control and critique, we should think carefully of what we might mean when associating these concepts with each other. It is undoubtedly tempting to see the all-encompassing control mechanisms of contemporary capitalism as a totalitarian system of sorts. However, such an association must be tested against Roberto Esposito's argument that as hermeneutic paradigms, totalitarianism and biopolitics are 'mutually exclusive in their presuppositions and effects on meaning' (Esposito 2008, 635). Totalitarianism, he notes, depends for its definition on the notion of democracy, and it can be traced back through a chronological and 'traditional philosophy of history' either via an Arendtian return to the Greek polis or via Jacob Talmon's searching for its origins within the same democratic tradition it supposedly opposes (Esposito 2008, 636). A biopolitical perspective, on the other hand, opposes such philosophical historicism because it does not understand modern history as a chronologically determinable succession of liberal-democratic and totalitarian regimes but as nonlinear and multidirectional politics that lie outside the conceptual apparatus of democracy altogether. Biopolitics that, as we have seen through Foucault, is a politics that functions directly on biological life, does not need the detour around the idea of the rights of the disembodied individual and rational will so central to democracy.

By the same token, biopolitics breaks up the possibility of theorising what is commonly seen as the two largest totalitarian efforts in history — communism and Nazism. While the former is a continuation of the logic of democracy, Esposito suggests, the logic of the latter is based on biopolitical principles. From this perspective, it makes no sense to bring them together and discuss 'biopolitical totalitarianism or a totalitarian biopolitics' (Esposito 2008, 635). It does make sense, however, to divide biopolitics into the biopolitics of the state on the one hand (Nazism) and the biopolitics of the individual on the other (liberalism) (Esposito 2008, 642). Opening up for a revaluation and a resituating of the concept of totalitarianism, Esposito implicitly indicates the error of Slavoj Žižek's argument that the concept of totalitarianism is a 'stopgap' that relieves or even prevents us from thinking and understanding historical reality (Žižek 2001, 138). Žižek and Esposito both notice how the concept has worked to clump together left- and right-wing politics. Žižek insists also that this has constituted a convenient means for a liberal-democratic hegemony to undermine critique from the Left by positioning it as a twin of Fascist dictatorship. There is little use, he argues, in attempting to redeem the concept by pointing out the differences (Žižek 2001, 3). Esposito, as we have seen, takes a different route by differentiating between totalitarianism and biopolitics and thereby actively working towards rethinking historical reality. Here, I would like to take a third route, formulated as a question. If we cannot discuss biopolitical totalitarianism without blurring the borders of their fundamental presuppositions, as Esposito suggests, how are we to analyse and conceptualise what nonetheless appear as distinct totalising tendencies of contemporary control society?

In general, Sheldon S. Wolin notes, capitalism 'is not solely a matter of production, exchange and reward. It is a regime in which culture, politics, and economy tend towards a seamless whole: a totality' (Wolin 2010, 269). In order to account for the logic of what he calls the Superpower—the power systems predominant in the contemporary United States and many Western countries—Wolin coins the phrase 'inverted totalitarianism'. It is telling that this phrase does not exist in the first version of his classic study *Politics and Vision* published in 1960 but appears in the extended edition of 2004 intended to account for and theorise the 'strikingly different forms of politics and theorizing' that have emerged during the second part of the twentieth century (Wolin 2004, xv). In such Superpower, empire and corporate capitalism are superimposed on democracy. What holds governance and the authority of the State together is not idealism so much as corporate culture. 'The dynamics of Superpower', he argues, 'are far stronger than those of earlier empires because it is conjoined with the dynamics of globalizing capitalism' (Wolin 2004, 591). Thus capitalism has 'come of age' and with it has come 'a new corporate aspiration, not just to exert political influence but to absorb and "incorporate" the political and transform it, tacitly abandoning the ideal of commonality' (Wolin 2004, 588). Important characteristics of Superpower are that it has no formal constitution, that there is no a priori structure and authority underlying this system, and that it exists outside and exempt from the constraints of constitutionalism (Wolin 2004, 591). As such, what may still be officially named democracy becomes increasingly 'devoid of democratic substance'. Central tenets of democracy—participation, inclusion, and mass empowerment—now come in the shape of mass consumption, workforce, and consumer sovereignty. These sublimations create 'the combination of the illusion of individual freedom and power with the encapsulation of the individual in a cocoon from which escape seems an incoherent idea' (Wolin 2004, 588). In this light, democracy, as an ideal and historical philosophical paradigm at the opposite scale of totalitarianism that Esposito discusses, is transformed to a point at which the totalitarian remerges in a new shroud. Wolin notes that unlike the totalitarianisms of the kind that puts the intentionality of shaping society into a preconceived totality to the fore, 'inverted totalitarianism is not expressly conceptualised as an ideology or objectified in public policy'. Instead, it seeps into society, furthered both by power holders and citizens who are not necessarily aware of their own complicity (Wolin 2010, xviii). Even if he does not discuss it in those terms, the Superpower that Wolin describes is aligned with the biopolitical system of control society. This becomes apparent in his comparisons with Nazism.

As we saw, Esposito finds the biopolitical at odds with totalitarianism as it stands outside the scale and the historical philosophical paradigms from which it emerges. However, the 'inverted totalitarianism' that Wolin describes is inverted exactly because although it draws from a setting of liberalism and democracy, it actually represents a form of political power more akin to Nazism. In fact, he argues, inverted totalitarianism is 'Nazism turned upside-down' (Wolin 2004, 591). While Nazism is a totality driven by ideology of a master race, the Superpower strives towards an ideology of cost-effectiveness—'by the material rather than the "ideal"'. While Nazism worked to endow the masses with a sense of collective power and confidence, inverted totalitarianism promotes political apathy via a sense of collective futility and a 'privatization of the self' (Wolin 2004, 591–92). While capitalism was ultimately subordinated to state control in Germany, corporate power has become predominant in the contemporary US political system. One of the key reasons for evoking inverted totalitarianism in relation to Nazism despite these differences is the way a focus on individual development and excellence has been replaced by standardisation and corporate control over education and propaganda (Wolin 2004, 594). In other words, the attitude towards its citizens is a question largely released from democracy and even the underlying principles of democracy altogether.

In the light of Esposito's rejection of the link between totalitarianism and biopolitics on the grounds that they are fundamentally different systems, where the former can be conceptualised in relation to a chronological history of shifts between democratic and totalitarian forces while the latter cannot be situated in such a history, our ideas about what constitutes a totalitarian regime must shift. Centrally, Esposito places communism as a totalitarian model but Nazism, as we have seen, as a biopolitical one. Fundamentally, this has to do with the direct way in which the former relies on an inversion and, it has been argued, a fulfillment of democratic ideals by means of 'its excess of egalitarianism' (Esposito 2008, 638) while the other builds on a radically different type of (bio)power that is related directly to life. Biopolitics, Esposito argues, 'is incompatible with the conceptual lexicon of democracy' (Esposito 2008, 644). In effect, Esposito calls for a rethinking of political history that gives space to recognising the way biopolitics exists as a transversal force that is radically different from democracy, communism, and totalitarianism. Because Nazism must be situated on the side of biopolitics, as we have seen, and because our contemporary logic must also be placed on this side, we not only have to rethink historicist conceptualisations of history but we also have to question the possibility of conceptualising the present in terms of an opposition between democracy and totalitarianism.

If Nazism is not a totalitarian power but a biopolitical one, as Esposito suggests, then one might argue that present-day politics should not be understood in terms of an inverted totalitarianism so much as a development of biopolitics. This development is one in which biopolitics as a rejection of democracy is replaced by a biopolitics dressed up as democracy. In this light, however, the concept of inverted totalitarianism may still be useful. Even if we would take on Esposito's argument of the radical difference between totalitarianism and biopolitics, the concept of inverted totalitarianism alerts us to ways in which, just as contemporary power has let go of its links to democracy, contemporary totalitarianism has let go of its links to idealism. Instead, both have become directly hooked up to the economic system. Without this link to idealism, it also becomes possible to link the political dimensions of totalitarianism, or rather inverted totalitarianism, to the more philosophical dimensions of the notion of totality. The totalising tendencies of contemporary control society are not based on any ideological preconceived political system. Rather, these tendencies emerge directly from the effects they have on the very nature of information, communication, and expression. In other words, these tendencies are not premeditated and geared towards an ultimate 'totalstaat' but emerge, rather, as an effect of the development and intensification of biopolitics during the past decades.

In this light, the crisis in critique that we began to outline above can be understood as a struggle to respond to a culture whose totalising tendencies cannot be separated from the culture itself. When Virilio describes the all-encompassing dissemination of power on all levels of society as a shift from totalitarianism to 'globalitarianism' he points exactly to this impossibility of an outside to present-day control systems. His concept of globalitarianism fills an important function as it underlines how these tendencies encompass larger territories than the Western countries under analysis here. But also on a more local level, such globalitarianism at least partly explains the totalising tendency by which an earlier counterculture positioned outside the mainstream—that is, outside the enclosed spaces of discipline—is increasingly made a part of the constitutive modulations of control society itself. Control is not so much about controlling what may be articulated in society but rather, as Nathan Moore suggests, pre-emptively determining what it 'will be possible to think and say' (Moore 2007, 441). Thus, political as well as cultural critique is not only drained of its oppositional force but also frequently put to work to perpetuate the very system it critiques. Where Marcuse mourned the way in which 'high culture' loses its power as it is inscribed into one-dimensional society, we can see today a curious flip through which contemporary mainstream culture tends towards an internalised cultural and political observation. At least in some sense, this might be the ultimate evidence that critique is finally fully absorbed into the system. This would certainly be Baudrillard's viewpoint. Baudrillard writes, for example, that the film *The Matrix* not only projects but also participates in the dissemination and refraction of the monopolitistic superpower it represents (Baudrillard 2005, 203). More recently, but on a similar note, Mark Fisher notes how the Disney film *Wall-E* (2008) portrays an earth spoiled by capitalism and consumerism while, rather than being an effective critique, performing 'our anticapitalism for us, allowing us to consume with impunity' (Fisher 2009, 16). Seen from Baudrillard's perspective, contemporary culture thus comes to offer but a 'mirage of critique', as Sylvère Lotringer puts it in his introduction to Baudrillard's *The Conspiracy of Art* (Lotringer 2005, 11), a way of expressing political resistance that is really only part of the system. It would, of course, be disastrous to simply observe this alleged disappearance of critique. Instead, we must interrogate what this internalisation of critique and control does to questions of representation and power and how we might need to review our 'critical arsenal', as Latour puts it (Latour 2004, 230).

Burroughs, as Deleuze notes, was one of the first to identify 'control' as the name of this 'new monster' (Deleuze 1992, 4) and also one of the first to attempt a cultural resistance against its politics. In his novels, Burroughs recurrently explores the intersection between political power and the individual in capitalist America. His entire literary oeuvre, Timothy S. Murphy notes, is defined by a long-term engagement with the notion of control that begins with a sense that control is inescapable in his earlier works but that develops in his later fiction into a more revolutionary ambition of finding escape routes from 'the linked control systems of capital, subjectivity, and language' (Murphy 1997, 4–5). One of Burroughs's key points is the duplicitous nature of language as that which controls meaning. Theorising control, Deleuze seems clearly inspired by this understanding of communication as something that has been corrupted. Perhaps, he suggests, the key would be to 'create vacuoles of noncommunication, circuit breakers, so we can elude control' (Deleuze 1995, 175). And this is clearly one of Burroughs's strategies. Language as that which controls communication is also that which constitutes his very own tools of resistance. His characteristic cut-up method is an attempt to break up the control of sense and information that centrally characterises the monster he has identified. Other writers have developed Burroughs's method; for example, Kathy Acker, who uses her method, associated with cut-up as well as postmodern intertextuality, to play around with and challenge the meanings preempted in textual as well as physical bodies. J. G. Ballard, as another of Burroughs's inheritors, works, in his more experimental fiction such as *The Atrocity Exhibition* (1970), to disrupt information in a media-based landscape. The popular 'critique' of contemporary politics in focus in the present study, however, belongs to a very different cultural tradition than that of Burroughs and his inheritors. It may, at least as a general trend, be seen as part of the 'new monster' rather than as part of its critique. So how are we to approach it?

If the danger of biopolitics of today lies exactly in its two-faced interiority, as identified both in the literary tradition of Burroughs and in the commodified culture at large as theorised by Baudrillard and many others, then so, presumably, does its potential. The two sides, folded into each other, should mean that just as critique is absorbed into the system, it is also within the system that we must locate the desire for change. As control society has abandoned the molds of discipline in favour of continuous modulations, as Deleuze notes, a critique from the outside must be replaced by new weapons (Deleuze 1992, 4). The intensification of the one-dimensional society that Marcuse theorised has also made it clearer than ever that it is futile to look to dimensions outside it for help. If Marcuse's contemporaneity still allowed him to grasp for, even as he mourned, weapons that lay beyond one-dimensional society, the nature of control society in the new millennium seems to point, rather, inward. This is also why Negri argues that we need a new critique in the place of the by now classic cultural critique performed by Adorno and Horkheimer. Adorno and Horkheimer, Negri notes, locate the commodification and seductions of the American culture industry as coextensive with European fascism. The dialectic tendency of the Enlightenment can be located exactly in its tendency to transform itself to its opposite. The subjection of the masses by means of the culture industry was seen as but another version of the fascist antithesis of Enlightenment ideals. The developments in the culture industry since the 1940s but confirm the ontological status of the world that Adorno and Horkheimer theorised. The problem Negri finds with Adorno and Horkheimer's dialectical model is not that it has been proven wrong, but that the once-innovative analysis of the relation between the culture industry and the seduction of the masses that it enabled is becoming tautological. The model 'has exhausted itself' and no longer suffices as cultural critique—it has become repetitive, and even banal (Negri 2007, 48).

Nealon takes this questioning of the validity of classic cultural theory one step further, arguing that the kind of cultural critique that Adorno and Horkheimer propose is not only banal but historically misleading. Their critique builds on an old set of maps according to which it is still politically or ethically useful to reveal homologies between cultural and economic production and thus to seriously question the value of cultural production. While Adorno and Horkheimer could critique the culture industry as an extension of a Fordist mode of production, the collapse of the cultural and the economic that they to some extent predicted but which was still in coming in the 1940s makes the present moment one in which value floats freely across material practices, be they economic or cultural. Thus, it is pointless, if not anachronistic, to point to a homology between the two. Instead, Nealon argues, like Fredric Jameson, we need to build our cultural critique on new cognitive maps, maps that charter, instead, this new ground (Nealon 2012, 176). As we have seen, Negri suggests that rather than repeating the critique of the commodification of culture, we need to recognise a 'new terrain' that must be negotiated by remaining within expression itself (Negri 2007, 50). Within the endless production of images, within the infernal machine that globalises culture, within the abstraction of signs, and within the self-sufficient circle of cultural communication, Negri identifies an 'insurgent spirit', a subjectivation of the multitude that reclaims some of the desire the infernal machine itself needs to function (Negri 2007, 49). Such expression is not born from a synthesis but from an event, and this new production of desire is not about interpretation but about transformation. Such cultural critique would be about rebellious production within the system itself—a production of images within the endless production of images, of new figures of expression within life itself, a monstrous innovation (Negri 2007, 51).

What both Deleuze and Negri recognise, then, is the potential that emerges by remaining within. For them, the act of doing away with the notion of an outside and abandoning a dialectical mode of interpretation activates a notion of immanence that is potentially enabling. The question of a potential without an outside is crucial. As Hardt puts it, 'Analyzing the new techniques of social control is only worthwhile to the extent that it allows us to grasp also the new potentialities for contestation and freedom emerging with this new paradigm' (Hardt 1995, 41). The present book chooses to remain 'within' in two ways. To begin with, it centers, not around 'alternative' modes of cultural expression such as that of Burroughs's, although it does return to Burroughs briefly in the concluding chapter, but on a more mainstream culture and the propensity for popularised critique that we have observed in it. It recognises that while it is still highly relevant to look at Burroughs and other 'enfant terribles' of literature and culture, a move from an Adornian critique of the seduction of the culture industry to an interrogation of the events of change within it makes it necessary to look directly at the internal and formal conditions of the products of this industry. Interrogating as one of its core questions the possibilities of critique from the inside rather than the outside, the book takes a close look at the contemporary tendency to incorporate cultural and political critique in mainstream literature and cinema. Second, the book resists the temptation, and maybe illusion, of trying to create 'new weapons' and chooses, rather, to 'grasp for potentialities' within a formalist tradition of literary and cultural theory itself. As I flagged in the introduction, and as we see in the next chapter, there is political potential in the formalist tradition previously denounced for its lack of it.

NOTES

1. Plant's study of the Situationist movement, *The Most Radical Gesture: The Situationist International in a Postmodern Age* from 1992, has been heavily criticised for striving to synchronise Situationist practices into one coherent theory and for failing to recognise the specificity of their historical moment (McDonough 1997, 8–9). While the present context does not warrant an in-depth discussion of these long-term tensions and debates, I have tried to avoid consolidating tendencies while relying on Plant's ambitious and useful study for explication and exemplification.

2. Although the debates are not central to the present argument, it is worth noting that both Adorno's conception of totality and Jay's description of it have constituted a source of contention not the least for Jameson, who suggests that both Jay and other interpreters of Adorno tend to simplify matters (see Pizer 1993, 129).

TWO

Formalism/Allegory/Totality

Parallel to the crisis in critique and the intensification of biopolitics outlined above, literary criticism has been opening for a way of reestablishing formalism by pointing towards its potential to engage with ethical and political questions. A general discontent with 'the turn against form' during the final decades of the twentieth century and the inability to recognize how form matters is evinced in a 2000 special issue of *Modern Language Quarterly* (Wolfson 2000, 8). As Susan Wolfson outlines in her introduction to this issue, the common complaints against formalism as being historically and politically disinterested were somewhat ambivalently contrasted with the recognition of the social, historical, and ideological impact and function of form itself by critics such as Harold Bloom, Terry Eagleton, and Jerome J. McGann during the 1970s (Wolfson 2000, 2–3). For them, in different ways, an interest in form would be of relevance only if it paid attention to its ideological and sociohistorical functions. At this time, this meant wrestling form from new critical explication and claiming it in a new historicist context. As Wolfson puts it: 'To read form was to read against formalism' (Wolfson 2000, 3). However, Wolfson indicates, such 'activist' formalist impulses were lost during the transformations of literary studies in the following decades (Wolfson 2000, 2). When W. T. J. Mitchell suggests that we are heading towards a new notion of form and new kind of formalism, as I noted in the introduction, this constitutes a recovery of such impulses. Mitchell notes how the intensified focus on structure during the past decades responded to a demand for an ethical and political purpose of texts that the commitment to form as formalism, as an instrumental focus on the means, seemed unable to achieve. Thus, what was seen as an apolitical and idealist attention to syllables, line lengths, and emphasizes or, even worse, a decadent aestheticism of the beauty of art, was largely replaced, from structuralism onward, by a focus on the social and political constructedness of texts. The shift in literary criticism from natural beauty and internal form to artificial structures and sociocultural constructivism, Mitchell notes through John Carlos Rowe, can be directly linked to the shift in Western economies from the industrial and material to information and service. However, he suggests, it is exactly because of this shift in political structures that we need a rethinking of form as well as commitment in literature. What he points to is how these shifts enable, and indeed require, an attention to how form is linked to political practice.

Mitchell's proposal is taken up in a 2004 article in *New Literary History* where Jim Hansen continues to build on the argument that formalism is returning to North American criticism after decades of exile in favour of structuralism and poststructuralism. The opposition between formalism as an immanent critique centring on the internal architecture of the object on the one hand and transcendent criticism such as Marxist, feminist, and postcolonial readings of its ideological implications on the other rests, Hansen suggests, on a neglect of the cultural and political in the case of the former and a disregard for the particular in the case of the latter (Hansen 2004, 666). Put simply, he argues, this opposition poses two critical alternatives, one that analyses the rhetorical and stylistic strategies of the art object and one that approaches the art object as a product intimately related to the ideology from which it is born. Positioned in such an antithetical relation, formalism puts its trust in ahistorical, universal meaning regardless of the position of the interpreter while transcendent criticism works with notions of social construction and change. Hansen notes, however, that while the opposition between immanent and transcendent critique is central to literary criticism, Theodor W. Adorno argues that such opposition is based on a reified consciousness that misses the fact that 'form is always already imbricated with the sociohistorical' (Hansen 2004, 666). The internal contradictions of a work of art reflect the contradictions of its historical, cultural, and social context. 'The artwork', as Hansen articulates it, 'falls short where the social world from which it springs falls short' (Hansen 2004, 667). Part of most formalist criticism, Hansen notes, is determining the extent to which the critic figures the immanent form of the art object 'as a reflection of the sociohistorical or philosophical finitude of human understanding and practice tout court'. Formalism indicates the boundaries of what can be discussed and harbours assumptions about the order existing outside the art object that the critical consciousness cannot reach but which implicitly shapes human action (Hansen 2004, 667). Hansen takes on Walter Benjamin and Paul de Man as two critics who made formalist practices central to their work. But both of them, he notes, 'often begin with formalism only to end up as its malcontents, articulating its various philosophical, social, and aesthetic paradoxes' in order to illustrate how the key quarrel with formalism—that its preoccupation with form is at the expense of the political—is inaccurate (Hansen 2004, 664). In different ways, Hansen suggests, both Benjamin and de Man consider aesthetic form by means of 'the dialectic of immanence and transcendence, the internal and the external'. As they are both thus committed to thinking about form beyond form, their different techniques point to contrasting but powerful ways in which the political and theoretical interventions are made possible by means of formalist strategies (Hansen 2004, 665).

The return to and renewal of form as a political tool is further underlined in a 2007 article in the *PMLA* called 'What Is New Formalism?' published in the section 'The Changing Profession'. Here, Marjorie Levinson delineates the development of this return to form which, she notes, is not a theory or method so much as it is a movement (Levinson 2007, 558). This movement she divides into two categories. To begin with, there is the kind of new formalism that aims to reinstate a focus on form to the historical readings that once took its place and rejected it. Second, there is a new formalism that wants a sharp division between history and art and between discourse and literature and that wants this division to be recovered by means of form. In other words, she states, building on Wolfson, there is the new formalism building on new historicism (what she calls 'activist formalism') and a 'backlash new formalism' ('normative formalism') (Levinson 2007, 559). A common concern, she argues, within both these kinds of formalism is that we have missed out paying attention 'to the processes and structures of mediation through which particular discourses (literary genres, for example) come to represent the real. By the same stroke, we have contributed towards establishing that empirical domain *as* the real, a process that entails the eclipse or exclusion of other contenders for that title' (Levinson 2007, 561). The critical process has thus come to treat artworks carelessly in terms of historical and cultural content without paying attention to how this content is determined by its form. As she shows, and if the more normative formalism is a 'backlash', there is also a strong tendency to strengthen the ties between the attention to form and a Marxist tradition consisting centrally of Adorno but also of others such as György Lukács, Louis Althusser, and Fredric Jameson. Levinson points to how critics work to show how the supposed divide between a structuralist attention to content and context and a formalist attention to form is not as radical as it has been made out to be. She also notes how an alliance between these camps can work to engage the role of form, not only as a productive part of the text more generally, but also to illuminate its links to extraliterary systems (Levinson 2007, 563, 566). The ambition of Levinson's essay, as its position in *PMLA*'s section on the changing profession suggests, is to trace and clarify new formalism in relation to its earlier formalism as well as in relation to the new historicism that has preceded it. It thus aims to give the profession some insight into a movement that has increasingly come to influence literary and cultural studies over the past decade. Discussions of this

revived attention to form and its possibly quite considerable role in relation to contemporary preoccupations in literary studies—as indicated
also more generally by these debates in major literary journals: *Modern
Language Quarterly, New Literary History, PMLA*—have also been taken as
a cause to revisit both the historical and current rationales of major literary journals such as *New Literary History* and *American Literary History*
themselves as forums that in different ways consider literary studies as a
field. This new formalism, David Palumbo-Liu argues, potentially enables new ways of theorising literary history and its relation to current
preoccupations with transnational and global configurations of literature
(Palumbo-Liu 2008).

Apart from these centralised and disciplinary debates on new formalism, this revived attention to form has also been picked up for further
analysis not only in transnational studies but also in many other fields
such as posthumanist and feminist studies (see, for example, Wolfe 2008
and Wolosky 2010). In the context of the present study, it is picked up
specifically as a tool to analyse the relation between allegory and critique.
Taking my cue from this revival of form, the following chapters explore if
such a critical mode may assist in the search for the 'new terrain' for
critique that Antonio Negri calls for. Negri's call, as we saw earlier, is
born from the tendency of what has been identified as control society to
incorporate opposition and critique within itself. The fact that mainstream culture readily offers allegories of capitalism and control society
speaks to a sense of imprisonment in a system capable of employing
resistance to its own advantage. As such it speaks to the sense of loss
outlined in earlier sections—a disappearance of critique that Marcuse
began to observe already in the 1940s or 'the conspiracy of art' noted by
Jean Baudrillard in more recent years. But while Baudrillard expresses
little confidence of recovering any sense of political agency in a world in
which resistance is immediately integrated into the equation (Baudrillard
2005, 203), Negri, as we have begun to see, does not stop at his observation about the difficulty of cultural critique but continues to point towards new possibilities. While old modes of critique have lost their
force—largely because the exteriority they tried to defend is now completely engulfed in the system it wants to critique—Negri suggests that
we give up on any project of standing outside and insist, instead, on
remaining within expression.

I would like to explore what such a new terrain of critique would look
like when informed by a politically informed formalist criticism. If the
disappearance of the outside is a central theme of theoretical work on
control society, we can take the motif of the outside as our central concern and position it in relation to classic literary and especially formalist
ways of approaching representation by means of allegory. What happens
with this concept that is so intimately bound up with tension between
reality and its reflection, reality and representation, and reality and the

outside, when faced with the increasing disappearance of the outside in control society? De Man notes how the polarities of inside and outside that shape conceptions of form can be reversed. When form is seen as an external frame for the intrinsic meaning of the artwork, it is considered as superficial or even expendable, but when it is seen as 'a solipsistic category of self-reflection', meaning is positioned as extrinsic (de Man 1979, 4). In other words, form is seen either as that which must be unlocked to disclose the meaning trapped inside the text or as that which must be transcended to reveal the structural connection between the text and its outside, that is, its referential meaning. De Man, as I noted in the preface, notes how the 'inside/outside metaphor' upon which recurrent discussions of opposing intrinsic and extrinsic interpretation rely needs to be questioned (de Man 1979, 5). By bringing semiology and rhetoric together, and thereby complicating the differentiation between literal and figural meaning, de Man shows how the inside/outside model of representation and interpretation, whether it favours a formalist or a structuralist mode of reading, does not hold. With this in mind, what is the function of formalist devices such as allegory, and can Benjamin and de Man aid an understanding of the mechanisms of incorporation in culture and cultural critique today? In short, are there ways in which we can meet up Negri's call for new kinds of cultural critique by means of such old literary concepts? Believing that it would be in line with the nature of the immanent critique Negri calls for, the second part of this book tests 'old belaboured' formalist concepts on contemporary cultural expression in an attempt to respond both to Mitchell's claim that 'some new notion of form, and thus a new kind of formalism, lies before us' (Mitchell 2003, 324) and to Negri's suggestion that a critique of culture today must be born from 'the capacity to remain within' (Negri 2007, 50).

ALLEGORY AND REPRESENTATION

Allegory constitutes a key example of how the inside/outside model of representation and interpretation has been portrayed and theorised. Before going into detail regarding allegory as a formalist trope, let us walk this question of the 'inside/outside model' through some basic literary and philosophical devices. At the very center of questions of representation in Western literature, aesthetics, and philosophy we find the concept of mimesis. The history of mimesis, as Stephen Halliwell succinctly puts it, reflects 'the status of representational "appearances" in art and their relationship to worlds both real and invented' (Halliwell 2002, 5). Two main lines of interest, Halliwell notes, shape Plato's engagement with mimesis in his dialogues. The first one is interested in the relationship between the mimetic work and the world it (purports to) represent in terms of the complex issue of 'likeness'. Plato offers no single view on this point, Halliwell notes. In his different dialogues, the relation between mimesis and likeness is discussed in terms of a differentiation between mimetic works that stand in easily discernible relationship to the real world and those that do not (The *Cratylus*), the interaction between 'truth' and 'falsehood' (Books 2 and 3 of the *Republic*), the particular intensity of mimesis as dramatic enactment (Book 3), the possibility of idealistic mimesis (various passages of *Republic*), the implications of a 'mirroring' conception of mimesis (Book 10), the distinction between literal and viewer-dependent mimesis (The *Sophist*), and the complexity of determining mimetic 'correctness' in the face of different cultural traditions and aesthetic judgements. These various approaches, Halliwell argues, speak against the common tendency of seeing Plato and his dialogues as a unified doctrine of aesthetics (Halliwell 2002, 25). As our engagement with Plato here is not very extensive and by no means as extensive as Halliwell's, it is enough for us to notice these nuances while establishing that in all instances, the Platonic conception of mimesis relies on a fundamental distinction between representation and reality.

The two central, long-lasting, and contrasting conceptions of mimesis that Halliwell outlines both rely on this separation. The first is based on the commitment to depict a world outside the artwork itself, a world that is admittedly only partly accessible and knowable but one whose norms can be tested within the artwork. The second conception sees mimesis as being about the creation of a world—'an independent artistic heterocosm'—within the artwork itself, a world that may aim to express some 'truth' of reality as a whole but that does not hold this as its primary goal. The consequences of these contrasting conceptions, Halliwell points out, constitute a major reason why mimesis has been so momentous in the philosophy of art (Halliwell 2002, 5). The five categories of phenomena in which mimesis has been central—visual resemblance, behavioural emulation/imitation, impersonation, vocal or musical production, and metaphysical conformity—may be different in kind, but the usage within each category has in common the basic idea of a correspondence between the mimetic work and its assumed real-world equivalent, whether externally given or just hypothetically projectable (Halliwell 2002, 15). Through mimesis, whatever its kind, then, the artwork establishes an analogical relation to a world existing outside it. If the first point of interest for Plato is the relation between the mimetic work and the world it hopes to represent, the second point of interest is the relation between mimesis and the audience. Through its Greek inheritance, mimesis is fundamentally linked to the relation between the artwork and its capacity to affect its viewers. The mimetic qualities of a work of art are not only intended to create a representation of the world but also to elicit an emotional or psychological response to this world from its audience. As Halliwell notes, the ideal audience of the mimetic work is also that which is an engrossed witness of the world it portrays. Mimesis thus inevitably raises important questions 'about the relationship between the world *inside* and the world *outside* the mimetic work' (Halliwell 2002, 21). In this perspective, mimesis is linked to a 'mind-*dependent* reality' and its appeal linked to the particularities of the social and cultural context of the audience (Halliwell 2002, 25).

These two lines of engagement in Plato are related to our key concerns of the problem of cultural critique and the possibilities of a new formalism. If Plato's concern was multifarious, as Halliwell suggests, our concern here can be narrowed down to the way in which our conception of the relation between the artwork and the world outside it affects the political potential of art. More specifically still, we want to pick up on the well-noted way in which distinctions between representation and reality are wearing thin in contemporary society and see how it affects our conception of form and its relation to the world. This seems like a crucial part of any attempt of conceptualising cultural critique today. Mimesis is, of course, centrally about the representation of the world. But a key concern throughout the aesthetic and philosophical history of interrogating the conditions of representation is also that which cannot be represented. As has already begun to emerge with Halliwell's discussion of Plato, mimesis struggles to portray a reality that remains 'only partly accessible and knowable'. For Plato, of course, this is related to the world outside the cave, the reality of which we will inevitably fail to grasp. If the limitation of mimesis in the Greek context points towards an ontological conception of the distinction between representation and reality, mimesis is also limited by religious beliefs in transcendence. God remains inaccessible by humans who can never directly represent this dimension. From such tensions between the representable and that which cannot be represented and between the immanent and the transcendent, allegory emerges as a central formal mode of representation. Indeed, allegory may be said to stand at the heart of questions of immanence and transcendence in theology and philosophy as well as in literary theory.

'The interpretive dance of allegory', as Angus Fletcher puts it, 'is an ancient literary phenomenon' (Fletcher 2010, 12). The concept comes with a long and complex history, and its uses are full of contradictions. 'Wherever we encounter it', as Rita Copeland and Peter T. Struck note, 'it is trailing its entire cultural history behind it' (Copeland and Struck 2012, 10–11). Any attempt to summarise the various conceptualisations and histories of allegory is therefore bound to be ambitious, and such ambitions are also beyond the scope of the present book.[1] In its most general sense, allegory refers to the act of portraying one thing while alluding to another. As such, it is of course, as Ismail Xavier suggests, a very wide conception that not only covers all kinds of figures of speech but also quite a large part of literary expression (Xavier 2004). Similarly, the act of interpretation can be seen as allegorical in a very general sense. In his classic *Anatomy of Criticism* (1957), Northrop Frye suggests that 'all commentary is allegorical interpretation' (Frye 1957, 89). This suggestion is echoed some twenty-five years later by Jameson in *The Political Uncon-scious: Narrative as a Socially Symbolic Act* where he suggests that the dimension of interpretation itself is an essentially 'allegorical act'—a 'rewriting' of 'a given text in terms of a particular interpretive master code' (Jameson 1981, x). As a text is always understood in relation to the context of its recipient, Jameson argues, the allegorical dimension of any interpretation is inevitable. This notion is also problematised in terms of history and historical readings by Richard Halpern, who points to the 'double articulation' occurring in the reading of historical texts and events as diffracted by historical difference (Halpern 1997, 5).

De Man suggests that reading itself is allegorical. As soon as we accept the contradictions and problems of reading, he argues, reading must take its starting point in an 'unstable commixture of literalism and suspicion' that continually questions the extent to which 'the meaning *read* is destined to coincide with the meaning *stated*' (de Man 1979, 57–58). Even without actual representations of acts of readings, such as those de Man analyses in Proust, 'the allegorical representation of Reading' is 'the irreducible component of any text' (de Man 1979, 77). As Jacques Derrida notes, de Man situates allegory at the core of language. For him, allegory 'is not simply one form of figurative language among others; it represents one of language's essential possibilities: the possibility that permits language to say the other and to speak of itself while speaking of something else; the possibility of always saying something other than what it gives to be read' (Derrida 1989, 11). Importantly, this allegory at the heart of language is not, for de Man, about the representation of something outside of language—some extralinguistic meaning—but it points, rather, to the play of language as always existing in an exchange with itself. At the same time, de Man notes via Proust, Reading as an allegorical figure appearing in all texts also prevents us from reading Reading itself—it forever blocks access to a meaning it nonetheless continually calls out for (de Man 1979, 77).

De Man thereby puts his finger on the metalevel of what appears as an inevitable allegorical balancing act: the inherent instability of any one text creates a multiplication of meaning by the same token as it prevents us from determining it. Thus, the meaning of the text and the meaning of reading are both destabilised. This is where irony carries an important function in de Man's conception of allegory. Irony, as I began to outline in the introduction, emerges in the inevitable interruption of the illusion of unity and stable correlation between layers of meaning. While allegory itself constitutes a gesture, however vain, towards the possibility of correlations of internal and external meaning, its conjunction with irony illuminates how both allegory and irony ultimately function to demystify 'an organic world postulated in a symbolic mode of analogical correspondences or in a mimetic mode of representation in which fiction and reality could coincide' (De Man 2013, 529). Irony is thus more than a potential temporary interruption; it is everywhere in the narrative making it inter-ruptible at any point, a 'permanent parabasis' (De Man 2013, 542). In the hands of de Man, as I noted in the preface, allegory thereby becomes a tool to question any totalising conceptions of literature or history. Unlike Romanticists like Coleridge and many post-Romantic critics for whom the symbol captures the relation between subjective perception and the nature of the object while allegory remains limited, de Man works to reinstate allegory as a tool sensitive to the way in which temporality makes such analogical relations forever unstable.

De Man takes the second of the two routes beyond new criticism formalism outlined by Wolfson, the first being a new historicist claiming of form á la McGann and the second being a critique of closure through deconstruction (Wolfson 2000, 4). Indeed, de Man's insistence on the alle-gorical nature of all texts is in itself a deconstruction of logocentrism and metaphysics. For de Man, there is no such thing as direct denomination since each naming is always already an interpretation. This means that all narratives are allegorical. Every reading of a narrative brings something to it that refers to something more than what the text or the reader can control. Meaning is not stable and cannot be defined by means of a cor-rect reading but is produced, rather, by a process of inevitable 'misread-ings'. Allegory thus becomes one of de Man's main rhetorical devices to undermine the 'genetic' model of the text, or of the world for that matter, a model that can take different shapes but that essentially relies on pola-rities between appearance and Thing, truth and falsehood, essence and accident. He thus challenges the underlying assumptions of this model that the existence of 'an entity that can be said to be identical with itself and that would engender, through a process of mediation, an appearance of which it is the origin and the foundation' (De Man 1979, 90).

De Man's deployment of allegory as an illustration of the instability of meaning can be contrasted with the ways in which it has also been em-ployed to infer very concrete relationships of meaning. Where allegory is exactly that which undermines the intentionality of both the writer and the reader for de Man, Frye emphasises the importance of intentionality for what he names 'actual allegory'. For a work to fit this genre, as I noted in the introduction, the author needs to explicitly point towards the rela-tionship between the work's internal logic and some external precepts. The author thereby gives an indication of how the work should be under-stood. This kind of allegory, Frye notes, frequently elicits resistance in the critic whose freedom is restricted by such prescribed modes of interpreta-tion (Frye 1957, 90). Another example of a type of allegory used to con-struct firm relationships of meaning is the 'naïve allegory' that, Frye writes, 'is a disguised form of discursive writing' performed mainly in elementary educational literature. This kind of allegory is grounded in 'habitual or customary ideas' and comes in the shape of a 'transient spectacle'. As such it has strong connections to the pictorial arts. At its extreme, he suggests, naïve allegory grows 'so anxious to make its own allegorical points that it has no real literary or hypothetical center' (Frye 1957, 91). But of course Frye also acknowledges the existence and logics of more sophisticated allegories. Literature evinces a sliding scale, he suggests, reaching from the most explicit and naïve allegories to the antiexplicit or even antiallegorical. In between, we find for example the classic and continuous allegories of Edmund Spenser's sixteenth-century epic poem *The Faerie Queen* and John Bunyan's seventeenth-century text *The Pilgrim's Progress* and works 'in which the structure of imagery, however suggestive, has an implicit relation only to events and ideas'. In the work of William Shakespeare and other texts in which the poetic imagery becomes 'increasingly ironic and paradoxical', we find a type of allegory that avoids explicit statements and which the modern critic therefore tends to feel more comfortable with (Frye 1957, 91).

For Frye, then, allegory is essentially a 'contrapuntal technique' that more or less directly allows text and world to run parallel. As such, it carries an intimate relation to questions of representation not only in literature but also in ontology and religion. In allegory, Lukács notes, two contradictory ontological claims meet. On the one hand, allegory carries strong links to transcendence in that it posits meaning beyond the text, or the world, and on the other hand, it rejects such notions of transcendence (Lukács 2005, 409). Historically, the allegorical, with its strong ties to the religious, speaks to the meaning of the world as an analogy to a transcendent God. Early and influential texts such as Bunyan's *The Pilgrim's Progress* are indicative of the relation between a human 'Christian' toiling on Earth and the Christian God that transcends it. Baroque art, however, and as Benjamin shows and Lukács underlines, complicates allegory's analogical nature, and modernist literature annihilates it. Thus is created a form of allegory that corresponds to nothing—a negation of transcendent meaning. At this point of nihilism, allegory is, as Benjamin puts it, 'left empty-handed'. Evil, as in the absence of transcendent meaning or God, 'is, precisely, the non-existence of that which allegory purports to represent' (quoted in Lukács [2005, 411]). The ambivalence related to the contradictory nature of allegory thus purports on the one hand to a reverent recognition of the transcendence of meaning and/or God and thus the impossibility of expressing it/Him directly and on the other hand to a denial of such meaning and/or God. In the case of the latter, the modernist literature to which Benjamin and Lukács ascribe this process falls into nihilism. This nihilism pulls aesthetics with it into the pit of annihilation of meaning. Aesthetics is pulled into this pit through a 'destruction of traditional literary forms' and a 'negation of art' (Lukács 2005, 412). Without the transcendence implied in religious allegory, modernist literature suffers from a foundational loss of meaning and its details, characters, and relationships are reduced to 'abstract particularity' (Lukács 2005,

410). While the conceptions of transcendence that characterise allegory are thus deeply contradictory, they nonetheless continue to depend on a similar conception of aesthetics as that to which external meaning should be ascribed. Thus, they also rely on a sense of the representational force, or lack of force, of expression. As Lukács shows, the loss of such meaning itself is significant in shaping modernist literature. Franz Kafka, whose work Lukács posits as typical of modernist allegory, labours to fuse the particular and the general in a life devoid of transcendental meaning (Lukács 2005, 412).

Where de Man positions allegory as distinctly secular and profoundly deconstructive and, as such, as evidence of the impossibility of stable meaning, Benjamin's conception of allegory continues, even is his later and more politicised work, to carry a theological and nostalgic longing for a more permanent meaning. Allegory, Benjamin argues, confirms the existence of truth in the realm of ideas—'The mode of being in the world of appearances is quite different from the being of truth, which is something ideal' (Benjamin 2003, 36). Indeed, allegory is not only different but even opposite to truth, he suggests. Allegory has no aspirations towards the truth but rather 'reveals more clearly than anything else the identity of the pure curiosity which is aimed at mere knowledge with the proud isolation of man' (Benjamin 2003, 229). Thus, allegory, in Benjamin's conception, confirms the transcendent even as it lays no claims to it. It sticks to the realm of human knowledge while continually recognising the ideal realm of truth to which it has no access. As Bainard Cowan puts it, allegory 'could not exist if truth were accessible: as a mode of expression it arises in perpetual response to the human condition of being exiled from the truth it would embrace' (Cowan 1981, 114). As a result of the lingering theology in Benjamin, the interrelation between irony and allegory that we saw in de Man as the joint demystification of analogical correspondences takes a slightly different shape.

In his earlier work, which, as Samuel Weber notes, foreshadows the theory of allegory that he was to develop later, Benjamin differentiates between material and formal irony (Weber 2008, 27–28). The former is associated with Romantic subjectivity and serves to underline the sovereign freedom of the author. The latter, which is more generative, resides less with the author and more with the form and the way it inevitably undermines the illusion of the integrity of the author as well as the work itself. Unlike material irony, formal irony is not an intentional endeavour so much as it is the realisation of the paradox inherent in any attempt 'to demonstrate the work's relation to the idea in the work itself' (Benjamin, cited in Weber [2008, 28]). Emphasising the distinction between a material irony, which is associated with the symbolic form and unity of the Romantics, and the formal, profane irony that could neither contain nor be assimilated to the absolute, Benjamin's work on irony thus foregrounds how ideas of the absolute are not abolished but must be separated from an attention to profane form in order for the latter to carry critical force. This critical force emerges, not because the separation between profane form and the absolute can ever be completed—indeed, formal irony, Benjamin states, 'has to do with the approximation of the particular and hence limited work to the absolute'—but because it focuses our attention on the function of form itself. Alongside his increasing investment in Marxist thought, Benjamin also comes to relate allegory to the exile from 'thinglyness' that comes with commodity culture. The separation of the perception of the object in itself and its value as commodity—essentially between its use and its exchange value—is characteristic of the crumbling illusion of wholeness in the modern period. As Benjamin puts it, '"value," as the natural burning-glass of semblance in history, outshines "meaning"' (Benjamin 1999, 347). The Baroque allegory that Benjamin discusses in his *Trauerspiel* study precedes the late-capitalist commodification of culture, as Halpern notes, which means that the commodity cannot be positioned as a 'historical-materialist "explanation" of allegory'. Nonetheless, he suggests, the process of commodification can be seen to reposition the allegorical in modern times. In fact, Halpern argues, the commodity 'renders allegory obsolete by perfecting and globalizing the latter's logic of representation' and as such it becomes 'the phenomenology of the entire social-material world' (Halpern 1997, 13).

In its Benjaminian conception, allegory also has a constitutive relation to ruins. More specifically, it is intimately affiliated with the ruins of unity and totality. As we have just seen, Benjamin distinguished between material irony and formal irony in order to be able to rethink representation beyond the Romantic belief in unity. While the symbol, from Georg Friedrich Creuzer to the Romantics, is associated with the unity of idea and representation—an ideal and intuitive mode of expression that is in itself complete—the fragmentation of totality in modernity entails also a loss of belief in such unity and ideality. Thus, the ruin of totality makes place for allegory as a form of expression that is never capable of recovering the unity of the symbol but that has the capacity to produce meaning by means of an unstable but continuous tying together of fragments. As Jeremy Tambling puts it, in allegory 'there are no "natural" comparisons; all terms of comparison are non-natural, ideological, non-proper, catachresis' (Tambling 2010, 118). This disintegration of the symbol entails that the image is recognised as a fragment of which a whole cannot be recovered but which can nonetheless, through the dialectical relationship of allegory, become a meaningful mode of expression. Built on ruins, allegory is thus born from a mourning of totality, a self-conscious but inevitable nostalgia for a moment of unity that is recognised as forever lost. Allegory, as Jameson puts it in *Marxism and Form*, 'is precisely the dominant mode of expression of a world in which things have been for whatever reason utterly sundered from meanings, from spirit, from genuine human existence' (Jameson 1971, 71).

Along with Lukács's *Theory of the Novel*, Andrew Arato notes, Benjamin's *Trauerspiel* study of allegory becomes a key background text for the *Kulturkritik* of the Frankfurt School. Central Frankfurt School thinkers such as Lukács, Adorno, and Jürgen Habermas all come to see allegory as crucial to the interpretation of modern art (Arato 1985, 208). Centrally, the allegorical has served to provide a transcendent referent in periods in which intersubjective meaning is at stake. In civil society, such transcendence is under threat from the mechanisms of alienation and reification. Allegory, as Lukács puts it,

> is that aesthetic genre which lends itself par excellence to a description of man's alienation from objective reality. Allegory is a problematic genre because it rejects that assumption of an immanent meaning to human existence which—however unconscious, however combined with religious concepts of transcendence—is the basis of traditional art. (Lukács 2005, 408)

Allegory, as we have already seen, points towards a transcendent mode even as its very logic underlines its inaccessibility. Addressing the concept of natural history and its reliance on understandings of first and second nature, Adorno notes how Lukács presses the distinction between a meaningful and a meaningless world, the latter which is the conventional, reified, and alienated second nature that 'supplies neither a meaning for the subject in search of a goal nor a sensuous immediacy as material for the acting subject.' Adorno cites Lukács directly to show how there is no 'lyrical substantiality' to the human constructs of second nature as 'its forms are too rigid to adapt themselves to the symbol creating moment' (Adorno 1984, 118). Benjamin, Adorno suggests, uses allegory as the means to recover this second nature, not as arbitrary and meaningless but as the expression of a particularity. As such, allegory makes it possible to capture the relation between nature, as that which appears, and its transient meaning (Adorno 1984, 119). Adorno then pushes the discussion further, suggesting that second nature is 'illusory because we have lost reality'. Yet, he notes, 'we believe that we are able to meaningfully understand it in its eviscerated state'. The key to moving forward, he argues, is realising that 'second nature is, in truth, first nature'—reconciliation is given only when the world is 'immured from all "meaning"' (Adorno 1984, 124).

The intrinsic link between allegory and totality emerges here in an increasingly secular and politicised form. In this light, it further illuminates the already noted differences between the Frankfurt thinkers when it comes to the question of totality with a more specific eye to the function of aesthetics and critique. Adorno argues that philosophy must give up the illusion of being able to grasp 'the totality of the real' and in doing so, it must 'learn to do without the symbolic function, in which for a long time, at least in idealism, the particular appeared to represent the general'

(Adorno 1977, 127). Marcuse's continued belief in normative totality that we noted in the previous chapter entailed a continued belief in the symbol. Habermas, outlining some tensions between Benjamin and Marcuse, notes how the former's interest in allegory as 'a counter-concept to the individual totality of the transfiguring artwork' can be contrasted with the way in which the latter's orientation 'depends on a concept of aesthetic beauty in which essence appears symbolically' (Habermas 1979, 35–36). Thus, and while the fulfillment and positivity promised by the symbolic makes it attractive to someone convinced of the possibility of normative totality, this, as Habermas notes, appears as false pretenses to those who think of the world as necessarily characterised by irreconcilable fragments (Habermas 1979, 36). For Benjamin, the symbol is a ruse while allegory 'is critique itself' or at least refers to critique (Habermas 1979, 36). This emphasis on allegory as an important element of critique can also be seen in Adorno's later Benjamin-inspired work on form. Although he may not have developed an extended engagement with allegory in his published works, it recurs, as Roger Foster notes, not only in Adorno's essay on natural history but also in later lectures (Foster 2007, 79). Essentially, allegory becomes a way for Adorno to reinstall an otherwise reified expression with political import not by means of content but by means of form. As Foster puts it, allegory becomes the means for Adorno to 'formulate a view on language as expressive precisely in its failure to say the unsayable' (Foster 2007, 79). Form, in other words, becomes a central element in the struggle of locating meaningful expression in a commodified world.

ALLEGORY AND THE PRESENT

In the struggle with the dreams of lyric unity and the realities of allegorical necessity present in Lukács, Benjamin, and Adorno, we see different ways of coming to terms with and developing the Romantic heritage. This is a heritage in which Coleridge saw the symbol as an 'organic form' reflecting a natural relationship while rejecting allegory as a 'mechanic form' deliberately yoking together heterogeneous elements. For Coleridge, as Jonathan Culler puts it, the inherent meaning revealed through the symbolic operation and which was seen to confirm 'the power of the poetical spirit' was contrasted with the figural and analogical relation of the allegorical (Culler 1976, 263). As the allegorical reemerges in postmodernity, however, the ambition of uncovering natural relationships and organic forms seems to be long gone. Allegory, it has been argued, becomes so central at this point that we cannot properly account for postmodernist art without it (Owens 1980, 75). Building on Craig Owens's work, David Joselit even argues that the tendency towards self-referentiality and anticipation of the critic's function in postmodern culture makes allegory a rhetorical figure of postmodernism itself (Joselit 2003, 3–4). The idea of a symbolic unity has long since faded as has, largely, the mourning for its loss. Allegory, Jameson suggests, is 'congenial for us today' and suits us far better than 'the massive and monumental unifications of an older modernist symbolism or even realism itself' because of its fundamental reliance on heterogeneity and discontinuity (Jameson 1986, 73).

When Jameson situates allegory as an important mode of expression in postmodernity, he does so because he sees how the gradual but continuous dismantling of ideas of stable meanings and coherent narratives that has shaped the Western world from Benjamin until the present has made the world yet more impossible to overview. The attraction of allegory today is that it enables a production of meaning in the otherwise fluid context of global capitalism (Jameson 1992, 5).[2] A major reason for the return of the allegorical that Jameson postulates is that it seems to offer a solution to the form problems of how to represent the collective processes of the social totality of multinational corporate networks (Jameson 1992, 4). Allegory opens for a depiction of the system of global control and the challenges of transnational classes and global management through a figurative machinery of individuals and limited landscapes. In a response to the ample critique of his 'Third-World Literature in the Era of Multinational Capitalism' (1986), an essay criticised for reducing the complexity of the 'third-world literature' to which he refers and for producing an idealisation dressed up as knowledge of a totality (Ahmad 1987, 4, 23),[3] Jameson explains that the purpose of this essay was to draw attention to 'the loss of certain literary functions and intellectual commitments in the contemporary American scene' by comparing them to 'the constitutive presence of those things' (i.e., national allegory) elsewhere (Jameson 1987, 26). In the essay, he positions a refashioned allegory as a potential cure for the 'epistemologically crippling' point of view of a dominant American perspective that 'reduces its subjects to the illusions of a host of fragmented subjectivities, to the poverty of the individual experience of isolated monads, to dying individual bodies without collective pasts or futures bereft of any possibility of grasping the social totality' (Jameson 1986, 85).

Jameson's project in *The Geopolitical Aesthetic: Cinema and Space in the World System* (1992) is to make an inventory of what he calls 'conspiratorial texts', that is, texts that among their multiple meanings can be read as constituting 'an unconscious, collective effort at trying to figure out where we are and what landscapes and forms confront us in the late twentieth century' (Jameson 1992, 3). The geopolitical unconscious is an effect of the new world system in which national cultures are disappearing and in which all thinking is therefore also 'an attempt to think the world system as such' (Jameson 1992, 3–4). This is the point, he argues, at which allegory reemerges in the postmodern era and seems to provide a relatively satisfactory solution to the form problems that emerge as the individual story must be understood in relation to large-scale and non-overviewable collective processes. Instead of being positioned as isolated monads, partial subjects and their constellations are assigned to play roles in the world system (Jameson 1992, 5). Jameson discusses the form problem in terms of empirical and conceptual content. Only in Utopia, he suggests, in 'a landscape of pure immanence, in which social life coincided fully with itself' would the absolute fusion of form and content be possible. Without a Utopia there can be no such union, and things have to be 'patched together with allegory'. Without an absolute fusion, meaning must be infused, remotivated, added as a supplement of a symbolic nature, and narratives must remain allegorical since they aim to represent a social totality that 'cannot be made to materialize as such in front of the individual viewer' (Jameson 1992, 45–46). At the same time, allegory comes to carry a polyvalent relation to commodification since the autoreferentiality in the postmodern also means that culture acts out its own commodification (Jameson 1992, 5).

If allegory remerges in postmodernity, as Owens, Jameson, as well as the cultural trend under discussion here suggest, it does indeed seem to do so through attempts of making sense of a global world order that we struggle to overview. At the same time, the notion of totality too remerges as a seemingly anachronistic concept not long after it has been rejected by most poststructuralist thinkers. Trying to orient ourselves in systems too vast for us to grasp, questions of representation again come to be associated with the issue of totality or, rather, as Jameson specifies, representability,

> a term that raises in turn the fundamental question of the conditions of possibility of such presentation in the first place. It is a question that necessarily opens out onto the nature of the social raw material on the one hand (a raw material which necessarily includes the psychic and the subjective within itself) and the state of the form on the other, the aesthetic technologies available for the crystallization of a particular spatial or narrative model of the social totality. For it is ultimately always of the social totality itself that it is a question in representation, and never more so than in the present age of a multinational global corporate network. (Jameson 1992, 4)

Allegory, as we have seen earlier, is about making do without the lost unity implied by the symbol. Benjamin sees allegory as an attempt to try, while ever failing, to tie together the fragments of such lost totality, and de Man uses allegory to prove that such totality was never possible in the first place. When Jameson suggests that allegory is a privileged mode of representation in postmodernity, he falls back on Benjamin's eternal project of tying together fragments. Allegory, as Jameson puts it, provides the means to decipher meaning 'from moment to moment, the painful attempt to restore a continuity to heterogeneous, disconnected instants' (Jameson 1971, 72). In its postmodern instantiations, he notes further, allegory no longer strives towards some idea of 'one-to-one table of equivalences' since the signifying process is inevitably contaminated by modifications of meaning over time (Jameson 1986, 73). This has implications for the function of irony. The function of irony in allegory is, as we have seen in de Man and Benjamin, essentially linked to the necessarily failing ambitions of allegory towards unity and stability. In postmodernity, Jameson suggests, such ambitions are abandoned. Therefore, and despite the common perception of irony as a frequent feature of postmodernism, he argues, irony belongs to the modern rather than the postmodern. As 'the quintessential expression of modernism and of the ideology of the modern as it was developed during the Cold War', he writes, irony wants to have its cake and eat it in that it builds on the affirmation of politics while simultaneously affirming the impossibility of political practice. It wants to be 'within the act or commitment and outside it' (Jameson 2007, 177–79).

However, and even if postmodernity may have seen an increasing affirmation of heterogeneity, the postmodern configuration of allegory that Jameson points to and that functions as a means to envision totality in the midst of heterogeneity carries its own form of irony. Even if constituted differently in terms of its geopolitical emphasis, the very idea of a nonoverviewable world system combined with the ambitions to nonetheless think or represent it points back to the irony outlined by both de Man and Benjamin. In this instance, however, the totality yearned for pertains directly to the idea of a 'world system'. Jameson suggests that the dispersed mode of production that we often call late capitalism, the landscape of which it is difficult to overview, comes with a 'new representational situation' that old forms of knowledge, such as demographics, do not cover (Jameson 1992, 2). On the one hand, the information and visualisation of the distribution of wealth, for example, are easily accessible on our television sets (and here, we hasten to update Jameson's text to the present and note that this information is even more accessible via other communicative media today) and thus offer no 'problems of figuration'. On the other hand, this easy access fails to connect this information with the deeper systemic causes and thus disables 'what used to be called self-consciousness about the social totality' (Jameson 1992, 2). Jameson suggests that this is a knowledge we should and do strive for without necessarily being aware of the process.

Exploring contemporary allegories in the following chapters in the light of the conceptions of allegory and totality outlined in this and the previous chapter enables me to highlight some questions about relations of content and form in control society. Because many of the texts and films present allegories of a contemporary society that seems to be all about totality, the highlighted questions are as follows: Has the transition between disciplinary and control society entailed a reconfiguration of the conditions and possibilities of allegory? While rejected by most so-called poststructuralists as a useful category, does totality reemerge with control society and again become a concept to be taken seriously? Do these texts and films, with their seemingly current and political edge in portraying contemporary society, in fact rely on analogue relations that are no longer relevant to this same society? If so, are these texts, while portraying seemingly potent social and political critique on the level of content, really sending out reassuring but misleading messages about the nature of control as well as the potential resistance to it? Placing an analysis of the tendency for political allegory in contemporary Anglo-American culture in the context of the debates regarding the crisis in cultural critique and the conspiracy of art, as well as in relation to the questions of form, allegory, and totality outlined so far, the rest of this book discusses this paradigm and what it may mean for cultural critique in control society. Focusing on central components of any organisation of society, the following chapters interrogate these questions with a specific eye to their implications in terms of space, time, and vision, respectively.

NOTES

1. Anyone interested in such overviews may consult studies devoted more directly to making them such as, for example, Rita Copeland and Peter T. Struck's *The Cambridge Companion to Allegory* (2012) or Jeremy Tambling's *Allegory* (2010).

2. As part of his project 'The Poetics of Social Forms', Jameson has stated that he has a book forthcoming on allegory. Together with other books on myth and realism, this book aims at making 'a theory of the cultures of modes of production and also to concentrate various problems that exist throughout, like those of representation, of allegories and meaning and interpretation' (quoted in Cevasco [2012, 89]).

3. Apart from Aijaz Ahmad's critique in 'Jameson's Rhetoric of Otherness and the "National Allegory"' (1987), other examples of criticism of Jameson's approach to Third World culture includes Gayatri Spivak's argument that Jameson's yearning for an overviewable political unconscious glosses over the discontinuities and interruptions of imperialism (Spivak 1999, 208) and Imre Szeman's more positive appraisal of it in 'Who's Afraid of National Allegory? Jameson, Literary Criticism, Globalization' (2002).

THREE

Space, Allegory, Control

Looking at J. G. Ballard's novelistic production as a whole brings to mind one of those tricks of visual media where the destruction of a building or something else solid is played in reverse, so that the pieces and building blocks seem to fly up and reattach themselves to each other thereby gradually rebuilding the construction from its ruins. In what is a continuous engagement with political space and time from the early 1960s up until the publication of his last novel in 2009, Ballard's work evolves from the depiction of dystopic ruins to dystopic perfection. This development can be seen to reflect escalations and elaborations of mechanisms of control over the past decades. The intensification of control during this period, outlined in chapter 1, the periodisation of which I will also return to in the concluding chapter, has, as I have noted, entailed a crisis in critique that demands a rethinking of the relation between political structures and cultural expression. Ballard's work cannot be said to fall into the category of contemporary popular culture analysed in the following chapters, but it shares with the works in that category the speculative, the dystopic, the political, and, essentially, of course, the allegorical. By expressing an increasing sense of political control in parallel with an increasing dependence on allegory, I hope that Ballard's work, and, of course, my analysis of it, secures some tools to think about politics and form in a contemporary context. The particular focus on space in a Western context also serves to set the stage for the configurations of time and vision discussed in subsequent chapters.

Ballard's novelistic production falls into a number of interrelated but thematically bound periods, each of which carries its own implications in terms of political space and form. The first set, which includes *The Drowned World* (1962), *The Drought* (2008 [1964]), and *The Crystal World* (1978 [1966]), is preoccupied with postapocalyptic space. These novels all present surrealist dystopias following natural disasters in different ways. The worlds depicted here are covered by water, plagued by droughts, or crystallised by pollution. Agency in these novels has to be negotiated through the new conditions of living emerging as a result of new spatial configurations. On the level of content, Ballard seems less concerned with the causes for disaster and more with how the collapse of certain organising principles of human life opens life to new formations. On the level of form, the literal ruins portrayed on the level of content are contrasted with a refusal to recover meaning. Where Walter Benjamin's ruins constitute the birth of modern allegory as a response to the falling apart of totality, Ballard's ruins in these early novels seem rather to question the mourning and longing for lost coherency. As I develop further below, the ruins that characterise his earlier novels can be seen as ruins of representation in its more affirmative sense—not as a loss but as a new possibility. As such, the ruins do not signify the irreparable but rather the basic building blocks of immanent creation.

Ballard's second set of novels is characterised by investigating the effects of the increasing technologisation and urbanisation of human life. In novels such as *Crash* (2008 [1973]), *Concrete Island* (1974), and *High Rise* (2006 [1975]), asphalt, highways, and high rises dominate a decidedly urban and politically efficient space that the individual attempts to negotiate. Compared to the affirmative ruins portrayed in the earlier novels, the asphalt jungles of this second set are part of a dystopic social totality of production, technology, and power. At the same time, however, the very focus of each of these novels is the mental as well as physical spaces forgotten in the grand scheme of urbanisation and efficacy. As such, functional space is contrasted with dysfunctional space—not ruins so much as gaps. While Ballard's resistance to allegorisation is still apparent in his refusal to infuse these 'other' spaces with meaning, this contrasting of spaces leaves the novels open to possible allegorical readings. Thus, for example, the concrete island in the novel with that name and its protagonist's impossibility to leave it can be seen to stand for the isolation and desolation of modern capitalism.

Ballard's most recent and final novels, *Cocaine Nights* (1996), *Super-Cannes* (2000), *Millennium People* (2004), and *Kingdom Come* (2006), have settings that project some possible effects of the complete incorporation of human agency into the economic systems that organise the Western world today.[1] These worlds are not submerged under water, plagued by drought, or in the constant process of crystallisation. Neither are they tracing the precarious and increasingly murky borders between humans and technology. Rather, they systematically stage ways in which agency is built into the spatiotemporal coordinates of a contemporary Western society. These later novels portray a completely different type of dystopia. Where the first set of novels depicts the ruins of modern social systems and the second set is content to point towards their cracks, this last set of novels can be seen to portray a society in which the ruins have been patched up and gaps have been filled. Western society truly emerges as a totality as the vast condos of the rich stretch over endless horizons and the dirty work of production has been completely relegated to an invisible outside. As a last step in the reversal of destruction, then, there is, in these final texts, a horrifying and all-encompassing inside from which no alternatives emerge. At the same time, the allegorical impulse, resisted in the earliest novels and only half-acknowledged in the middle period, is reconfigured in this last period. Here, we witness what appears to be a triumphant reestablishing of a meaning-making that has become completely internalised into the control system itself. The simile of the destruction played in reverse that I have just outlined above only half works, however, since it is not the same construction that is being put back together but a distinctly modified one. Of course, the societies that are drowned, dried out, and crystallised in the earlier novels are not the same ones that begin to assert the power of technology and urbanisation in the second set, and they are definitely not the same ones that are so mercilessly all-devouring in the last. Rather, the destruction played in reverse should be understood on the level of form. The gradual intensification of control society is reflected in a gradual coming into allegory—a new configuration of totality in which allegory emerges not as a mourning of fragments so much as pure reflection.

As outlined in previous chapters, the function as well as the fundamental conception of allegory in its relation to transcendent meaning has developed throughout its history, and its development may be seen to come to a peak in a modern world struggling to make sense of meaning at all. From a Benjaminian perspective, the ruins that testify to the fragmentation of meaning and the loss of the transcendent unity of the symbol are irreparable, and allegory is but the forever insufficient means to tie together ill-fitting fragments. This modernist loss and the mourning inherent in it develop, in postmodernity, into a more affirmative abandonment of meaning. As compared both with the romanticist rejection of allegory in favour of the unity of the symbol and with the modernist acceptance of allegory as a means of handling its loss, allegory increasingly loses its links to transcendent meaning altogether. By the same token, it sheds its role as a necessary evil intended to replace something more valuable. Or, as Jeremy Tambling puts it, the 'assumption that it is an artificial device no longer seems so problematic' (Tambling 2010, 2). Instead of pointing towards transcendent meaning, allegory is secularised as it becomes less a means to recover lost meaning and more the means to grasp current political and social systems. Fredric Jameson notes how our 'new being-in-the-world' is characterised by the disappearance of more traditional national, cultural, and class demarcations and categories and the emergence of a social totality too vast to grasp 'by the natural and historically developed categories of perception with

which human beings normally orient themselves'. This ungraspability of
the social totality creates a representational problem that has a particular
association to space. The mapping of the social by means of clear geographical borders no longer holds as a means of comprehending the
mechanism and dynamics of the mode of production in late capitalism
(Jameson 1992, 2). This ungraspability comes with a set of form-problems
relating to how we might create self-consciousness about the social totality. Allegory, Jameson argues, constitutes one possibility. More specifically, a new, refashioned national allegory constitutes a means to approach
this new social totality. For Jameson, as I noted in the previous chapter,
all thinking today also necessarily constitutes an attempt of thinking the
world system. This adds to thought a fundamentally allegorical level
(Jameson 1992, 4). It is as if the individual position, landscape, or event,
when losing recourse to the more clear-cut identities, institutions, and
social systems of disciplinary society, is immediately coupled up to the
social totality of the world. Partial subjects, lacking a clear role in identifiable classes, come to stand in, rather, for larger forces in the world system. Allegory corresponds nicely to such machinery because it 'allows
the most random, minute, or isolated landscape to function as a figurative machinery in which questions about the system and its control over
the local ceaselessly rise and fall' (Jameson 1992, 5).

Unsurprisingly, Jameson's reading of postmodern allegory still speaks
to the inability to grasp meaning in any complete sense. This, however,
has less to do with transcendence and more to do with capitalist global-
isation. Ballard's works testify to this secularisation of allegory at the
same time as they illuminate its new formations and functions in control
society. Ballard's rich oeuvre shows how the reemergence of allegory in
the postmodernity that Jameson theorises can be illuminated in terms of
control society specifically. The development that his novels elucidate
results not only in a complete abandonment of transcendent meaning,
but also in a political system the very nature of which is grounded on the
lack of an outside. Put together, these novels, reaching from 1961 to 2009,
trace a development in terms of the relation between space, allegory, and
totality from disciplinary to control society. While being fictional, these
novels thus tell us something important about the role of form in relation
to control. Investigating the relation between inside and outside in terms
of allegory thereby enables a discussion of the relation between form and
the question of the inside and outside in control society. Before going into
the analyses of the texts in more detail, I will outline some of the theoretical investments in how the political employment of space has developed
during the modern period.

SPATIAL PREOCCUPATIONS

Space, as Henri Lefebvre reminds us, is not a neutral area in which time is played out, but needs to be recognised as a field on which all aspects of social practice are projected (Lefebvre 1991, 8). In addition, space is not only a passive field of projection; it plays an active and instrumental part in any chosen mode of production (Lefebvre 1991, 11). As a result, space is not only a means of production but also a means of control, domination, and power (Lefebvre 1991, 26). Rather than a *res extensa* of the subject, as earlier conceptions of space would have it, 'social space' plays an active political role. The fact that social space is a construct is hidden, Lefebvre argues, by a double illusion. First, there is the illusion of transparency—a sense of innocent and free correspondence between mental activity and it social realisation in space. Second, there is the realistic illusion that presupposes that space holds a substantiality, reality, and truth independent of the subject (Lefebvre 1991, 27–30). Beyond this double illusion, however, we discover that social space is not indistinguishable from mental and physical space. Therefore, the significance of the deployment of space in the construction of subjects and societies cannot be underestimated. The implications of Lefebvre's insistence that space is socially produced include a disappearance of the notion of natural space, that is, a space existing beyond social construction, and a recognition that each society, or rather each mode of production, appropriates space in its own particular way (Lefebvre 1991, 31).

To Lefebvre's theory of the production of space, Jameson ascribes a spatiality unique to the postmodern period. The particular spatiality of postmodernism that Jameson identifies in 1990 'is somehow *more* spatial than everything else'. Although other modes of production too are spatial, postmodernism posits space as 'an existential and cultural dominant, a thematised and foregrounded feature or structural principle' (Jameson 1991, 365). This is a spatiality characterised by fragmentation, confusion, and dislocation. It is a space that involves a turning from modernist experiments and investigations into the relation between temporality and subjectivity, between past and future, between history and the new to interrogations of the chaotic distribution of life in the present—a flattening of time. 'Postmodernism', Jameson famously suggests, 'is what you have when the modernisation process is complete and nature is gone for good' (Jameson 1991, ix). In this sense, the spatiality of postmodernism may be understood as the complete victory of social space—the abandonment of the illusions of transparency and realism that have hidden the fact that space is always socially constructed. Along with the disappearance of illusions of transparency and realism, the notion of an outside to the cultural, the social, and the political also has to be abandoned. The specific philosophical problem of whether the disappearance of such an outside is a specifically postmodern problem or if it is a permanent ontological condition—so, for example, whether it is meaningful to imagine, as do Lefebvre and Jameson, a nature that has disappeared as part of a historical development of modernisation or if this cultural condition is but a more transparent configuration of an ahistorical state of things—constitutes a question of its own. For now, let us settle for the fact that both in terms of culture and politics, historical, political, and cultural developments in the past decades have entailed new approaches to, and new constructions of, space that rely on an awareness and deployment of an all-encompassing logic.

If our contemporary cultural and political condition is created out of a redistribution of biopower from a distribution in space and ordering in time typical of disciplinary society to continuous, flexible, and all-encompassing modes of control, as we have seen via Michel Foucault and Gilles Deleuze, then the division of space in terms of an outside and an inside—and here, a simple example is the difference between information controlled by institutions and information distributed through networks—is necessarily reconfigured. As the political system adapts to a flexible employment and an all-inclusive construction of space, new political and geographical constructions of space emerge. These new dimensions are profoundly related to a technologisation and digitalisation that force us to rethink the function of spatial coordinates. For Jameson, as we have seen, the reappearance of allegory in postmodernity is related to such new geopolitical dimensions of space. As the very conditions of possibility of representability are challenged by what has essentially become an unoverviewable system, the allegorical becomes an 'aesthetic technology' that enables 'a particular spatial or narrative model of the social totality' (Jameson 1992, 5). Thus, for Jameson, 'space, representability, allegory' become useful theoretical and analytic tools for exploring films from 'that new world-systemic moment' of postmodernity or late capitalism in order to unearth the 'geopolitical unconscious' (Jameson 1992, 5). In other words, exploring the allegorical imperative in a contemporary context provides the means to understand how we are understanding, to map how we are mapping, contemporary political configurations. My ambition in this chapter is not to scan 'the world system itself' for this understanding, nor to offer arguments for a larger geopolitical unconscious. Rather, I scan a limited literary material that, in its historical development, provides useful tools to discuss the relation between allegory as an aesthetic technology and the models of social totality that it enables in the face of the political development of control society in the past decades.

CELEBRATING RUINS: *THE DROWNED WORLD,* *THE DROUGHT, THE CRYSTAL WORLD*

According to the image of a reversed deconstruction of a building that opened this chapter, Ballard's first set of novels would be the equivalent of the ruins at the beginning of the sequence. The construction has fallen apart, and it takes us a while to imagine what it might once have looked like. The simile of the sequence works quite well here because in these novels we do, in one sense, begin at the end, learning little about what has come before. The ruins Ballard depicts, rather than evoking nostalgia or mourning, come with a sense of estrangement as if it is not only the constructions that have crumbled but also our conceptions of the societies they enabled. The lack of nostalgia brings with it a lack of representative distance. The ruins refuse to stand as representations of lost worlds and instead pull us into new ones where meaning has not yet sedimented into permanent, or even semipermanent representations. This first set of novels—*The Drowned World, The Drought,* and *The Crystal World*—all engage with a postapocalyptic topography inspired by Surrealist aesthetics. The novels are characterised by painterly and dreamy descriptions that evoke the eerie beauty of new landscapes. These are the landscapes that appear once the ice caps have melted or the world has been flooded or when radioactive waste has destroyed the water and initiated a global drought. Ballard's postapocalyptic novels differ from many literary and cinematic texts about climate change. As Jonathan S. Taylor notes, Ballard's post-apocalyptic novels do not rely on the heroic survival of protagonists in the face of global disaster but depict, rather, characters accepting and adopting the new conditions even when they are lethal (Taylor 2002, 96). There is no clear separation between subject and external space and thus no polarised conflict between them. Rather, the inside and the outside are shown to be inextricable from each other.

Ballard's work is also, as W. Warren Wagar notes, 'fundamentally topographic'. Throughout his engagement with space, Wagar suggests, Ballard shows how we are conditioned by the external world and also how it is necessary to engage with and provoke this exteriority as the only means to move forward. Wagar also notes Ballard's relative lack of interest in the nuances of characters and interpersonal relations compared to his continuous interest in space (Wagar 1991, 53). Comparing him to a modernist writer like Henry James, Wagar stresses the limited attention to details of psychic and emotional set-up in Ballard's characters. A different way of putting this would be to recognise that Ballard's characters reflect a conception of selfhood that differs from James's modernist conception of consciousness and psychology. Even if James was certainly sensitive to the effects of artificial conventions and contexts on the individual, Ballard's interest in landscapes and the way they mirror or even help shape and organise the soul, as Wagar puts it, points to an understanding of agency that is less linked to ideas of internal human subjectivity and more to the specifics of the space through which it emerges.

The inextricability of inside and outside becomes evident from the very beginning of each of these first novels. They all open with distinctive and slightly defamiliarising descriptions of space. As *The Drowned World* opens, its protagonist stands on his balcony watching the sun, 'no longer a well-defined sphere, but a wide expanding eclipse that fanned out across the eastern horizon like a colossal fire ball' rise 'behind the dense groves of giant gymnosperms crowding over the roofs of the abandoned apartment stores' (*Drowned* 7). In the opening of *The Drought*, the protagonist wakes to find his houseboat beached, the 'slopes of mud, covered with the bodies of dead birds and fish, stretched before him like the shores of a dream' (*Drought* 4). *The Crystal World* begins as the main character enters the jungle on a river surprisingly black in contrast to the buildings on its sides, which gleam 'across the dark swells with a spectral brightness, as if lit less by solar light than by some interior lantern, like the pavilion of an abandoned necropolis' (*Crystal* 11). Opening his 'disaster novels' with such potent descriptions of space, Ballard not only provides the beginning of a setting for each novel—although the visual richness of these descriptions may remind the reader of establishing shots in films. Also, what makes them symptomatic of each of the novels as a whole is the way in which the verbal descriptions testify to an intense focus on the relation between postapocalyptic landscapes and the characters that emerge with them. If each of these first pages is suggestive of worlds gone awry, they all begin to indicate that there is something not quite stable in the relation between inside and outside. In the first book, the sun seems to escape its usual form and the gymnosperms, themselves indicative of a specific relation between inside and outside in their distinct trait of carrying their seed on the outside rather than within a flower, are taking over the apartment stores. In the second, the slopes of mud and fish are like the shores of dreams, and in the third, crystallised buildings seem to glow from inside out. Forms, shapes, buildings, and dreamscapes no longer seem to function to separate space and create borders between inside and outside. The landscapes and their climates are going through immense changes, but instead of placing his characters as human subjects fighting or struggling to escape from these cataclysms, worlds and selves transform together. As Jameson puts it, speaking of heat specifically in Ballard's novels, there is 'a kind of dissolution of the body into the outside world, a loss of that clean separation from clothes and external objects that gives you your autonomy and allows you to move about freely, a sense of increasing contamination and stickiness in the contact between your physical organism and the surfaces around it' (Jameson 2007, 268).

By this same token, the characters are not positioned as human heroes fighting a battle with nonhuman nature. Rather, they are increasingly stripped of the frameworks of meaning that would construct them as distinctly human. With the ruins of the human constructed societies come the ruins of representation and life emerges afresh. This way, Catherine in *The Drought* invites Ransom to help her 'teach the lions to hunt in packs' (*Drought* 65) as if all potential modes of being are up for grabs. In *The Crystal World*, distinctions between human, animal, and mineral diffuse as '[T]he two had become merged, the man himself, half-white and half-black, fusing with the dark jeweled beast. Their outlines were still visible as they effloresced through each other's tissues' (*Crystal* 166). The supposedly human need to master both the earth and its meaning is de-emphasised. While the characters do fight for their physical survival, they do not seem particularly attached to human modes of understanding. Instead, the fragments of society are taken at face value—as building blocks without assembly instructions.

Ballard's work can be seen to engage with constructions of meaning not just in terms of the human but also in terms of a particularly Western frame of reference. His long-standing interest in the relation between inside and outside space also speaks to a sensibility to the historicopolitical configuration of space as such. His work thereby comes to evoke a postcolonial perspective. Ballard, Jameson suggests, projects the historic collapse of the British Empire outward 'into some immense cosmic deceleration of the universe itself as well as of its molecular building blocks' (Jameson 2007, 269). In this context, the dissolution of the borders between self and space that these novels describe may be seen as the dissolution of a distinct separation between the colonial self and its Other. This is not a return of the Other as a threat to an otherwise stable self so much as a questioning of the very possibility of insisting on such a distinction. As Dennis Walder notes, Ballard's interest in inner space is not reflective of a stable and authentic selfhood built on a clearly identifiable history but rather of a collage of different and unstable perspectives, some of which need cleansing, such as the 'imperial and colonial delusions' lingering in the British major history (Walder 2011, 143). It is tempting, therefore, to read the deaths of the protagonists at the end of each of these early novels as fictive orchestrations of the end of colonial subjectivity. Compared to a central narrative of colonialism such as Joseph Conrad's *Heart of Darkness*, this is not the horror of spaces refusing to be fully conquered. Rather, the characters submerge themselves in the waters and crystals, becoming part of spatial conditions they never intended to conquer. It is the end of an era of mastery.

Ballard's surrealist imagination has been identified as a means of mobilising something more constructive in the face of the subjective fragmentation and wordly disintegration that he also portrays. This also becomes a way for critics such as Jeanette Baxter to question the common reading of his work as nihilistic and ahistorical and of Ballard himself as a voyeur mapping the destruction of the world 'with grim satisfaction' (Baxter 2009, 9). Baxter points back to Ballard's own expressed interest in surrealist techniques and their usefulness in the creation of constructive tools for dealing with a postwar world in which real and fiction is blurred (Baxter 2009, 4). Surrealist techniques provide the means to confront technological developments, consumer landscapes, and alienation. They also provide the possibility of exploring the relation between inside and outside as being neither nihilistic nor passive. 'The leading surrealists', Lefebvre notes, 'sought to decode inner space and illuminate the nature of the transition from this subjective space to the material realm of the body and the outside world, and thence to social life' (Lefebvre 1991, 18). I would suggest that while Ballard clearly adopts a surrealist imagination, as Baxter argues, his focus is also reversed. What he tends to depict is the transition or at least the interdependent relation between the material realm of the outside world and subjective spaces. Indeed, he states himself that he makes use of the fictive transformation of landscapes to reflect but also to 'marry' them with the internal transformations of the characters (Pringle, cited in Taylor [2002, 96]). While Ballard may thus share the postmodern disillusionment with the idea of a stable subject, he recuperates a surrealist engagement with the relation between self and space to offer alternative ways in which subjectivity can be modulated.

A discussion of the role of the construction of meaning in Ballard's early texts is thus inevitably colored by the surrealist expression with which they engage. Not only must allegorical readings of such expression take into account the particular ways in which reality tended to be configured in the Surrealist movement; also, the Romantic heritage that the Surrealists nurtured points towards a sense of unity of meaning that is better discussed in terms of the symbol. In marrying a Romantic notion of unity with a repudiation and resistance of modern capitalism, the Surrealist conception of totality is one that relies largely on the possibility and mobilisation of unity as a mode of resistance against the alienating effects of capitalist production. In other words, totality is conceived of as an open and essentially positive potential that would counteract the fragmentation of modernity. For this to be possible, however, it is necessary to break with any conceptions of meaning that separate it from being itself. As Benjamin puts it, André Breton was intent on 'breaking with a praxis that presents the public with the literary precipitate of a certain form of existence while withholding that existence itself'. A Surrealist life is worthy as such only when language becomes joyful by flows of sounds and images and leaves no crack open for 'for the penny-in-the-slot called 'meaning'' (Benjamin 1978, 177). It is also necessary to break with a conception of totality relying on Hegelian dialectics that continues to rely on contradiction. As Martin Jay notes, in the place of dialectics and its ultimate synthesis, the Surrealist process of totalisation relies on the emergence of a new whole by means of 'an unmediated juxtaposition of seemingly discordant elements' (Jay 1984, 286–87). As a weapon against alienation and reification, the clashing of forms is intended to disrupt bourgeois consciousness (Jay 1984, 287).

Even as they are, can, and have been read as dystopic depictions of futures shaped by climate change and environmental destruction and even as they can thus be seen to comment on the social and the political, the allegorical impulse, if indeed there is one in these novels, is not easily read in terms of the postmodern allegories that Jameson theorises. Rather than an employment of allegory as a means of attempting to grasp global capitalism—an attempt that, as we will see, becomes increasingly present in Ballard's later works—these early texts point towards an open-ended surrealist unity between the characters and their surroundings. The self that merges with space in these novels is not one that loses its access to meaningful existence in the ruins of totality caused by the alienating effects of modern life. Rather, the self that merges with space becomes part of a surrealist unity of meaning that cojoins the landscapes and topographies with the characters traversing them. Like for the Surrealists, meaning is not sought after in systems external to experience but is seen to emerge with it. This configuration of meaning relies fundamentally on a unity of meaning characteristic of the symbol rather than the allegorical. It seems, then, that even as they flaunt the ruins of society, Ballard's early work resists the allegorical impulse to tie together the fragments of lost unity. To return to the image of a destructed building being gradually reconstructed by reverse playback that opened this chapter, these first novels insist on stopping this playback and thereby invite another spatial as well as temporal arrangement. The fragments are not primarily presented as fragments speaking to past forms but are fragments with potential future expressions. As we see in the next section, however, this Surrealist totality, which resists alienation by celebrating discordant elements, becomes harder for Ballard to maintain as the reversed playback is allowed to continue into the next set of novels and the sociopolitical systems of contemporary society gradually stabilise.

FILLING THE GAPS: *CRASH, CONCRETE ISLAND, HIGH RISE*

Where the first set of novels opens with the typography of strangely beautiful postapocalyptic worlds, the novels in the next set, *Crash, Concrete Island*, and *High Rise* all open with terrifying descriptions of urban space. *Crash* opens with the death of a man in a rehearsed but misguided car crash intended to fulfill his dream of dying in a crash with Elizabeth Taylor. Instead, the crash kills him and a busload of airline package tourists as his car jumps the rails of the London Airport flyover and plunges through the roof of a bus (*Crash* 1). *Concrete Island* too opens with a crash as the protagonist Robert Maitland loses control of his car. The car then 'veers from side to side across the empty traffic lanes', its tyres leaving black strokes across the white lane markers, and ultimately crashing into the embankment from which he will be incapable of leaving (*Concrete* 7). If the first two make clear their interest in highways and concrete islands on their first pages, *High Rise* immediately reveals its spatial conditions as it opens with a man sitting on his balcony of his apartment building that contains 'forty floors and thousand apartments, its supermarket and swimming-pools, bank and junior-school' (*High* 13). While Ballard clearly continues to focus on landscapes and their relation to the individuals submerged in them, this second set thus portrays worlds not of water, heat, or crystals, but of metal, concrete, and technology.

The tensions and struggles emerge, in these novels, through a set of spaces particularly linked to a historical period in which the speedy development of technology and efficient spatiality is seen to fundamentally alter the kinds of subjectivities and agencies possible. Urbanisation seems complete in these worlds. Rather than the open postapocalyptic spaces of the first set of novels, space is here characterised by a dizzying and modern combination of speed and confinement. The lines on the road, the concrete island surrounded by highways, and the apartment buildings that you never have to leave all mark the quite concrete borders of a society that offers increasing efficiency for the citizens at the same time as it imprisons them in this same efficiency. The novels respond to what Jonathan Crary observes as the significant changes urbanism underwent in the late 1960s caused by the transitions in capitalism 'when the rationalization of built space became secondary to problems of speed and the maximization of circulation' (Crary 1986, 159). In this period, the 'antiterritoriality' of capitalism increasingly infringed on the same field that urbanism tried to make into intelligible space. Ballard's characters, it seems, are caught in a tension between the solidification of space—highways, high-rises, and embankments are concrete spaces that they cannot escape—and the intoxicating and uncontrollable speed of the cars and communications that these solid constructs enable. This tension, in other words, is one between the deceleration and acceleration of space.

Whether the new dimensions of space that come with technologisation and digitalisation open up new modes of resisting political developments or whether they primarily serve the interests of corporate capitalism, multinational trading, and the spectacle of consumerism is theorised in Marshall McLuhan's contradictory legacy. While it is relatively unproblematic to inherit McLuhan's essential claim regarding the relevance of communication technologies to our cognitive perception, his techno-optimistic claims about the freedom created by new technologies are controversial. McLuhan, as Gary Genosko shows, has come to be identified both with the development of business in accordance with the new possibilities of mass media—'the spectacle's first apologist' as Guy Debord calls him—and with resistance to the way consumer society has multiplied by means of these same possibilities (Genosko 1999, 9–11). Genosko shows how McLuhan's writing on the effect of increasing speed on social relations has been of importance to both Paul Virilio and to Baudrillard. Thus, for example, the latter have both been influenced by McLuhan's argument that the increasing speed enabled by developments in technologisation and communication causes an 'instant implosion and an interfusion of space and function' that profoundly alter the nature of social relations and capitalist conditions (McLuhan 1964, 93; Genosko 1999, 96).

As 'masters of implosion', as Genosko calls them, Virilio and Baudrillard are inheritors of McLuhan while also differing in their reading of how these new spatial conditions should be understood. Picking up on McLuhan's conception of speed, Virilio argues that place is supplanted by speed—a chronopolitics rather than a geopolitics. While McLuhan largely sees new possibilities of contact in the development of speed, however, Virilio argues that space collapses in the face of the increasing instantaneity and continuity of communication. For him, this collapse destroys the field of action causing profound inertia (Genosko 1999, 95–97). Baudrillard—a 'main carrier' of the McLuhan heritage, as Genosko puts it—also employs McLuhan's theories of implosion, but he translates McLuhan's more optimistic views of the positive potentials of communication into a more cynical conception of how mass media and technologisation undermine the social. For Baudrillard, this results in a 'renunciation of political intelligence and rational choice, the loss of interest in self-constitution, self-understanding, productive citizenship and social responsibility' (Genosko 1999, 95). As Genosko summarises, McLuhan's conception of the positive and expansive effects of information flows on interaction and connection is complicated, for Baudrillard, by a disbelief in the existence of shared codes across cultures (Genosko 1999, 121). In other words, then, while McLuhan believes in the positive effects of the expansive and inclusive potential of mass communication, Baudrillard not only questions the possibility of such inclusiveness but also finds that the expansive elements undermine rather than generate energy. Space does not expand but implode. Rather than an expansion reaching out to the outside, the outside is infolded to the point where all becomes simulacra.

Ballard's middle novels reflect these ambivalent attitudes towards the configurations of speed and space in late capitalism. On the one hand, speed itself is foregrounded as an accelerating movement in space—the speed of cars and highways. On the other hand, these novels depict the first signs of the inertia that follow in the wake of this same acceleration. The sense that there is nowhere to go is clearly foregrounded by the protagonist in *Concrete Island* who is unable and increasingly unwilling to leave the concrete island on which he is stranded. The way all needs and desires are built into housing in *High Rise* constitutes another central example. While these novels are frequently read in terms of the dissolution of subjectivity and self through the gradual disappearance of reality and the increasingly all-encompassing nature of society, it has also been suggested that Ballard does more than simply record these developments. Taylor argues, for example, that Ballard's *Crash* offers a social critique of the effects of technological change and socially constructed environments on the individual (Taylor 2002, 99). I would like to suggest, more specifically, that Ballard's ambivalent configuration of space reflects a key modulation of biopolitics in the transition between disciplinary and control society.

In the hierarchal modulations of the disciplinary society that Foucault outlines, power is enforced via the enclosed spaces and molds of institutions: schools, hospitals, prisons. 'In the first instance', he writes in *Discipline and Punish*, 'discipline proceeds from the distribution of individuals in space' (Foucault 1995, 141). Outlining the development of the distinct power structures of the sovereign to the distribution of power through disciplinary institutions to the increasingly governmental tactics of these institutions, Foucault also traces increasingly distributed but nonetheless ultimately identifiable and localisable modes of biopower. Disciplinary society relies on its own specific techniques of space: enclosure, location (or partitioning), and the functionality of specific sites (Foucault 1995, 141–44). As capitalist structures come to override all other principles, however, the influence of disciplinary models and governmentality seems to weaken. In control society, Deleuze suggests, the factory is replaced by the corporation, and minted money in a vault is replaced by floating exchange rates (Deleuze 1992, 4–5). If we imagine the walls of an institution as emblematic of the borders that localise power and in relation to which identity and agency can be negotiated, the redistribution of power entails that these walls have been exploded and multiplied. In disciplinary society, Deleuze notes through Foucault, the individual is passed from one closed environment to the other—the family, the school, the factory. In control society, this molding of the individual is replaced by the constant modulations that permeate society as a whole (Deleuze 1992, 3–4). The borders of control society are thus no longer best compared with the walls of institutions but rather with a distributed and continuously shifting order of codes and passwords. As the biopolitical is less linked to specific governmental apparatuses and more to the modulations of information and capital, the borders are reconfigured and spatial control comes to be distributed horizontally rather than vertically. As power is distributed throughout the spatial field rather than centralised through institutions, it becomes harder to identify positions outside the system.

This lack of an outside constitutes one of the main reasons why Mark Fisher finds it necessary to supplant Jameson's conception of postmodernism with the term 'capitalist realism'. In the late 1990s, it is still possible for Michael Hardt to elaborate on Deleuze's brief essay on control society by expanding on its relation to a Jamesonian postmodernism (Hardt 1998, 141). Fisher's term, however, while having much in common with postmodernism as Jameson theorises it, also emphasises how the development since the 1980s context in which Jameson's conception was first articulated has entailed a crucial difference exactly in its conception of and relation to the outside. Back then, Fisher points out, there were, at least by name, still alternative political systems to capitalism in place, an outside, if you will, to the capitalist system. The term 'capitalist realism' captures the all-inclusive capitalism that has emerged since then. It is 'realism' because it is exhaustive. Even in the face of the rapidly disappearing outside indicated by a cultural logic based on the pastiche, repetition, and surface that Jameson identified, our current state, Fisher argues, mirrors 'a deeper, far more pervasive, sense of exhaustion, of cultural and political sterility' (Fisher 2009, 7).

Ballard's middle set of novels is written in the mid-1970s and as such, in a period that, in the midst of technological development, is still able to see an outside 'if only by name'. As the concrete island comes to stand for the last possible gap in the increasingly all-devouring efficiency of capitalist production, the absurd delimitation of this space serves largely to underline the disappearance of such alternatives. This ambivalence foregrounds Virilio's description of a society that is increasingly built on a logic, or logistics, where '*everything arrives without any need to depart*' (Virilio 1999, 20). The fact that cars play an important part in both *Crash* and *Concrete Island* is indicative of this tension, or in-between stage, characterised by what Virilio understands as the '*vehicle mutation*' that will take us from 'unbridled nomadism to the definite inertia or sedentariness of whole societies' (Virilio 1999, 20). The automotive vehicle has not yet been outrun by the audiovisual vehicle, as Virilio would put it, and therefore movement in space is still important. However, and as the purposeful crashes in *Crash* seem to indicate, going somewhere in particular is of less value. Virilio's 'polar inertia' is gradually setting in. 'The car', as Baudrillard puts it is his essay on *Crash*, 'is not the appendix of a domestic, immobile universe, there are no more private and domestic universes, only figures of incessant circulation' (Baudrillard and Evans 1991, 314). The erasure of any clear boundaries between interior and exterior space that we saw already in the earlier novels takes on a different meaning here. Here, the infolding of exteriority is not characterised by a postapocalyptic destruction of human-made spaces or by the disintegration of a postcolonial claim to a conquerable outside. Rather, this infolding is characterised by the impact of technological development on the construction of space and the individuals emerging with it. The prospect is rather bleak. In the reversed playback of my central metaphor of a gradually reconstructing building, Ballard's middle period depicts a society that is progressively building itself into capitalist perfection. It is not yet complete, but finding the gaps is becoming increasingly difficult.

At the same time, the allegorical imperative is strengthened. There is an urgent need to make sense of space in this middle period that is not present in the same way in the earlier set of novels. Even if the earlier novels too are intensely spatial, as my reading of them suggests, this spatiality is portrayed as a merging of inside and outside in symbolic unities that escape rather than entangle themselves in preestablished meanings. As I suggested, these earlier texts are not about sense as much as about symbolism. The tensions between inside and outside in the middle novels, on the other hand, are deeply implicated in structures of human-made meaning. The result, it seems, is a sense of meaninglessness and alienation. In this context, allegory becomes a viable way of responding to the fragments of lost totalities in the Benjaminian sense as well as to the new totalities of the global world in the Jamesonian sense. The societies that Ballard portrays here seem to be torn between two different forms of totality—that ideal one infused with a sense of unity, belonging, and meaning and that modern society has undermined, and the totality of late capitalism that reunites all the fragments by means of its own logic. Regardless of how we read it, allegory has become indispensable in a way in which it previously was not. When Robert Maitland is unable to cross the road and thus to leave the concrete island on which he is forever stuck, he is also our modern-day version of Bunyan's allegorical Christian. He is an everyman on a mission to reconnect with the outside, a mission that, in line with its postmodern context, will forever be aborted. In other words, the anxieties of political and technological developments are directly reflected in physical spaces, physical spaces that immediately offer themselves up to allegorical readings.

For Baudrillard, Ballard's work constitutes an excellent description of the hyperreality that the former theorises in his early work.[2] Fully aware that Ballard himself understands his own work differently, Baudrillard reads *Crash* as at least partially intended as a warning against the 'brutal, erotic, and overlit' margins of the developments of technology. He also reads it, however, as one of the first novels to describe hyperreality beyond value judgement or moral message (Baudrillard and Evans 1991, 319). One effect of hyperreality, according to Baudrillard, is the disappearance of perspectival and panoptic vision. We can no longer assume a point of perspective from which the gaze emanates and from which surveillance is maintained—a transparency of control. Instead we find ourselves in a space where it becomes impossible to determine 'one instance of the model, of power, of the gaze, of the medium itself, because *you* are always already on the other side'. There is no determining what is the real and what is the model and to distinguish between who is watched and who is watching as space becomes simulacra (Baudrillard 1994, 29). As 'the first great novel of the universe of simulation', Ballard's *Crash* shows us the world 'with which we will all now be concerned' (Baudrillard 1994, 119). I look more closely at the changing role of vision in control society in chapter 5, but for now, we can establish that here, the merging of inside and outside space, of technologies and bodies, is, perhaps unsurprisingly, read as symptoms of the postmodern world.

Another example of how the configuration of space is positioned as both a literal and an allegorical representation of the contemporary world can be found in Laura Colombino's reading of *Concrete Island*. She suggests that while Ballard engages with the way in which the subject is integrated into the capitalist economy, he not only depicts this process but also mocks it (Colombino 2006, 616). While the concrete imprisonment of the protagonist on a concrete island certainly reflects the inescapability of the *'architectural armature'* of modern society, there is also a sense in which the unclaimed space of the concrete island constitutes a rupture within capitalist space, a 'crevice' in the urban texture that enables the ungovernability of space, the body, and individual experience to reemerge (Colombino 2006, 617). Even here, though, Ballard does not escape the association to Baudrillard, albeit a Baudrillard of a slightly more hopeful note. Colombino finds *Concrete Island* closely resembling a late admission of Baudrillard's that there may be 'secret images' within the 'smoothly visible', that is, spaces radically other and that offer alternative perceptions (Colombino 2006, 617). Possibly a trace of his affinities with the Situationist movement, a link that we explore further below, the idea is that the capitalist construction of abstract space is not as seamless as it appears. Baudrillard's recognition of potential gaps means recognition, also, of potential resistance. In the face of Ballard's merciless depictions of the concrete conditions of an emerging consumer and control society in this middle set of novels, it would thus be possible to find not only disabling forces but also enabling moments of resistance.

As Baudrillard's and Colombino's readings indicate, Ballard's middle set of novels engages directly with contemporary concerns in a different way from the earlier set. The earlier set also addresses contemporary anxieties, such as concern for environmental change and the changing postcolonial landscape, but as I have tried to show, Ballard seems to resists the temptation to address these issues by means of allegory. This is also why these early novels, while clearly dystopic in some senses of the word, to some extent escape the nets of meaning and ideologically infused messages that otherwise tend to inform this genre. Totality reemerges here as a posthuman possibility rather than as a political threat. By the time we get to Ballard's second set, however, his engagement with urbanisation and technologisation on the level of content seems to call for a formal engagement with allegory. The spatial conditions of the postmodern urban landscape seem to come with an inevitable destruction of normative unity and the threat of a totality of a more menacing kind. In the process of identifying spatial gaps in this increasingly all-encompassing capitalist logic, relations in space inevitably come to carry a signifying relation to society as a whole. Watch the building blocks of the ruin as they reattach themselves to each other.

COMING INTO ALLEGORY: *COCAINE NIGHTS, SUPER-CANNES, MILLENNIUM PEOPLE, KINGDOM COME*

When Wagar found Ballard's work 'fundamentally topographic' in the early 1990s, the last set of novels, *Cocaine Nights, Super-Cannes, Millennium People,* and *Kingdom Come,* had not yet been published. The topographics of surrealist postapocalyptic worlds in the first set and the landscapes of technologised alienation in the second develop, in the third set of novels, into geographies of apparent perfection. These later novels, as Andrzej Gasiorek notes, mark a shift from the collapse of social systems explored in Ballard's earlier texts to a depiction of the implications of the success of social systems (Gasiorek 2005, 20). This is a completely different type of dystopia—the nightmare of the ultimate success of capitalism, or, as Baxter puts it, 'the alliance of neo-fascism and global capitalism across a shifting contemporary Europe' (Baxter 2012, 386). Instead of taking place in dystopian wastelands, these later novels are set in spaces in which all human needs, as Gasiorek puts it, 'have been anticipated, and the entire social mechanism has been calibrated to minimize friction and disturbance' (Gasiorek 2005, 21).

As in the two other sets of novels, the first page of each of these last novels is indicative of the relation between space and agency that will come to be played out in each of them. In the first lines of *Cocaine Nights,* the protagonist declares that crossing frontiers is his profession. He presents an ambivalence between on the one hand, the way the 'strips of no man's land between the checkpoints always seem such zones of promise', and on the other, how the custom's checking his luggage makes him feel like they are 'trying to unpack my mind and reveal a contraband of forbidden dreams and memories' (*Cocaine* 9). The protagonist in *Super-Cannes* enters the 'intelligent city' of the Eden-Olympia business park and the 'waiting madness, like a state of undeclared war, [that] haunted the office buildings' (*Super* 3). In *Millennium People,* we first find the protagonist waiting like 'a visitor to an abandoned film set' outside the middle-class Chelsea Marina listening to a 'reassuring medley of car stereos and ambulance sirens' (*Millennium* 3). 'The suburbs', *Kingdom Come* opens, 'dream of violence. Asleep in their drowsy villas, sheltered by benevolent shopping malls, they wait patiently for the nightmares that will wake them into a more passionate world' (*Kingdom* 3). These openings, and each of the books as a whole, share with the others a translation between internal and external space. The rummaging through luggage that is like rummaging through dreams, the office buildings that seem to exude madness, the reality that feels more like a film set, and the villas that are in a state of drowsiness all indicate that while the spatial conditions have changed yet again in this last set of novels, the translation between inside and outside remains key in Ballard's work.

In contrast to the second set of novels in which the intersection of speed and space was central, these last four novels portray a Western world in which intense progress has, seemingly paradoxically, been translated into a pacifying stagnation. When the middle set of novels portrays how the speed of technological evolution builds the characters into the spatial conditions that enable such speed, there is still a sense of a border in relation to which characters can act and identify themselves. The concrete island in the novel with that name is emblematic: it might not be possible to cross the border, but it still exists there. As such, it marks a line in relation to which the protagonist can build his identity and determine his mode of action. In this last set of novels, however, the borders have become invisible, which results in a sense of profound inertia. The paradoxical tendency towards polar inertia in the face of the speeding up of communication and movement in the middle set of novels is completed in the last set as speed has maximised and rendered movement redundant. The worlds that the characters inhabit seem to have stopped revolving at the same time as groundbreaking science is conducted and immense riches are accumulated. Each of the novels discloses a similar story—characters who are benumbed by comforts and whose needs are preempted by the system to the point where movement has become superfluous. Again and again, Ballard pursues what seems to be a determination to explore angles on and implications of the 'suburbanization of the soul' that 'has overrun our planet like the plague' (*Super-Cannes* 263). The settings of the dystopian landscapes of the disaster novels and the urban nightmares of the middle books have been supplanted here by the smooth spaces of contemporary control society.

What these novels portray with some clarity is a world in which the fragmentation and heterogeneity associated with postmodernity and late capitalism, and which the middle set of novels depicts so powerfully, is being patched up by the mechanisms of an even later capitalism. In the later capitalist system portrayed here, biopolitics is increasingly unhampered by institutions and stable meanings and has become a free floating but intrinsic part of every element of society as well as of every dimension of the individual. The concrete island has been replaced by comfortable 'capsules' for the rich in which the shadows on the walls become a 'substitute for thought' (*Cocaine* 215). The association of Ballard's work with Baudrillardian dystopian simulacra emerged, as we have seen, with his middle set of novels. These convey an anxiety sparked by the speed with which the construction of urban space seems to produce a social and political totality and ensue in a deep-seated sense of alienation. Arguably, the last set of novels portrays an intensification of these kinds of spaces. If we want to continue reading Ballard through Baudrillard, we may say with the latter that they portray how 'we are accelerating in empty space' (Baudrillard 2005, 104). All 'of the ends of liberation (of production, progress, revolution) are already behind us', argues Baudrillard. 'What we are haunted by, obsessed with, is the anticipation of every result, the availability of every sign, every form, every desire, since everything is already liberated' (Baudrillard 2005, 104).

The sense of availability of every sign, form and desire that emerges as 'everything is already liberated' is underscored in Ballard's last novels. As compared to the middle texts, where this liberation causes confusion and alienation, the later texts point towards an unmooring of meaning from content to the point where it becomes directly coupled up to the flow of capital. What characterises these novels is not confusion and alienation so much as complete abandon. Instead of a mourning of a lost totality, we can discern a yielding to a new sense of totality. When Jameson suggests that allegory reappears in postmodernity as a means of restoring continuity to heterogeneous instants, as we have discussed earlier, this is a response to a world that, to refer to a worn but central conceit of postmodernity, has lost the grand narratives that kept the world together. Thus allegory becomes the new narrative in a sense—not grand maybe, but still attempting to be so—a secular attempt at unifying experience. Ballard's last set of novels could be seen to depict the reemergence of a very particular and distinctly unitary narrative, one in which capitalist production no longer needs to take the route via the factory but feeds straight into being itself. This narrative, as it emerges here, is coextensive with a new sense of biopolitical totality—one that does not need beliefs, convictions, or institutions but that reproduces itself automatically by means of the all-encompassing control systems of the contemporary Western world.

In the place of disciplining institutions and factories, Ballard locates a set of differing modes of control and immaterial production. In each of the texts, the organisation of space underlines an interlinked set of implications of what appears as a set of political time-space configurations based on class. In this new biopolitical context, the more uniform spaces of factories and institutions are transformed into a more distributed political use of space. As Hardt and Antonio Negri note, in the contemporary West, labour is not necessarily executed at the assembly line but is constituted by all activities perpetuating capitalist production—culture, shopping, leisure (Hardt and Negri 2000, 402). In this light, Ballard's novels and their focus on different classes provide a prism in which to explore and rethink the distribution and nature of political space in control society. Each of the late novels presents an organisation of modern-day labour in which different classes of society are hooked up to the totality of control. Where *Cocaine Nights* explores the rich, *Super-Cannes* explores the elite in terms of education and science. In *Millennium People*, it is the comfortable middle class that is put to the test, and *Kingdom Come* portrays the negotiations of space by the working class. I have already discussed elsewhere how these novels stage the relation between the mechanisation of life and the deadening temporality that comes with it through a set of class-based contemporary time-space configurations. There, I argued that this focus on class provides an interesting prism in the light of recent theorisations of temporality and production in control society.[3] Here, I would like to bring a stronger focus to how the changing nature of work from the streamlining effectiveness of linear time of the factory to a more distributed immaterial labour affects the production of space.

Ballard's targeting of different social groups, or classes, is mirrored in the spatial setting. In different ways, these social groups all live in cages of perfect life, designed to absolve them not just from work or other exterior demands but also from agency itself. In the luxury condos of the rich, the business parks of the educated elite, the housing estate of the middle class, and the shopping malls of the lower-class workers respectively, class appears more than anything as a distinction of physical spaces. While the spatial set-up is thus differentiated on the level of class, all the different spaces promote inertia. Estrella de Mar in *Cocaine Nights* is described as a place of unreality and surface, an 'affectless realm' (*Cocaine* 35) where the miles of white cement erases memory and 'abolishes time' (*Cocaine* 34). Similarly, the nearby Costasol complex builds its inhabitants into 'prisons' disguised as luxury condos designed for people to do nothing (*Cocaine* 220, 213). This is a limbo for those who can afford it, a place where the redundancy of time and movement is literally built into the structure of existence. Space not only serves as a container for passive life but even seems to be endowed with more life than the characters themselves, as the beach furniture is described as waiting 'like the armatures of the human beings that would occupy them that evening' (*Cocaine* 215). If the patient waiting of the beach furniture symbolises the total subsumption of agency into space for the residents of Estrella de Mar and Costasol through the perfection of leisure, the business park in *Super-Cannes*, Eden-Olympia, marks the subordination of bodies to the progression of science through the spatial organisation of home and office. The homes, which are constructed as part of the business park, are 'service stations' for the body 'to be fed and hosed down, and given just enough sexual freedom to sedate itself' (*Super* 17). The significant space, instead, is the offices, which are all glass and titanium, high-tech, the architecture of executive efficiency, the model for 'executive-class prison' (*Super* 133). This distinction between home and office is indicative of the way in which this 'intelligent city' (*Super* 16) completely dominates the people working in it. The design of the park is also the design of the characters.

With a moral order engineered into the system, the characters, like the business park, are beyond leisure, beyond social life, and without any 'emotional trade-offs' that would give them a sense of who they are (*Super* 255). Where agency in *Cocaine Nights* is diffused by the white walls, agency in *Super-Cannes* is subsumed into hyperorganised action. Like the glass and titanium, the aim is so clear that human contingencies are made superfluous. The middle-class characters in *Millennium People*, largely imprisoned by their breeding into docile civic-mindedness (*Millennium* 292), have their docility accommodated and reinforced by the comforts of Jacuzzi bathtubs and upholstered sofas. The enormous aluminum dome of the Metro-Centre, the giant shopping mall in *Kingdom Come*, is described as 'a cathedral of consumerism' that dominates and usurps the surrounding landscape as well as the people (*Kingdom* 15). As one of its critics say, 'we might as well be living inside that ghastly dome. Sometimes, I think we already are, without realizing it' (*Kingdom* 31). The Metro-Centre's complete usurption of its surroundings both in terms of time, space, people, and meaning seems to echo quite directly Baudrillard's description of consumer society:

> Work, leisure, nature, culture, all previously dispersed, separate, and more or less irreducible activities that produced anxiety and complexity in our real life, and in our 'anarchic and archaic' cities, have finally become mixed, massaged, climate controlled, and domesticated into the simple activity of perpetual shopping. (Baudrillard 2001, 38)

In each of the novels, then, space is depicted as a concrete challenge to the agency, freedom, and power of the characters. White concrete condos, glass and titanium business parks, affluent gated communities, and shopping malls are constructed not only to accommodate for but also to contain the rich, the scientists, the middle class, and the workers. As the four novels thus come to depict capitalist society as divided into a set of class-bound spatiotemporal configurations, they, put together, point to a distributed but ultimately all-encompassing system.

Important to note is that one element remains invisible in this system. As immaterial labour has completely engulfed the system of production in these Westerns spheres, the production of material goods—the factory and the discipline—becomes a blatant elsewhere. As we move from novel to novel this elsewhere becomes increasingly apparent in its absence. This way, Ballard's portrayals of contemporary societies come to demand not only an understanding of time and space adjusted to the kinds of 'work' taking place in contemporary Western society. They also suggest that while work and play may be configured differently in different layers of society, they all rely on the fact that the 'work' associated with production of goods is outsourced to the invisible and missing masses. As such, they confirm the way in which the past decades have enforced a new shift in the employment of space also on a global level. On the one hand, David Harvey notes, technological advancements and the shift from a stationary Fordist mode of production to a more flexible accumulation have entailed an increasing collapse of spatial barriers. On the other hand, and seemingly paradoxically, an effect of this collapse is that the significance of space is growing. The lack of fixity in space, Harvey observes, has consequences for the potential power of a continuous working-class community to negotiate its conditions. It also has effects on the capitalist identification and exploitation of the most generative geographical spaces globally (Harvey 1990, 294). As capitalists are growing more, not less, aware of the specific advantages of specific geographical locations, such locations develop an incentive to distinguish themselves in terms of their own potential attraction force on capital (Harvey 1990, 295–56). While it is possible to argue, like critics such as Virilio, that space is disappearing as an effect of mechanical technologies, it is thus also possible to identify ways in which these developments have stimulated a more informed and more instrumentalised awareness of the particularities of different geographical spaces. This development makes it necessary to ask that if the relation between inside and outside is necessarily reconfigured by the changing conditions of the construction of space, as I have suggested earlier, what is the 'other' or the outside in relation to a spatial configuration that 'exploits a wide range of seemingly contingent geographical circumstances, and reconstitutes them as structured internal elements of its own encompassing logic' (Harvey 1990, 294)?

As in Andrew Niccol's *In Time*, which is discussed in the next chapter, the all-encompassing nature of control society, like the disciplinary society before it, is based on a division of space. In this instance, however, the space of linear production does not constitute a key framework for the logic of society but is rather hidden away. Ballard's later novels underline how the division of time is not so much taking place within society or within the individual life but is rather separated spatially by the global and national distribution of work and leisure. While they all reflect specific class-based spatial prisons, what they clearly have in common is that none of them portray the West as a space of production but only as a space of consumption. Or, rather, they illustrate how consumption is the new labour. As such, the linearity of Lefebvre's space of production in modernity is minimised. At the same time, the cyclical nature of what he calls 'lived time' reemerges, not as a universal human cycle but as class-based. As the cyclical reappears in the twenty-first century, Ballard's novels suggest, there are no longer any 'natural' bodies, adjustments to seasons, or acknowledgements of the phases of life and death. Emptied of the premodern cyclical mode as well as of the linear time of factory production, a third temporality emerges that corresponds to the immaterial labour of consumption. While the four books all portray such labour, the differences between them underline that the distinction between hours, days, seasons, activity, and rest is not universal but must be differentiated depending on geopolitical configurations of space and time. The body usurped by sun chairs in *Cocaine Nights* is an irritating inconvenience in *Super-Cannes*. The well-groomed body merging with the bourgeoisie comforts in *Millennium People* is a commodity among others in *Kingdom Come*. What the temporalities of these bodies have in common, however, is that they are fully integrated into their respective spatial order and as such, utterly passive. The problem to be addressed in each novel is the need to revive people, to free them from their specific spatiotemporal prisons. The possibility of opting out has been abolished by the complete colonisation of space. 'We're building prisons all over the world and calling them luxury condos. The amazing thing is that the keys are all on the inside' (*Cocaine* 220).

Especially when read together, the systematic portrayal of the different but interlinked spheres of a late-capitalist Western society in these novels emerges as a powerful totality based on the logic of the all-encompassing logic of control society. The political employment of space on the level of class presents us with a totality in which all levels of society are incorporated into what is ultimately the same logic. At the same time, there seems to be no doubt that the different groups and locations portrayed in each of the novels portray and comment on developments in the contemporary world. Compared to the resistance to allegory suggested in the first set of novels and the ambivalent relation to it in the second set, the perfected spaces of the last set can be read not just as portrayals of the ultimate success of capitalist control but also as a yielding to the inevitability of allegory. This is where, to return once again to the figure of the reversed deconstruction of a building that opened this chapter, the building becomes completed. The fragments are now cemented together so neatly by the allegorical that you would need to look closely to identify the seams. The building is perfected, a capitalist totality is achieved, and the allegorical form reaches its peak. As we recall, however, the very fundament of allegory, at least in its Benjaminian instantiation, depends on the ruin rather than the completion of totality. If unity was complete, there would be no need for the allegorical. And indeed, the totality portrayed in Ballard's novels may be perfected in terms of the system, but as we soon notice, the persistence of the fragment is the threat that the allegorical will consistently try to recuperate.

TOTALITIES, ALLEGORIES, AND REVOLUTIONS

In each of the novels, there is a precarious balance to be struck between efficiency and passivity. The larger system has to make sure that its subjects perform what is expected without disturbance. And yet, the lack of disturbance in these perfected spaces is exactly what threatens to bring them down. The catatonia of dead time in *Cocaine Nights*, the tyranny of the efficiency of linearity in *Super-Cannes*, the well-adjusted everyday life in *Millennium People*, and the consumer torpor in *Kingdom Come* are all portrayed as in different ways causing extreme passivity. But whereas the reasons are different, the novels all provide the same answer to such decay of agency. Rather than lateral movement in space, it is clear that any possible solution to this passivity of comfort must be found internally. Here, we can return to Fisher's note about the shift in capitalism from the process of capturing energies from outside to handling the complete success of this capture and function without an outside. While Baudrillard finds that all true events seem to belong to history and that what is left is but a 'fatal indifference' (Baudrillard 2005, 105), Fisher, as his connection with the CCRU (The Cybernetic Cultures Research Unit) and Accelerationism suggests, sees the nostalgia for an outside to capitalism as a danger. He finds it more enabling to search instead for strategies based on an acceptance of what he, as we have seen, calls capitalist realism. And indeed, Ballard's work is claimed as a precursor of contemporary Accelerationism by Robin Mackay and Armen Avanessian. As they put it in their introduction to *#Accelerate: The Accelerationist Reader*, this Accelerationism insists that 'the only radical political response to capitalism is not to protest, disrupt, or critique, nor to await its demise at the hands of its own contradictions, but to accelerate its uprooting, alienating, decoding, abstractive tendencies' (Mackay and Avanessian 2014, 4).[4] Ballard's last set of novels does portray capitalism as a system that it has become impossible to step outside. Importantly, they also depict how this apparent 'success' is both its strength and its weakness. Without an outside, without transcendence, without challenge, the system may seem safe, but at the same time, it now has to find ways of keeping its energies in circulation internally. The movement that has been built out of space needs to be reinstated.

For this to be possible, Ballard quite overtly evokes an anticapitalist Situationist politics based on orchestrating breaks with the society of the spectacle associated with the 1960s. To see the relevance of this, we must remind ourselves of these politics but also recall how they constituted a direct response to a very particular historicopolitical moment in time. Only a few decades ago, the political construction of space theorised by post-Marxists such as Lefebvre inspired strategies of resistance based on the rupture of politically delimiting spaces. At this point, these delimiting spaces were largely the concrete spaces of cities and institutions. Following upon Lefebvre's understanding of space as a politically configured tool for regulating behaviour, Situationist tactics aimed at disrupting organised space. The intention was to resist the capitalist organisation and colonisation of space and meaning, and the tactics involved approaching the environment in ways that would liberate the desires otherwise repressed by it. The material environment gives rise to particular kinds of behaviour, Debord declares (Debord 2006, 38), and a politics of change is therefore necessarily about unsettling the way we approach the environment. Even if they were later to reject Lefebvre's take on politics, the Situationist group, as Michel Trebitsch notes, found much of their theoretical inspiration in his work and not the least in his theory of moments, which lay the grounds of their theorisation of situations. Lefebvre, they found, provides the means to critique the contemporary world but not the means to make a radical change (Trebitsch 2002, xxiii). 'What you call "moments," we call "situations"', Lefebvre recounts them saying, 'but we're taking it farther than you. You accept as "moments" everything that has occurred in the course of history: love, poetry, thought. We want to create new moments' (Ross 1997, 72).

Like Lefebvre, Situationist theories took the social construction of space to be a central aspect of the capitalist order. *Psychogeography*, the study of how the specificities of the geographical environment affect the moods and behaviour of individuals, became a central aspect in their struggle to grasp the forces of the construction of space and to resist them. Some of the central strategies evoked in this context include the construction of *situations* and the opening up of organised space through *dérive*. A *situation*, as the core activity of this group of 1960s French activists, is the deliberate construction of an event. Intended to clarify desires that are otherwise repressed by functionalism and commerce, the situation accommodates for 'a temporary field of activity favourable to these desires' (Knabb 2006, 49). Such a situation is always transitory and always intertwined with their immediate environment as the actions are 'the product of the décor and of themselves' (Knabb 2006, 49). The larger purpose of a situation is to bring to the surface that which is suppressed and concealed in the society of the spectacle. The spectacle transforms lived experience into representational space and disables the directly lived as it mobilises all energy as part of its own image. But as time and space are approached in a manner different from what is prescribed new possibilities of changing the conditions of being emerge. As the preoccupation with time and space suggests, and as the theoretical indebtedness to Lefebvre explains, Situationist theories see the spectacle as built into the very architecture of society and the environment as promoting certain kinds of behaviour. A politics of change, as we have seen Debord argue, must therefore be about unsettling the way we approach the environment.

The question that Ballard's last set of novels evokes is if such strategies of resistance can still be of use today. Baxter, as we saw earlier, identifies and analyses the Surrealist influence on Ballard's work and she also provides an outline of the Situationist movement as a background to her reading of Ballard's earlier novels. She does not resume this reading in relation to Ballard's later books, however. Such a move is important as it adds some tension to our discussion of totality and allegory as means of analysing contemporary Western politics through its current time-space configurations. In the face of the all-consuming nature of the society of the spectacle that Debord theorises, he and many other of the Situationist movement long continued to believe in the possibility of transcending the spatiotemporal grid of everyday life. Today, however, and as Fisher notes, the tension between *détournement* and recuperation that sparked earlier modes of resistance seems hard to maintain. Although commodification has played an important role in the production of culture also in the twentieth century, the new society in which we live is no longer simply about incorporation but about *precorporation*, that is, about 'the pre-emptive formatting and shaping of desires, aspirations and hopes by capitalist culture' (Fisher 2009, 9). As the political construction of space is shifting from more stable and identifiable units in urban planning to flexible and modulating employments of global space it becomes harder to challenge political constructions by moving differently in space and to encounter the new. Fisher indicates that the period between the 1960s until the present marks a crucial shift. While 1960s and 70s capitalism grappled with the question of how to capture energies from outside, contemporary capitalism grapples rather with the opposite problem— 'having all-too successfully incorporated externality, how can it function without an outside it can colonise and appropriate?' (Fisher 2009, 8). In this light, one may ask if Ballard's novels portray the ultimate incorporation of what were once revolutionary strategies aimed at breaking with capitalist commodity culture. Alternatively, one could ask if they could also be seen to position such strategies as the means of accelerating the internal tendencies of capitalism towards its absolute domination of the sociocultural fields.

When Ballard evokes Situationist tactics in his last novels, he evokes the contrasting kinds of totality theorised by Theodor W. Adorno and Herbert Marcuse, as we saw in chapter 1. Such conceptions of totality are also at the heart of Situationist theory. While the very target of Situationist tactics, at least in their Debordian instantiation, was the totality of the society of the spectacle, the aim of their revolutionary tactics was to break through this spectacle and arrive at the social totality that the former disabled. In other words, Situationist ambitions, while increasingly disillusioned about the possibility of achieving it, retained the idea of a normative totality in the face of the empty totality of spectacular imagery. The tactics of *dérive* and *détournement* were intended, as Sadie Plant puts it, 'to conjure a totality of possible social relations which exceeds and opposes the totality of spectacular relations' (Plant 1992, 3). Reading Ballard's last four novels with these contrasting types of totality in mind helps bringing out the political function of the allegorical in relation to a politics of control. Most likely aware of Situationist activism if not directly associated with it and with joint links to Surrealism and post-Marxism, Ballard seems to agree with the influence of space on the behaviour of its inhabitants and also with the necessity of exploring the possibilities of unsettling space as a mode of resistance. Already in his earlier works, Baxter notes, Ballard reworks the Situationist politics of psychogeography, *détournement*, and created situations and aligns it with the earlier Surrealism as well as the neo-avant-garde (Baxter 2009, 5). The later novels in focus here present a series of situations that, at least on the surface, have a number of things in common with the Situationist model.

Like the Situationist model, the situations constructed in Ballard's texts all have a temporary *'director'*, a few *'direct agents'* living out the situation set for them, and a number of passive *spectators* who are forced into action (Knabb 2006, 50). Like this model, the events orchestrated by Ballard's characters are temporary and like this model, the events are intended to force 'play' back into functionalist society. In each of the novels, a central character puts a number of agents to work to construct events by creating the right ambience and ultimately force others into action. Thus, for example, the denizens of Costasol, like those at Estrella de Mar before it, who are on a passive and complacent journey of 'inward migration' (*Cocaine* 216) are shaken alive by the set of arbitrary and provocative acts staged by Bobby Crawford. By means of petty burglaries and random violence—'anything that breaks the rules' (*Cocaine* 245)— Bobby and his crew force these people into recovering their drive by reminding them that 'time is finite' (*Cocaine* 244). Similarly, the elite in *Super-Cannes* are salvaged by the psychoanalyst Walter Penrose, described on the first page of the novel as an 'amiable Prospero, the psychopomp who steered our darkest dreams towards the daylight' (*Super* 3). In this 'Eden without a snake' (*Super* 258) where the contingent world is an annoyance built out of the system (*Super* 19), the inhabitants start suffering from what is best described exactly as the lack of contingencies. Prescribing psychopathy to the inhabitants of Eden-Olympia, Penrose is convinced that only meaningless violence and gratuitous madness can rescue this super-efficient elite from the malaise of efficiency and help them discover who they are. Thus madness, prescribed in carefully monitored doses, becomes the cure rather than the disease. 'Meaningless violence', as Penrose explains, 'may be the true poetry of the new millennium' (*Super* 262). The acts that Penrose prescribes—physical violence typically directed at arbitrary people outside the business park, robbery, drug dealing—seem to have no other purpose than to keep the perpetrators sane and they are carefully monitored, 'like a vitamin shot or an antibiotic' (*Super* 259).

But if these staged events have a number of similarities with the idea of the creation of 'situations', what makes them radically different is not just the violent cynicism of the events themselves but also, more fundamentally, their underlying purpose. If the Situationist idea is to intervene in the predominant ruling forces of commercialism and commodification and their 'situations' are part of a strategy to challenge the totality of the spectacle, the objectives behind the meaningless acts in Ballard's novels speak to different agendas. In the first two novels, *Cocaine Nights* and *Super-Cannes*, these acts work not to upset but rather to keep the systems going, although with slightly differing articulated purposes. Bobby Crawford yearns to bring people back to life (*Cocaine* 219) and wants to make people feel again (*Cocaine* 246) while Walter Penrose claims to want to rescue people from the malaise of the complete sanity of capitalism. Ultimately, however, they both assist in the perpetuation of the system they seemingly resist. In *Super-Cannes*, the meaningless acts that Penrose prescribes are not ultimately about challenging the existing system but about supporting it. As the minor issues ailing the executives begin to endanger their efficiency, the willed madness of his organised 'rattisages' proves to be the best medicine. What look like small disruptions within the perfected construction of efficient space really constitute ways of maintaining it. Missing out on what emerges as inconvenient but ultimately necessary 'emotional trade-offs' (*Super* 255), the characters are 'salvaged' by Penrose's measured psychopathy at the same time as the system is saved by this diversion of the reactions which might otherwise have been turned against it. In both these novels, then, the illegal acts of madness that on surface level seem to stand outside the functionalism of their respective societies are ultimately proven to be part of them. As such, these arbitrary acts are best understood in terms of the total subsumption of energy back into the system. As such, they speak to a Baudrillardian meaninglessness in which any negativity or revolutionary perspective is immediately inscribed and put to work in service of the system. The outside is not truly such but rather an integral part of the system. This is what Benjamin Noys, through Baudrillard, calls 'the murder of alterity', the ultimate nightmare where what is staged is 'both the danger of simulation leading to the internal collapse of a social system and the way in which those who manage the system recognise this risk and "re-inject" alterity' (Noys 2007, n.p.).

Another way of understanding this mechanism is by means of allegory. If we return to the Benjaminian notion of allegory as a patching up of the fragments of lost totalities and juxtapose it to Ballard's evocation of Situationist tactics and the two conceptions of totality associated with it, it becomes possible to discuss two different functions of allegory. We have already looked at the way in which allegory becomes a somewhat nostalgic form in which a desired unity, once expressed through the symbol, is patched up. But the spectacular totality that the Situationist tactics evoke brings out how the means of tying together loose ends that allegory provides may also be employed towards solidifying, or at least strengthening, the all-encompassing nature of control society. As such, it plays on the longing towards unity and normative totality only to strengthen the power of the spectacle itself. As Plant puts it, looking through Situationist eyes,

the spectacle propagates the image of participation and invites everyone to 'join in' with the happy whole whilst at the same time ensuring
that this totality is illusory and unattainable: a strong, appealing, but
empty image. In principle, one can have anything, do anything, be
anything, and go anywhere, but one cannot choose or define the whole
in which these abundant choices are made.

As such, the longing for unity is married to the commodification of pleasure since it 'is only in the context of the advertised whole, the image of
spectacular unity, that the commodity has meaning' (Plant 1992, 25). In
this light, the Situationist tactics in *Cocaine Nights* and *Super-Cannes* are
themselves coopted and put to work for the kind of totality they were
meant to resist.

In *Millennium People* and *Kingdom Come*, the situation is slightly different. Like the first two novels, both portray characters struggling with a
sense of meaninglessness but unlike the first two, they both in different
ways include characters determined to use this meaninglessness to make
a political change. In *Millennium People*, characters who have 'never had
the central heating turned off in their lives' (*Millennium* 67) and whose
bodies 'had been pummeled only by their lovers and osteopaths' (*Millennium* 201) begin to perform meaningless terrorist acts as a reaction
against 'the regurgitated vomit people call consumer society' (*Millennium*
81). The discontents of too-high parking tolls, school fees, maintenance
charges, and mortgages convince these architects, journalists, and academics that they 'know why the miners went on strike' (*Millennium* 80).
Their weapon against meaninglessness is meaninglessness itself, as if
nothing and nothing makes something. But as they declare in words that
clearly echo Breton's description of the 'simplest Surrealist act' of 'dash-
ing down into the street, pistol in hand, and firing blindly, as fast as you
can pull the trigger, into the crowd' (Breton 1972, 125), the search is not
for nothingness but for a new kind of meaning:

> Blow up the Stock Exchange and you're rejecting global capitalism.
> Bomb the Ministry of Defence and you're protesting against war. You
> don't even need to hand out the leaflets. But a truly pointless act of
> violence, shooting at random into a crowd, grips our attention for
> months. The absence of rational motive carries a significance of its own.
> (*Millennium* 194)

The meaningless acts have a distinct purpose, which is to 'shock the
bourgeoisie out of its toilet training' (*Millennium* 138).

As in the earlier novels, *Kingdom Come* portrays willed madness and
'elective psychopathy' as the cure against the dangers of boredom (*Kingdom* 102). Worrying about the immense boredom of a perfected consumer
culture and the fascist state such boredom could ultimately lead to, a
group of people come together determined to keep the boredom under
control by stunts of voluntary madness. Like the art that Baudrillard

finds is ultimately promoting society even as it claims to critique it, this is 'the most efficient way of locking out all genuine alternatives' (Baudrillard 2005, 203). And like the prescribed psychopathy in *Super-Cannes*, this part of the revolt is but 'a *trompe-l'oeil* negativity' (Baudrillard 2005, 203) ultimately aimed to maintain the current order. At the same time, however, there is another group of people in *Kingdom Come* who are 'deliberately re-primitivizing themselves' in desperate attempts to escape the rationality and boredom of consumerism (*Kingdom* 103). If the *trompe-l'oeil* psychopathy is but part of the system of control, there is also an increasing resistance against the Metro-Centre and the all-encompassing consumer society it epitomises that seems more genuine. In the latter case, the irrational comes to stand as a break with and freedom from 'all the cant and bullshit and sales commercials fed to us by politicians, bishops and academics' (*Kingdom* 105). In a Situationist *détournement* style, the slogans, the sales tactics, and even, ultimately, the Metro-Centre itself are claimed and put to use in an attempt to effect a break with the seemingly inevitable obliteration of agency in the face of complete consumerism. Pearson, an ad-man, is put to work repurposing a TV presenter named David Cruise who, like the consumer society he represents, is 'a complete fiction, from his corseted waist to his boyish smile' (*Kingdom* 93) for the cause. People's worship of the Metro-Centre and the consumer culture it stands for is employed as the Metro-Centre is sieged and the people become hostages in its new republic: 'a faith trapped inside its own temple' (*Kingdom* 218).

Ballard's final novels are characterised by spaces where need and necessity no longer fuel people's desire to participate actively in their own lives and where, as a result, not only political agency but even a more basic sense of individual will seems to wither. While these last novels and their problematics are clearly differentiated in terms of social class, they all underline a sense of individual agency becoming superfluous as leisure, progress, culture, and consumerism are built into both time and space. Where the behaviour and agencies of the characters in *Crash, Concrete Island*, and *High Rise* were conditioned by the speed built into the concrete environments of cityscapes and highways, the characters in these last novels are determined by the increasing inertia of postindustrial societies. The characters are not making use of the sunbeds, upholstered sofas, and consumer durables so much as they are subsumed by them. By exploring what it takes to make characters wake up from the coma of well-being, Ballard's novels also explore the chances of recovering agency in extremely class- but non-production-based societies that they project. Together, the novels point to a sustained engagement with a politics determined to explore the possibility of renegotiating the smooth and powerful spatiotemporal conditions of contemporary capitalist society. Reading the meaningless acts constructed in each of his last novels through the prism of Situationist politics underlines the question of whether all exits from what appears to be the all-encompassing system of control of the contemporary West are barred or whether there is still room for rebellious movement within the existing political construction of space.

While the four last novels share the deadening of space, the strategies of unsettling this totality move in opposite directions. The first two— *Cocaine Nights* and *Super-Cannes*—ultimately depict the radical acts of meaninglessness as quite purposeful ways of sustaining the system. As such, they may at best be described as performing a perverted kind of *détournement* of such Situationist acts of rebellion. The revolutionary tactics are coopted by a capitalist world that has discovered in them the ultimate way of maintaining its own system. When the productivity of immaterial and affective labour is put at risk by the inertia that according to both Virilio and Baudrillard characterises the spatial conditions of late capitalism, selective psychopathy sustains a desired degree of mental functionality. Selective psychopathy becomes an artificial outside—a way for capitalism to handle its own all-too-successful incorporation of the outside and negotiate energies from within.[5] In the last two novels— *Millennium People* and *Kingdom Come*—on the other hand, the random acts of violence are depicted, not as a mechanism of maintaining the logic of the spectacular totalities they portray, but rather as an urge to break free. Where the first two speak to a Baudrillardian hyperreality in which divisions between those empowered and those disempowered in the Marxian sense are diffused through a logic that undermines a Marxist politics of revolt and where all acts are ultimately subsumed under the logic of late capitalism itself, the second two novels seem to speak rather to a Situationist will to change. Ballard's last two novels, then, stage the Situationist tactics somewhat differently. The politics in *Millennium People* certainly seems preposterous when the revolution is articulated by means of olive ciabattas and parking slots but, nonetheless, the disruptions are at least intended to challenge rather than maintain the system. The main orchestrator of events in this novel, Richard Gould, really believes that pointless acts can 'challenge the universe at its own game'. The failed revolution is celebrated as such. Even if everything ultimately returns to status quo, the book ends with a sense, if not of hope, then at least of life. *Kingdom Come*, as the last of the four novels, performs a *détournement* of the consumer logic that governs the society and the potential fascist state that the novel depicts. The shopping mall mutiny has made a difference, its 'seismic jolt' unsettling the ground beneath their feet (*Kingdom* 279). Previously, the Brooklands suburbs have been increasingly dominated by violence, racism, and hooliganism—a 'new kind of fascism, a cult of violence rising from this wilderness of retail parks and cable TV stations' (*Kingdom* 258)—but along with the burnt down Metro-Centre, racist attacks and post-football-match violence vanish into thin air and the fascist threat is at least temporarily defeated. There is no radical break with the politics that have created it but at least a temporary respite. As such, it is suggestive of some degree of agency and possibility for change. As the motif of the burned-down shopping mall as a volcano that may one day revive suggests, the defeat of the potential fascist state is not definitive. But the final lines of the novel, which also turned out to be the last words Ballard wrote in the novelistic form, call us to a revolutionary future: 'the turnstiles of its beckoning paradise' may be resisted if the sane wake up and rally themselves (*Kingdom* 280). However, and while there are thus some differences between these two sets of the last novels, and while the Situationist tactics revoked in all of them may seem seductively rebellious, the potential for critique that we are looking for is not locatable on the level of content so much as it is on the level of form.

CULTURAL CRITIQUE AND FORM

In the first section of this book, I pointed to the return to formalism in recent literary criticism and to the suggestion that developments in political structures call for an increased attention to arguments about how form is linked to political practice. Where the critique of and decline in formalism during periods characterised by Structuralist and Poststructuralist theory emerged from an intensified concern with a more direct link between political content and context, the new formalist interest is one that is particularly invested in the politics of form. The early resistance to but increasing affirmation of allegory in Ballard's long-standing oeuvre provides us with an opportunity to address the politics of form in relation to developments in political systems. On the one hand, and as I have argued in this chapter, the increasing level of allegorisation in Ballard's novelistic oeuvre can be seen to follow the development of the depiction of the system of production. With an increasing level of control comes an increasing sense of totality. As every level of society and its inhabitants is monitored and regulated, not by institutional reinforcement and subject constitution but by a more direct modification of affects and desires, the Western world increasingly appears as a totality that is neither the normative totality of a community of fulfilled subject theorised by early Frankfurt School theorists such as Max Horkheimer nor simply the oppressive one-dimensional homogeneity of the totality identified by Adorno and Horkheimer a bit later on. Although a relative of the latter, this new totality differs from it in its intensified configuration of affects and desires. This intensification entails that it is no longer possible to even identify 'man's alienation from objective reality' as György Lukács puts it, because these two categories—'man' and 'objective reality'—are no longer self-evident. In this light, allegory appears not as a preexisting subject's expression of its mourning of totality so much as a representational tool for weaving affects and desires into the system of production itself. In this respect, Jameson's explanation of the upshot of allegory in postmodernity as a means of trying to grasp a global system that is otherwise too large to comprehend may need to be expanded to include also a biopolitical dimension. Understood through Ballard's late novels, allegory becomes not just the means of understanding control society but an aid in constituting it.

So how are we to understand the gradual victory of allegory in Ballard's work? To return one last time to the imagined video clip playing the destruction of a building in reverse that opened this chapter, the last novels depict the completed building, the disappearance of the ruins, the completion of control. As we saw in this last set, a reinforced sense of totality configured by a system of comfort and control relies on a possibly inadequate but frequently convincing sense of unity of a system without an outside. Such a system is strengthened by an allegorical binding that hides the fragments that may otherwise threaten to challenge it. This is what the cooption of a Situationist tactics in the first two of Ballard's last novels illustrates so well—how the system itself needs to shatter a few glasses in order to control both the breaking and the patching up. In this light, the resistance to allegory in the earlier sets of novels could be read as a political gesture—a repudiation of the systems of representation and explanation that make us think we can conceptualise 'the world system as such' and thereby create a false sense of agency in a system that consistently strives to deny it. The engagement with Surrealist aesthetics in the first set of novels provides, as I argued, a way of resisting the allegorical impulse as a means of political explication. The fact that the world and its referential systems have crumbled in these novels is presented as an emerging potential of a posthuman and postsignifying world that the unifying struggle of allegory would disturb. This becomes particularly clear when compared to the second set of novels in which the alienating structures of modern society seem to demand the allegorical. With this second set emerges the sense of allegory as a necessary evil in the face of the gradual disappearance of the outside. In the last set of novels, finally, allegory helps align all desires with the new capitalist totality it seems to support. This is a totality that is neither longitudinal nor normative but seems rather to be an inevitable result of an all-inclusive system.

However, and this is on the other hand, the different configurations of Situationist tactics in this last set of novels suggest that what is allegorised in these novels is not just a political system but resistance itself. This is where irony remerges with some force. In these novels we can see how a sense of an all-encompassing political system matched with an all-encompassing allegorical mode of representation is placed alongside the constant potential for interruption of the analogical correspondences that irony carries with it for both Benjamin and de Man. The irony here resides in the way in which its potential interruptions are orchestrated. One could read the coopted Situationist tactics in this last set of novels as an allegory, not only of control society but also of the crisis in cultural critique itself as analysed by Baudrillard, Bruno Latour, Negri, and Jeffrey T. Nealon that I account for in chapter 1. As we saw in that chapter, Baudrillard argues that contemporary art and culture, even when it seems to portray political critique, ultimately work to perpetuate the system. Applied straight onto Ballard's last novels, this approach would suggest that they offer but a 'simulated real' that makes it possible for us to tolerate the suffering of nihilism (Baudrillard 2005, 202). Or, more disturbingly still, they may be read as a set of *trompe-l'oeils* that methodically functions to satisfy and thereby placate any sense of need for radical change. But if we read them, instead, as allegorising this very tendency, the allegory no longer primarily functions to support the sense of unity of control society but rather to illustrate its mechanisms.

As I began to map in the first parts of this book, a major challenge today when it comes to political as well as cultural critique is how to locate positions from which to question and interrogate what we, via Fisher, began to call 'capitalist realism'. How to find a cultural or political voice that is not always already preempted and internalised by the all-encompassing structures of control society? I noted earlier how a post-Marxist politics of critique and subversion has been linked to an alternative cultural expression locating itself as 'other' to the society it critiques. I also noted that such a politics of resistance needs to be rethought in the face of a society of control. The Situationist tactics that are repeatedly evoked in Ballard's last novels constitute a good example of what was once such an 'alternative' critical practice. Here, however, these once-revolutionary tactics have become modes of 'emotional trade-off' to keep characters motivated enough to persist in their perpetual immaterial labour. In other words, resistance is positioned as a constitutive part of the very process of recuperating resistance. This way, the depiction of the cooption of these practices for the purposes of control in the last novels emerges as affirmative of irony as it positions these texts as allegories not only of the political system itself but also of the crisis in cultural critique it has generated. As such, they may be read, not just as allegories of the crisis in critique in contemporary culture but also as examples of the new terrain for the critique of culture that Negri calls for. As we noted earlier, Negri suggests that such a critique must be one that builds on 'the capacity to remain within, to hollow out language from inside and make the material desire for transformation emerge' (Negri 2007, 50). As I hope to have shown in this chapter, Ballard's work indicates that an attention to form in general and an attention to allegory in particular enable discussions of the politicisation of form. Such politicised formalism may in turn provide one example of such internal cultural critique. That such attention to form constitutes a crucial part of a new terrain for critique becomes clear in the next two chapters because without it, the mainstream political allegories analysed there function, instead, to disarm the critique they purportedly articulate.

NOTES

1. Similar identifications of these different periods in Ballard's oeuvre have been made before. See, for example, Taylor (2002). It is also worth adding that these sets are not exclusive—other novels could also fit in, such as Ballard's very first novel, *The Wind from Nowhere* (1961), which would fit with the first set, and *The Atrocity Exhibition*, which could fit with the second.

2. Indeed, Ballard's fictional universes are often associated with Baudrillard's theories of postmodernity. As Bradley Butterfield points out, the two have been seen virtually as prototypes of postmodernist aesthetics and theory; 'the killer B's', as they have been called. Ballard has responded ambivalently to the intrusion of theories of postmodernism into his sci-fi aesthetics. 'You are killing us!' he writes in a debate about his and Baudrillard's work in the early 1990s as he sees theory devouring science fiction, 'rolling its jaws over an innocent and naive fiction that desperately needs to be left alone' (see Butterfield 1999, 65). He is clearly reluctant to accommodate for the tendencies of letting his work serve as a prototype for postmodernist theory. We return to the question of Ballard's postmodernity later.

3. See Beckman (2013).

4. The CCRU was a group of theorists, writers, and artists that came together during the 1990s at the University of Warwick in the United Kingdom to explore possibilities of collapsing capitalism by its own means. This group, which included theorists such as Nick Land and Sadie Plant and later on students of this duo such as Mark Fisher, Robin Mackay, and others may be seen as the starting point for Accelerationism, or Neoaccelerationism as some would call it, acknowledging a trajectory reaching from the theories of Karl Marx and the writings of Samuel Butler through modern French philosophers such as Gilles Deleuze and Félix Guattari, Jean-François Lyotard, and Gilles Lipovetsky through the cyberculture theories of Land and Plant in the 1990s to the contemporary convergence of 'new theoretical enterprises that aim to conceptualise the future outside of traditional critiques and regressive, decelerative or restoratice "solutions"' (Mackay and Avanessian 2014, 6–7). This Neoaccelerationism has emerged in the twenty-first century as a response to what it sees as the challenges and possibilities of a contemporary global, neoliberal capitalism and includes proaccelerationist texts such as Alex Williams and Nick Srnicek's '#Accelerate: Manifesto for an Accelerationist Politics' (2014), as well as antiaccelerationist ones such as Benjamin Noys's *The Persistence of the Negative* (2010) and *Malign Velocities: Acceleration and Capitalism* (2014).

5. The fact that Ballard already in *The Atrocity Exhibition* from 1969 pointed to the importance of preserving the psychopathic as a 'nature reserve, a last refuge for a certain kind of human freedom' (Ballard and Self 2006, 380) makes this capitulation of the psychopathic into the capitalist conformity particularly unsettling.

FOUR

Time, Allegory, Control

The gradual intensification of control indicated on the thematic level in J. G. Ballard's oeuvre is, as I tried to show in the previous chapter, paralleled on the formal level by an increasing allegorisation of space. As control society tightens its grip over the West, these novels seem to indicate, the fragments of an always already politicised space that once constituted possible openings for resistance are subject to an immediate translation back into totality. Having thus addressed a possible way of analysing some spatial implications of control society as well as ways in which attention to form can help us to better understand such implications, this fourth chapter turns to time as an even more central dimension of this intensification of control. Always central to production, the political modulations of time have continued to change with the advancement of modernity and, as movements such as Accelerationism have underlined, neoliberal capitalism now moves us with a blinding speed towards 'ever-accelerating catastrophes' (#Accelerate 01.3).[1] Unsurprisingly then, perhaps, time itself has returned as a thematic preoccupation in contemporary culture. While Fredric Jameson famously characterises postmodernism as a period when time has been flattened into space, and as a point which has 'forgotten to think historically' in the early 1990s (Jameson 1991, ix), the first decade or so of the new Millennium has witnessed the emergence of a visual culture intensely interested both in history and in temporality. First, historical narrative has emerged as a distinct trend in contemporary American television and film. TV series such as *Carnivàle* (2003–2005), *Deadwood* (2004–2006), *Mad Men* (2007–), and *Masters of Sex* (2013–) and films such as *J. Edgar* (2011) and *Lincoln* (2012) just to mention a few suggest an intense interest in revisiting and reconstructing, not only history generally, but American national history specifically. Second, there is a distinctive preoccupation with different and differ-

73

ing conditions of temporality. In TV series such as *Carnivàle* and *Pushing Daisies* (2007–2009) and in films such as *The Butterfly Effect* (2004), *Inception* (2010), and *In Time*, the conditions and determinations of time and temporality are under close interrogation. Through their preoccupation with time, these series and films rekindle questions of subjectivity, identity, and agency in the light of new technologies and communicational tools that have emerged and become part of control society. While some of these series and films focus on how a differential conception of time affects subjectivity, agency, and memory on a personal level, such as *The Butterfly Effect*, others, like *Inception* and *In Time*, are concerned with the relation between the organisation of time and the organisation of economy and politics. Time, as an important key to understanding what we are and what we are becoming, reemerges here in the light of contemporary modes of production. Time 'is a corporate asset now' as one character explains to another in Don DeLillo's *Cosmopolis*. 'It belongs to the free market system' (*Cosmopolis* 79). This current preoccupation with history and time in American culture seems to respond to a society in which the temporal conditions of capitalism are changing.

That several different organisations of time exist simultaneously constitutes an inevitable condition of political life. In our current world, however, the spatial distribution of these systems is, as I began to note in the previous chapter, conditioned by a global capitalism that, as Ballard's work portrayed so neatly, makes increasingly sharp distinctions between the immaterial labour of the Western world and the outsourcing of the production of material goods to a frequently invisible elsewhere. The supposed collapse of spatial barriers enabled by digital communication systems and global capital can, as I noted via David Harvey earlier, be contrasted with the way in which the mobility of capital and production has enabled an increased attention to the generative specificity of different geographical spaces. The experience of temporality and the way it conditions existence thus comes to vary broadly across different systems of production. While time may very well belong 'to the free market system' as the DeLillo character puts it, this market system includes everything from the temporality associated with the Fordist line of production that continues to shape some parts of the globe to the milli- and nanoseconds of the electronic stock market, including algorithms for high frequency trading (HFT) that enable computers to make use of fractions of seconds when trading. Somewhere in between we find the fluid temporalities of the ever-present affective and immaterial labour that characterises and fuels contemporary Western societies. These new configurations of time underlie and condition the logic of control society and demand further attention.

TIMELY PREOCCUPATIONS

The conception of time that has dominated Western history for centuries builds, as Giorgio Agamben notes, on the one hand on the cyclical temporality of Greco-Roman antiquity and an Aristotelian understanding of time as 'a precise, infinite, quantified continuum' (Agamben 1993, 93) and on the other, on a secularised Christian, and a modern Hegelian, conception of time as 'homogeneous, rectilinear, and empty' (Agamben 1993, 96). While circular in its earlier conception and rectilinear in its later version, the two have in common an understanding of time as measurable, quantifiable and, essentially, beyond the grasp of man. '"Great men"', as Agamben puts it through Georg Willhelm Friedrich Hegel, 'are merely instrumental in the forward march of the universal Spirit' (Agamben 1993, 99). Karl Marx's conception of history, Agamben notes, opens for a different understanding of time based in rather than beyond man. Irreconcilable with both the Aristotelian and the Hegelian conceptions of a time that dominates man, Marx's understanding of history sees it as emerging from man by means of *praxis*, that is, by means of concrete activity that generates time (Agamben 1993, 99). Although Marx does not sufficiently develop this theory of time to correspond with his understanding of history, Agamben maintains, the latter makes it possible to think a temporality of production rather than negation, that is, a time within rather than beyond reach (Agamben 1993, 100). Still, Cesare Casarino argues, Agamben does not fully take into account Marx's considerable engagement with time. Such an engagement, he suggests, emerges rather through Antonio Negri's writing (Casarino 2003, 189).

Negri's understanding of time, like Agamben's, takes its starting point in a critique of the Aristotelian-Hegelian logic of spatialised and quantified time. Unlike Agamben's, however, Casarino argues, it pursues the Marxian notion of the productivity of time with more care (Casarino 2003, 189). All time equals productivity in Negri's Marxist reading. 'Production is life itself', as he puts it. 'It is by virtue of this fact that everything that lives is part of the system of production' (Negri 2004, 62). The project of the capitalist logic is to subsume time to ensure that this productivity is controlled and harnessed in the service of a capitalist extraction of surplus value. In other words, the goal of late capitalism is to reduce time to zero, that is, to make sure that no time escapes its own logic (Casarino 2003, 190). This seems to be becoming an increasingly all-encompassing fact. As the Accelerationist manifesto suggests about our present point it time, 'We may be moving fast, but only within a strictly defined set of capitalist parameters that themselves never waver' (#Accelerate 02. 2).

Failing to consider the reconfigurations of political temporalities is, as Agamben notes, a crucial error (Agamben 1993, 93). A central question today, and that can be linked back to what already emerges as a set of 'traditional' post-Marxist scholars such as Henri Lefebvre, Louis Althusser, and Walter Benjamin as well as to a more current set of researchers such as Agamben, Michael Hardt, and Negri, is how we can begin to theorise the temporalities of a contemporary capitalism in which the conditions of production have changed. These changing conditions are central to the transition between disciplinary and control society. Through Lefebvre, we have seen how the production of premodern, precapitalist times was adjusted to the circular time of bodies following the rhythm of day and night, spring and fall, and birth and death and to the specific conditions of different places and ways of living (Lefebvre 2002, 49). Through him, we have also seen how life in modernity introduces a spatial and temporal uniformity that accommodates for the linearity of capitalist production (Lefebvre 1987, 7). These two temporalities, Lefebvre's analysis of everyday life suggests, intersect and create a modern-day time in which the linear continually cuts through the circular. Following up on Althusser's proposition that the specifics of any type of labour time influences also how temporality is perceived and experienced in society at large, Jameson notes that while the difference between agricultural and industrial society makes the link between modes of production and temporality fairly straightforward, the pursuit of the same principle in the present necessitates more subtle differentiations between distinct modes of production as well as affective labour, or what he, via Raymond Williams, calls 'structures of feeling' in culture and everyday life (Jameson 2003, 707–8). In Negri's work as well as in many other post-Marxian theories of temporality, the organisation of time is not only an effect of the organisation of labour and capital, but rather, it is a constitutive element of the political system itself. But as the linear production of the factory is increasingly replaced with the nonlinear and continuous immaterial labour that informs all aspects of modern life in the West, the link between temporality and production is reconfigured.

Hardt and Negri note how the gradual transition from a disciplinary society based on institutions and linear production to a society of control in which production is dispersed in space and time brings with it an alteration of temporality. While an increasing amount of the production associated with linear time such as factory work has been located in non-Western countries, the contemporary West has seen the emergence of a new stage of capitalism where labour is no longer mainly characterised by factory work and other types of measurable activities. As Gilles Deleuze notes, while modern-day capitalism relegates production to the Third World, its first world is characterised by

> a capitalism of higher-order production. It no longer buys raw materials and no longer sells the finished products: it buys the finished products or assembles parts. What it wants to sell is services and what it wants to buy is stocks. It centers not on production so much as on the

> product and its selling and marketing. Thus, the system is essentially dispersive, and the factory has given way to the corporation. (Deleuze 1992, 6)

Instead of the streamlining effectiveness of linear time and uniform space of the factory, new temporalities emerge as a response to a more distributed spatial and digital production. These temporalities depend rather on the biopolitical merging of production and reproduction and the immaterial and affective labour that characterise societies of control. When Deleuze notes that control society is not dependent on the spatial organisation and division of labour, this is only half true since this mode of organisation in the West continues to rely on linear modes of production, although these are increasingly pushed beyond national borders and located in an elsewhere the recognition of which is limited. In a Western context, however, it seems correct to argue that where the disciplinary society that Michel Foucault famously theorises functions to 'distribute in space; to order in time; to compose a productive force within the dimension of space-time whose effect will be greater than the sum of its component forces' (Deleuze 1992, 3), the society that is gradually succeeding it brings with it a crisis in such organised and closed environments, a dissolution or, better, a redistribution of such streamlined spatial and temporal mechanisms of control. Instead of molds, as Deleuze puts it, there are modulations—a continuous and flexible mode of control that no longer needs institutions to regulate behaviour according to set models but that relies, rather, on codes and flows of information. As labour is not limited by material or corporeal production but includes the immaterial and the intellectual, time, as well as value, becomes increasingly hard to measure. As Hardt and Negri put it: 'there are no time clocks to punch on the terrain of biopolitical production; the proletariat produces in all its generality everywhere all day long' (Hardt and Negri 2000, 403).

The developing relations between time and value cause Negri to question the continuing usefulness of Marx's theories on value and time. If Marxist theories of subsumption saw how the employment of the 'socially combined worker' pointed towards a social whole subsumed by capital in a one-dimensional combination of production and reproduction, how does time constitute a measure of social labour? A crucial question in the present context is if this reconfiguration of time and production opens up for a new kind of totality, one that relates specifically to organisations and perceptions of time beyond the institutions and factories of disciplinary society. The fact that Negri's *Time for Revolution* (2005) revives the concept of totality after its rather consistent rejection by the poststructuralist thinkers of the last decades of the twentieth century, and the fact that it does so specifically in relation to temporality and contemporary political organisation suggests as much. As Negri himself puts it: 'If social labour covers all the time of life, and invests all of its regions, how can time measure the substantive totality in which it is implicit?' (Negri 2005, 29). In other words, the development of labour in the contemporary period brings with it a reconfiguration of the relation between time and totality. In the following, I analyse this shift by returning to a Ballard story from the 1960s and comparing it with a contemporary film. With the ambition of simultaneously saying something about the possibility of cultural critique and the political implications and employments of allegory, I have purposefully chosen to contrast a story securely situated in a more alternative 1960s counterculture with a film that corresponds to the current trend of mainstream political allegories outlined in the introductory chapter.

IN AND OUT OF TIME: 'CHRONOPOLIS' AND *IN TIME*

Andrew Niccol's film *In Time* from 2011 is an allegory of contemporary capitalism in which time and space are presented as a seamless whole. As we will see, it centrally relies on a figural move of transforming the conflation of money and time from a metaphor to a quite literal and physical reality. This produces a sense of totality that at least on an immediate level serves to illustrate the complete usurpation of time into the social and affective realms. While thus speaking to the questions of control society, allegory, and totality central to the present study and doing so specifically regarding the question of time, we must not lose sight of the fact that it belongs to the current mainstream trend of political allegories and needs to be explored on that level. Niccol has been involved as a director or scriptwriter for films such as *Gattaca* (1997), *The Truman Show* (1998), and *The Terminal* (2004), films that all in different ways deal with the relation between technology and economy and between politics, space, and culture. Like these earlier films, *In Time* is a fairly straightforward contemporary mainstream film. It features sexy characters and car chases, it features good guys and bad guys, it features heavy doses of hold-your-breath excitement and romantic moments, and it features singer and actor Justin Timberlake and model and actress Amanda Seyfried in the lead roles. At the same time, and like Niccol's earlier films, it depicts a highly dystopic version of society. In the world projected in the film, the overpopulation of the Earth has been solved by a predetermined longevity. When you turn twenty-five, your clock—visible through the skin on your wrist—starts ticking. At this point you get one more year to live. In this world, time is not the measure of currency but the thing itself. You are paid in time for your work and you pay for everything with time. One minute for making a phone call. Four minutes for a cup of coffee. One hour for taking the bus. Although this system is said to spring from a need to manage overpopulation, this explanation is later exposed as a partial truth, at best. More poignantly, it constitutes a way of controlling the work force and ascertaining a system that guarantees an increasing accumulation, and control, of time.

The film perfectly illustrates Jameson's positioning of allegory as a means by which to survey the landscape of late capitalism. As we saw in chapter 2, Jameson explains the reemergence of allegory in postmodernity as related to attempts of pinning down and portraying a contemporary global world that has grown too complex to otherwise envision. In *In Time*, the fluidity of global capitalism is portrayed as such while at the same time being contained within an identifiable system. Two central allegorical devices, relating to time and space respectively, are used to enable such 'tying together of fragments'. To begin with, the clocks that govern production are built into the very bodies of the workers. This way, the fluidity of value—released from permanent values and central organising institutions—is represented exactly in terms of physical—but not individual—temporalities. For the working classes, however, this reconfiguration of time does not entail a great deal of difference compared to, say, the analogue clocks of earlier modes of production. Quite on the contrary, the organisation of life for the factory workers in the film continues to be strictly determined by linear production, and any escape from this linearity is efficiently prevented by means of the limitation of time itself. The film's protagonist, Will Salas (Timberlake), has grown up in this area and has hardly ever had more than a day's worth of time on his clock. Like the other workers, he is so busy staying alive that there is no time to even think about the system and how it came into being, no less to plot a revolution. As Will's voiceover says at the very opening of the film: 'I don't have time. I don't have time to worry about how it happened. It is what it is.' Being kept on a very short leash in terms of the time they have left, the fact that many of the poor run out of time seems part of the system: 'For a few to be immortal', as one of the protagonists is told 'many must die.'[2] For the wealthier classes, on the other hand, the reconfiguration of time to some extent entails a reconfiguration of living. They have plenty of time in store and since they do not have to worry about making it to the next day, they can spend their time making more time. Their potential to live forever would be threatened only by an accident to their body or, on a larger scale, by a radical overturning of society, which, the system has ensured, seems highly implausible. What is brought out by this direct translation of money into time is that while the developments of society resulting from digitised time and the spread of immaterial and affective labour constitute a potential in the contemporary world, this development has not fundamentally changed the conditions of those still chained to the production line.

A second allegorical device can be found in the film's handling of space. Here, the allegorical mode enables the representation of the contemporary global world as an overviewable spatial totality as it fits an entire world system within the framework of its one fictional society. The time zones in *In Time* are distributed across the society portrayed and based on how much time you have. The poorest—the factory workers who struggle just to earn enough time to survive another day—live in the roughest area called 'the ghetto' or 'the Time Lines' while those with plenty of time live in 'New Greenwich'. The name 'New Greenwich' clearly positions the city as an imperial standard. To begin with, it is obviously a reference to Greenwich Mean Time as the global standard of measuring time. Second, and relatedly, it can also be read as a reference to the town of Greenwich in England, a historical site for the Prime meridian that was incorporated during the eighteenth century into the broader cosmopolis of London as a centre of temporal, navigational, and thus horological innovation and control. Third, it establishes a link to the affluent Greenwich Village in Manhattan in New York City, United States. Thus, the New Greenwich of the film comes to stand as an unequivocal landmark of the intersection of imperial spatiotemporal power. New Greenwich is, of course, located numerous time zones away from the Time Lines, and because you have to pay in time to move between time zones, there is a clear spatial separation between the workers and the people who benefit from their work. In other words, the spatial distribution of power is controlled by means of time. The geopolitical distribution of time that the film portrays and that its allegorical overview of a political landscape underlines points towards a fluid global capitalism that identifies temporality as a key to totality.

Temporality and totality are, of course, closely linked theoretically. Even on the most fundamental level we can see how longitudinal totality, in its trust in the possibility of knowing history, is suggestive of a linear and essentially mappable temporality. Normative totality, in its constant ambition, is irrevocably linked to the future. But how these notions of totality and their political potential are understood comes to depend largely on the conceptions of temporality that underlie them. Thus, Hegel's Absolute Spirit reflects how his conception of time as unidirectional but also coinstantaneous enables a particular conception of totality in the present that is impossible to conceptions of an open-ended temporality such as those of Immanuel Kant's and the Romantics in which totality was always postponed into the future (Jay 1984, 56). Totality, for Hegel, was in this sense constantly reaffirmed in the dialectical play between subject and object. At the same time, Hegel's conception of linear time created problems for his Marxist inheritors in terms of longitudinal totality because it relied on a reflective moment after. The Hegelian owl of Minerva, which flies only at dusk and thus enables knowledge only after the event, points to a link between temporality and production that is problematic, as Martin Jay shows, to a Marxist tradition directed not just towards reflection but towards the making of history—*praxis* (Jay 1984, 36).

Post-Marxist thinkers of course relate to Marx's Hegelian heritage in different ways. György Lukács, for whom the concept of totality was central if ever-changing in his work, found a way to employ Hegel to ward off his early doubts about the possibility of totality and to create an expressive conception of totality exactly by including the intentionality of the subject thus seeing the whole as a product of praxis (Jay 1984, 109). This entailed an active conception of totality that stressed the possibility for change (although Lukács's understanding of totality came to grow more pessimistic again in his later work). For other, less-Hegelian post-Marxist thinkers, the role of time in relation to totality plays out different-ly. Many resisted the continuous temporalities proposed by Hegel. The Frankfurt School thinkers, inspired, as Jay notes, by Benjamin, pointed towards complex temporalities that in different ways put pressure on the notion of totality (Jay 1984, 414–45). In Benjamin's work we can see how experiences of time as shards, fragments, and moments are threatened or undermined by ideas of totality as an overviewable and continuous whole. Such conceptions elucidate with some clarity how totality can be related to ideology as well as modes of production and representation. The idea of continuity causes severe misrepresentation of both history and memory. Benjamin sees, for example, how progressive linear narra-tives represent a totalisation of experience that does not reflect the dis-junctions and fragmentations of lived time. Modernity tends to resist such totalising representation. As Michael P. Steinberg notes, Benjamin sees the work of art as taking an ethical position 'only in its self-conscious status as a fragment, in its refusal to claim totality' (Steinberg 1996, 14). At the same time, then, as totalisation emerges as a totalitarian impulse, the rejections of progressive, linear time challenge and potentially under-mine also the more positive notion of normative totalisation. By the time we arrive at contemporary political thought and the development of bio-political strategies and modes of organisation, Negri suggests that we are facing a tautology that

> after presenting itself *intensively* as the impossibility of distinguishing the measure of the differentiation of the substance of value, reproposes itself *extensively* as the impossibility of distinguishing the totality of life (of the social relations of production and reproduction) from the total-ity of time from which this life is woven. When the entire time of life has become the time of production, who measures whom? (Negri 2005, 29)

Ultimately, Negri revokes totality and situates it in a present in which time is but a 'transcendental schematism accomplished because presup-posed'. Because the time of production has been redistributed and is no longer linear but relies on a multidirectional, 'ecstatic' present, 'the ana-lytic of capital operates on a *totality without genesis*' (Negri 2005, 80).

By means of its two central and interrelated moves—building econo-my into the body in a quite literal sense and elucidating the differential temporal conditions on which global capitalism rely—Niccol's *In Time* reminds us that any conception of totality today must acknowledge that the global redistribution of production comes with a reconfiguration of totality. Negri notes that 'No analysis of the contemporary State is pos-sible that fails to recognise it as completely invested by the social totality, by the collectivism of life, by the socialisation of life—to the point of the transformation of constitutionalism into totalitarianism—but also as tra-versed by a global antagonism' (Negri 2003, 133). Taking this one step further, we see the conditions of possibility for totality no longer primari-ly linked to the State institutions of a disciplinary society but linked, rather, to the pure flow of money in a society of control. This reconfigura-tion of totality as linked to a floating but all-encompassing global capital-ism means that we have to rethink the link between inside and outside and between institutions and individuals. From one angle, this dissolu-tion of more unitary political State systems may be read as the ultimate breaking down of the social totality that Negri points to but from another, it may be seen as its ultimate triumph—a capitalist totality based on the total integration of the shards and fragments that once seemed to threat-en it.

The allegorical structure of Niccol's film creates a concrete means of envisioning this integration of shards and fragments. We can see this if we compare how the different modes of production at play in the film are positioned in relation to the idea of a limit. Elucidating the different temporal conditions of the Time Lines and New Greenwich respectively, the film positions this difference as a distinction between how time is, or is not, related to the limit. The experience of time and space, Harvey argues, is 'one singularly important mediating link between the dyna-mism of capitalism's historical-geographical development and complex processes of cultural production and ideological transformation' (Harvey 2006, iix). In the Time Lines, the limit is conditioned by a very concrete temporal linearity governing every minute of the day. With hardly ever more than a bare minimum of time, Will and the other denizens in the Time Lines are literally facing this limit every day. While the temporal conditions of the factory seem to be infinite, the workers who constitute its cogs are confined to a limit experience that forces them to keep up speed or they will be expulsed by the system by means of death. Bodies that have 'timed out' are not an infrequent sight around the factory. That direct engagement with the limit constitutes a part of an everyday econo-my here can also be exemplified by an event where Will's mother gives Will enough time to have lunch before he goes to work despite the fact that this leaves her with just enough to last her until they meet in the evening. At this point, he will have earned some time to give her back. When she gets on the bus to meet him, however, the bus fares have increased—two hours instead of one—which means that she does not have enough. Instead, she is forced to run in a literal struggle against time, running out of it the second before she reaches Will. To infuse the everyday even with the smallest pleasures, such as giving someone you love time for lunch, is inevitable tied to the possibility of death. Juxtaposed to such temporal conditions, the endless time of the people in New Greenwich seems to open up towards equally endless possibilities. That Will raises suspicion when he runs, rather than walks, on the streets of these wealthy sections a little later in the film illustrates how the limitless capital of time here makes speed or urgency superfluous. The languid speed of people here is efficiently contrasted with the panic of Will's running mother a few scenes earlier.

Returning to Lefebvre's theorisation of a precapitalist circular time adjusted to days and seasons and the capitalist linear time of production that cuts through it, it becomes quite clear that the temporality governing New Greenwich is regulated neither by natural cycles nor by linear production. As the disciplinary system of power is efficiently outsourced to the Time Lines, the labour characterising New Greenwich is best illustrated by a set of control systems. To begin with, there are digital maps providing overview of the flow of time. So while the importance of linearity is severely diminished, the flow of time nonetheless remains under control. Second, there is the control of emotion that is needed to ensure that no one does 'something foolish' as the female lead, Sylvia (Seyfried), puts it. As the daughter of the wealthy businessman Philippe Weis, she is emblematic of this system that on the one hand leaves nothing to be desired and on the other leaves nothing for desire. As she explains to Will, the limitless time available in New Greenwich means that only an accident can end your life. You can live forever as long as you do not expose yourself to any risk. This also explains the necessity of the many checkpoints between the poorer and the richer areas—the urgent needs of the workers constitute an obvious threat to the safely guarded eternity of the inhabitants of Greenwich Village. It is not enough, however, to protect these inhabitants from the workers, but they also need to be protected against themselves. It soon becomes apparent that the possibility of eternity works as the ultimate means of control since the inhabitants are effectively prohibited from any kind of living that is not closely monitored. There is simply too much to lose. In short, then, and if the agency of the workers in the Time Lines is curtailed by the permanent lack of time, the agency of the citizens in New Greenwich is undermined by its affluence. Just as the film brings out the conditions of living on the limit for the poor, it brings out the pacifying force of a temporality constructed, not by means of a limit, but by means of free-floating control. The 're-lease' from the temporality of production, the film seems to suggest, means a capture into a different system based on security, comfort, and consumption that effectively eliminates real pleasure and desire. As Sylvia puts it, 'The clock is good for no one. The poor die and the rich don't live.'

The concept, then, is quite simple. In Niccol's film, time has become money in a literal sense, and the distribution of wealth equals the distribution of time. This allegory is not just of the Western world but of a late capitalist geopolitics in which parts of the world that still rely on the conditions of a linear temporality of material production are contrasted with other parts in which such time is no longer a major organising principle. The distribution of different forms of labour across the planet is neatly fitted into an allegorical city. The separation between workers and those benefitting from their labour is, of course, a long-standing political issue as well as a classic theme in allegorical and dystopian fiction reaching back at least to the spatial separation between the Eloi and the Morlocks in H. G. Wells's novella *The Time Machine* (1895) and the division between the towers of the well-to-do intellectuals and the working classes down below in Fritz Lang's film *Metropolis* (1927), to mention but a few classic examples. In the light of this tradition, Niccol's film may be said to bring such spatial distinctions of labour to our time. Like Blomkamp's *Elysium*, mentioned in the introduction, which may be said to draw more extreme spatial dividing lines between the working poor and the wealthy leisure classes by means of planetary segregation, *In Time* too focuses on the spatial separation of workers and nonworkers, but it also explores more explicitly the temporal implications of such separation. The film's time zones succinctly represent a redistribution of labour that has pushed disciplinary modes of organisation and Fordist linear production to a periphery that is more or less invisible to a Western control society where labour is rather about consumption and immaterial modes of production. It portrays a Third World still governed by linear production and contrasts it with a First World in which the linearity of time is becoming increasingly irrelevant. On an immediate level, the film seems to allegorise this transition between disciplinary and control society discussed above quite directly. As we will see in a moment, however, the portrayal of the revolution at the film's ending complicates this political currency.

That the distribution of labour in the film corresponds to the logic of control rather than disciplinary society becomes all the more apparent if we compare it with some earlier allegories of time and production. Anxieties and concerns about the ways in which human life and bodies have come to serve the temporalities of production have, of course, been reflected in literature throughout the modern period. Marcel Aymé's short story 'The Ration Ticket' (1943; 'La Carte' in the French original. Also translated into 'The Life Ration') opens with the rumor that '[i]n order to ward off shortages and insure greater output from the laboring element of the population, there will supposedly be executions of non-productive consumers: the elderly, the retired, those of independent means, the unemployed and other non-essential persons' ('The Ration Ticket' 1). The characters are allocated differing number of days to live per month depending on their 'usefulness'. In Harlan Ellison's 'Repent Harlequin said the Tick Tock Man' (1965), the amount of time any one character can have can be regulated by means of a 'cardioplate'. 'And so it goes goes goes goes goes tick tock tick tock tick tock and one day we no longer let time serve us, we serve time and we are slaves of the schedule, worshippers of the sun's passing, bound into life predicated on restrictions because the system will not function if we don't keep the schedule right' ('Repent Harlequin' 5).[3] In terms of allegories of totality and time, a useful comparison, which is therefore worth a little more of our time, is that between Niccol's film and Ballard's short story 'Chronopolis' from 1960. These two works, of course, have a number of important differences. They are expressed through different media—written fiction and film; different periods—the 1960s and the 2010s; and different countries—the United Kingdom and the United States. These differences are interesting exactly because the two stories also share a number of pertinent qualities. Both texts share an intense preoccupation with clocks and the political construction of time and both are blatant allegories of the relation between temporality and political control. Both outline what seem to be perfected temporal systems based on attempts to institute the ultimate employment of time. While Ballard's 1960s story may be said to portray a socialist dystopia, Niccol's recent American film depicts rather a dystopic version of capitalism. We will have reason to return later to the notion of 'dystopia' itself. For now, however, let us focus on how the differences in the context of the making of Ballard's and Niccol's works open up the question of allegory, totality, and cultural critique.

Ballard's story is written in a Cold War Europe and in a post-Wellsian and Orwellian Britain characterised by anxieties of socialist totalitarianism as well as of the increasing alienation and commodification of modern life under capitalism. The story is set thirty-seven years after a revolution against the linear time of production in which the organisation of the work force into different time zones and time groups has well-nigh perfected a Taylorist engineering of labour productivity. Supposedly because of overpopulation, this enormous city was organised like a giant organism. 'Only by synchronizing every activity, every footstep forward or backward, every meal, bus-halt and telephone call, could the organism support itself.' Each and every move needs to be controlled perfectly, '[l]ike the cells in your body, which proliferate into mortal cancers if allowed to grow in freedom' ('Chronopolis' 159). While this system was extremely limiting as each day was organised by means of elaborate schedules for every 'permitted' activity on any one day, it was also supposedly enabling, as this organisation also meant being 'served quickly and efficiently' ('Chronopolis' 161). In one sense, the city appears as a socialist utopia and on the other, as emblematic of the horrors of historical socialist reform. The protagonist, Conrad, who has grown up after this system has been overturned, has problems understanding the reason behind the revolution as he sees only beauty in a system 'engineered as precisely as a watch' ('Chronopolis' 161), but his teacher maintains that this was a system that denied people integrity, will, and freedom.

In the postrevolutionary state, clocks have been banned and Conrad, who keeps finding traces or parts of clocks and watches without initially knowing what these objects are, begins to investigate the cause of this prohibition. The answer his teacher gives him is quite simple—clocks are dangerous weapons because you can time how long it takes people to do something—and then you can make them do it faster ('Chronopolis' 153). The same teacher takes him to see the city—Chronopolis—that was abandoned after the revolution. Here, clocks are everywhere—'at every street corner, over every archway, three-quarters of the way up the sides of buildings, covering every conceivable angle of approach' ('Chronopolis' 157). These clocks are colour-coded and have numerous hands. The colours and hands indicate time zones of different professional categories and 'consumer shifts' ('Chronopolis' 158). This teacher also observes that 'there is usually one revolution each century, and that successive revolutions receive their impetus from progressively higher social levels. In the eighteenth century it was the urban proletariat, in the nineteenth the artisan classes' ('Chronopolis' 162). The revolt against the clocks in Chronopolis, in turn, was executed by the white-collar office worker caught up in an economic system that denied him 'all freedom of will or personality' ('Chronopolis' 162). It seems apt that in this city where everyone is a cog in the wheel, it is not the working class demanding change but the group of people who would be most used to a 'freedom of will or personality' that the system denies them.

What is central to 'Chronopolis' is that it tries but struggles to envision an outside to the controlled temporalities of production. After the revolution, the city is abandoned and the people start a simpler life outside it and, this is the idea, outside the tyranny of clocks. The merciless temporalities of the city are thus contrasted with the less regulated life after the revolution. However, and poignantly, the nature of this postrevolutionary state of being is not elaborated to any great extent in the story. It seems clear, however, that the temporality governing the postrevolutionary society is not necessarily more enabling than the order of the city. In this world, clocks have been supplanted by 'a whole variety of timers' that enables people to know when they are due at work and at school. At least from young Conrad's narrative perspective, this is an ambitionless world. Even if Conrad, whose fascination with clocks colours most his actions, may not be a very reliable focaliser in this respect, it does seem that the organisation of life by means of timers in effect entails a pacification of people as their lack of overview means that they cannot make plans. If the tyranny of the clocks meant a perfect regulation of the work force, so does the tyranny without them as the people become subject to a time they cannot fully see. Thus, as the life of Conrad and his family is described, 'Time unfolded at its usual sluggish, half-confused pace. They lived in a ramshackle house in one of the amorphous suburbs, a zone of endless afternoons. Sometimes he went to school, but until he was ten he spent most of his time with his mother queuing outside the closed food stores' ('Chronopolis' 151). Even though the disciplinary society of the city is abandoned, the power that determines the setting of the timers and the movement of the time police that enforces the prohibition of clocks remains beyond grasp. This is reflected also in how the characters become, in a sense, passive wind-up workers waiting for an external call for action. 'What if it was half past three, as the old reckoning put it, if you weren't planning to start or finish anything then?' ('Chronopolis' 152). Ironically, then, the very 'freedom of will or personality' that the white-collar revolutionaries fought for seems as unrealisable after the revolution as before it. Without the clocks (and the city) there is nothing to fight against—no time for revolution, to borrow from Negri, no time to overturn. Time has become, in a sense, invisible. The strength and irony of this move is underscored at the end of the story when Conrad, ultimately imprisoned for his illegal adventures in Chronopolis, finds his prison cell adorned with a functioning clock. Part of his punishment, clearly, is to see time. The 'insanely irritating tick' of this clock also reminds us that this political logic is still analogue ('Chronopolis' 168).

When it comes to the potential of time, Ballard's story is what Jameson would call anti-Utopian rather than dystopian. If a more general conception of dystopian fiction sees it as a dark projection of where current developments would lead us if allowed to continue—for example, in terms of pollution and technological change—Jameson argues that a distinction needs to be made between works suggestive of an essentially hopeful conception of the social possibilities of mankind and works that lack belief in the positive force of humans. He proposes the term 'critical dystopia' for the former, noting also that it constitutes a 'cousin' to the utopian fiction with which it would share its positive conception of humankind. The latter he calls anti-Utopian as it serves to warn against the illusion of political utopian projects, such as communism and socialism, as they rest on an unrealistic view of the possibilities for a positive development (Jameson 2007, 198–99). Ballard's 'Chronopolis', in which the revolution against linear time leads only to another and less visible form of external management, seems essentially doubtful not only about the positive potential of humankind but also about the possibilities of more enabling employments of time. It is as if, having pushed the consequences of linear production to its limit, it remains impossible to envision an alternative. In this early story, Ballard's imaginary world remains analogue. As we saw in the previous chapter, he later came to develop his fictional worlds to include the distributed temporalities of control society, but at this point, the narrative remains dependent on the national, the analogue, and the linear logic of discipline.

While the societies portrayed in Niccol's and Ballard's texts, respectively, have in common a markedly spatial organisation of time as power in terms of time zones, factories, and banks and thus both display an organisation of power in terms of the inside and outside of institutions and identities characterising a disciplinary society, the film internalises the clocks that remain external in the short story. Read together, these two texts can be seen to allegorise the transition, not just between disciplinary and control society, or between the national and transnational, but also, and quite foundationally, between the analogue and the digital. By the same move, the separation between inside and outside typical of institutions and factories is transforming into a more distributed division. Deleuze matches the evolution of machines with the evolution of societies and of capitalism. While societies of sovereignty employed simple machines such as levers and clocks and disciplinary societies used machines of energy, societies of control are governed rather by computers (Deleuze 1992, 6). Along with this development, both the spatial and the temporal conditions of capitalism change. That this change brings with it a fundamental intensification of biopolitics can be illustrated by our comparison between the two narratives. Where Ballard's story portrays a society that is still based on analogue machines as run by, but physically separable from, the workers, Niccol's film points to the way in which the integration of capitalist time in the body constitutes an intensification of power and capitalist production as it comes to infiltrate all aspects of life. The film thereby updates the 'above ground wealth and underground worker' theme of much dystopian political allegory to a modern control society.

When it comes to the central dimension of revolution, however, this updating no longer holds. To begin with, the logic of the revolution with which the film culminates is structured according to more disciplinary modes of power and resistance. With Will and Cynthia as a modern-day Bonnie and Clyde robbing banks and distributing the time to the poor, the film falls right back into a logic of identities and institutions that the control society it seemed to have staged was supposed to have surpassed. Disciplinary power, Patricia Clough points out, engages in a politics of representation where the constitution of subjects can be ascertained through ideological apparatuses. Such a politics, she notes, which relies on representation and institutions, also to some extent makes space for resistance by transgressing institutional norms and established identities (Clough 2003, 360). When *In Time* falls back on such structures, the poor exploited man and the bored upper-class woman robbing banks and redistributing wealth, the central conceit of the translation of money into time is exposed as banal. Despite its potential to illuminate the more intimate reconfiguration of control and temporality in the light of an increasing digital and immaterial production, this conceit ultimately does not entail a shift in the construction of affectivity and resistance that the digitalisation and intensification of control would require. On the level of content, we can see this as a ruse of agency based on the sense that we, regardless of the shifts and intensifications in power, could still model our resistance on clearly identified identities and institutions. Second, the very staging of this revolution and the feel-good ending it entails bring us back to the formal question of what the popularised representations of revolutions in the present do. This is where the real control takes place. As compared to Ballard's short story and its reluctance to portray the revolution itself, Niccol's film and many of the others exemplified in the introduction, such as, for example *Equilibrium*, simply position the revolution as the new happy ending. Where Jean Baudrillard argues that '[w]e have added enjoyment of the spectacle of servitude to servitude itself' (Baudrillard 2005, 192), these films suggest that what has now been added is the spectacle of revolution to servitude. As such, the disciplinary style revolution is deceptive not only in its reliance on old models of resistance but also in its performance of, and thereby placating of, to return to Mark Fisher, the impulses of political resistance themselves. As such, the most acute form of control is not on the level of content but on the level of form.

CULTURAL CRITIQUE AND FORM

Niccol's film is made in a period in which the nature of control, communication, and consumption has intensified and evolved. However, and whereas Ballard writes in an earlier tradition of counterculture writers, not the least in the spirit of William S. Burroughs as a central figure in fictional writings on control society, Niccol's action movie is decidedly part of a mainstream culture industry. As a representative of the tendency to incorporate critique in the mainstream, or to provide its illusion, as some would argue, *In Time* elucidates the problems of allegorisation and cultural critique in relation to the conditions of control society that I introduced in the first sections of this book. While Niccol's film seems to provide elucidating commentary on contemporary capitalist structures, there are also several disturbing elements in this allegory. To begin with, and to return to the Jamesonian allegory outlined earlier, there is something slightly unsettling about the way it seems to propose a rather direct allegory that could be read 'against some one-to-one table of equivalences' and as such with 'a one-dimensional view of this signifying process'. As such, and if we are to continue reading it through Jameson's eyes, it speaks to a relation between reality and representation which the postmodern world has largely done away with. As I have noted earlier, a political allegory such as George Orwell's *Animal Farm* could be organised according to a fairly stable set of equivalences because it referred to an outside that, first, consisted of a more easily identifiable set of institutions and, as such, as bearing a particular relationship to external precepts and systems, and second, that was analogous to the novel because it was so clearly positioned as separate from it. Neither of these conditions is still in place in a contemporaneity based on a dissolution of meaning, a rethinking of representation, and a fluidity of control. This first disturbing element, then, can be identified as a tension between the upgrading of time and totality by means of content and an outdated version of the same by means of form.

As we noted via Marjorie Levinson in chapter 2, part of the new formalist tendencies in contemporary literary theory is a reawakened attention to how structures of mediation single out particular discourses to represent the real. It becomes apparent that there is something to gain from combining a structuralist attention to content and a formalist attention to form. If formalist critique was once rejected because of its supposed apolitical attention to formal detail, it seems naïve, especially after decades of more explicitly political approaches to literature and art, to suppose that form could somehow be excluded from the political. In fact, and we may assume that this is partly the reason behind the new formalist interest, a development of a society in which distinctions between representation and reality are under question combined with intense theoretical scrutiny of how reality is imbricated and shaped by representation makes it absolutely necessary to return to and critically investigate how and what forms are given priority to shape this reality. Form itself must be seen as a political practice. If we situate the tendency towards political allegory in mainstream culture in relation to arguments that form can be seen 'as a reflection of the sociohistorical or philosophical finitude of human understanding and practice', as Jim Hansen suggested in chapter 2, this allegorical imperative emerges as a reflection maybe not so much of the finitude of our understanding—although allegory as a specific example does, of course, have links to this finitude on a different level—but as part of a political shaping of this understanding.

The stability of the allegory on which Niccol's film is built, relying, as it does, on presumptions of direct referentiality, seems to speak to a sense of political as well as representational transparency that we might want to question. Rather than reflecting the dissolution of stable meaning, the straightforward allegorical mode that the film employs encourages a direct and transparent understanding of politics and society. By the same token, the film positions itself as separate from a reality from which, many theorists of contemporary politics and visual culture would argue, it is in fact inseparable. If the updating of Theodor W. Adorno and Max Horkheimer's cultural critique that Negri calls for builds not on the inaccuracy but on the redundancy of their argument, as I outlined in chapter 1, this is partly because the commodification and seduction that the

Frankfurt School theorists identified in the 1940s only begins to explain the way in which culture has become an ever-present part of the immaterial labour that now makes up a central part of production in control society. If the culture industry was seen as a constitutive element of a politics of commodification for Adorno and Horkheimer, the increasing indistinction between reality and representation suggests that the manner in which it is constitutive has evolved. As we explore further in the next chapter, the separation between the screen and the viewer, which the idea of the exhausted worker in front of the television that Adorno and Horkheimer evoke suggests, is exchanged for a continuous modulation of visuality and representation that builds exactly on the impossibility of making this separation. The problem with the explicit and straightforward political allegory of *In Time* is that while the film seems to critically portray a number of features of contemporary society in terms of content and as such may be perceived as conveying a radical political message, its allegorical form curtails this portrayal and brings it back, rather, to structures of meaning and representation that are decidedly at odds with this same society.

The allegorical mode, as we have noted earlier, relies fundamentally on the dissolution of unity. Emerging as a way of responding to the fragmentation of totality in the readings of Benjamin, allegory constitutes a way of making sense without transcendent truth. When Jameson reads the reappearance of allegory in postmodernity as a means to make sense of an essentially fragmented world, he builds on the idea of allegory as a comforting, if forever inadequate, salvaging of meaning in a modern world. *In Time* corresponds nicely to Jameson's observation about the trend in allegory generally while also employing it to construct 'one-to-one' equivalences that are not part of the postmodern allegory he identifies. This way, the film, along with a number of other texts to be discussed later, lays bare an allegorical mode that is not only an attempt to portray a global world but is also, in effect, a way of containing it in structures at odds with this world. What gives *In Time* away, and what thereby undermines its political message on the level of content, is the way in which its narrative is framed by a formal structure that points towards constructions of meaning that are untenable. The modulations of power, neatly portrayed through the geopolitical organisation of time and production in the Time Lines and New Greenwich, respectively, and the literal incorporation of time into the body politic through the central metaphor that translates money into time may indeed illustrate some of the essential developments taking place in the transition between disciplinary and control society. However, the production of knowledge, also tidily conveyed through the neatness of its allegorical form, relies, if we choose to continue employing Deleuze's terminology of disciplinary and control society, less on modulations than it does on molds. In this sense, the film's form speaks against its content as the former points towards the possibility of equivalences that the latter seems to try to unpack. If allegory works so well in the context of global capitalism because it enables a production of meaning in the face of fluidity, as Jameson suggests and as we have seen earlier, *In Time* suggests that this 'geopolitical unconscious' is skewed in its nostalgia for a coherent production of meaning.

Now, allegory, not the least in its de Manian conception, inevitably comes with a temporal disjunction. The irony inherent in allegory resides exactly in the 'distance and difference' that forever keeps it from capturing totality. This 'truly temporal predicament' entails that the portrayal of a forever-inaccessible anteriority can be repeated indefinitely and with increasing consciousness, but it will also be 'endlessly caught in the impossibility of making this knowledge applicable to the empirical world' (de Man 2013, 528–29). In this sense, the disjunction outlined in reference to *In Time* is unsurprising. However, and as I have begun to suggest, there is also a more political dimension of this disjunction, one that has less to do with the inherent impossibility of concurrence and more with a more instrumental employment of this gap. As the clear-cut bodies, institutions, and identities in the film are reflected in what appears to be a rather direct allegorical exposition, the irony does not primarily reside in the awareness that the whole cannot be captured in the midst of attempts of doing just that, but rather in the exact opposite, that is, in its very projection of a 'knowledge applicable to the empirical world'.

This projection is in turn related to the second disturbing element of the film, which we find in the way in which this mainstream action movie, along with the many others mentioned in the introduction, takes it upon itself to criticise the capitalist system. As I noted in the introductory chapter, the fact that mainstream films of this kind seem to take on the burden of an, albeit superficial, commentary on capitalist exploitation of time seems itself worth considering. For Baudrillard, and as I began to discuss in chapter 1, a film like Niccol's would most likely be seen as but a 'mirage of critique' (Lotringer 2005, 11), a way of expressing political resistance that is really only part of the system. By means of the attention to form that we learned through the reading of Ballard's oeuvre in the previous chapter and that we can now apply to the reading of the function of allegory in *In Time*, we can develop and concretise this observation. The 'mirage of critique' can be located in the tension between the critique performed on the level of content and the specific use of a form that dislocates, or at least confuses, the political message. This is not to suggest that this constitutes a purposeful choice on behalf of the director or others involved in the making of the film. Rather, and especially as it can be situated as part of a larger trend of political allegories in mainstream culture, it may be seen as part of a larger system of control the very nature of which is to manipulate and exploit a sense of freedom beyond State and institutionalised politics.

In the control society that Deleuze begins to outline, I noted earlier, the configuration of power by means of institutions and identities, and thus of an inside and outside, that characterised Foucault's disciplinary society are shattered into an all-encompassing dissemination of power on all levels both within a specific society and in the world. Instead of more identifiable units of control, be they on the level of societal institutions or individual bodies, control comes to be distributed across and through all relations, and the line between inside and outside becomes increasingly blurred. While the integrated temporal system in Niccol's film, especially in comparison with the external system of power in Ballard's story, points to the indetermination of the inside and outside characteristic of control society, its formal elements continue to signal a separation between the two and thereby to point to the idea of control as an identifiable system separable from reality. Ultimately, then, and to return to the questions outlined at the beginning of this chapter, the film mirrors the reconfiguration of totality in our contemporaneity on the level of content at the same time as it relies on a formal construction that is at odds with this configuration. Because it points towards a mode of representation that resists rather than acknowledges the fragmentation of unity that stands at the bases of central conceptions of allegory, the mirage is not only thematic but also formal. The concomitant irony here is formal in the general sense of Benjamin's conception in that it works to approximate the particular work to the absolute but also in a more directly political sense in its particular envisioning of this absolute. The nature of this mirage and its function within control society is, as we see further in the next chapter, fundamentally linked to the logic of hiding the political in full view.

NOTES

1. The renewed interest in Accelerationism in recent years itself has an interesting relation to temporality building its response to contemporary neoliberal capitalism on late-nineteenth-century thinkers and writers such as Marx and Samuel Butler while producing 'accelerationism "itself" as a fictional or hyperstitional anticipation of intelligence to come', as Robin Mackay and Armen Avanessian put it (Mackay and Avanessian 2014, 8).

2. This built-in lifespan is reminiscent of Philip K. Dick's modern classic *Do Androids Dream of Electric Sheep?* (1968) and its adaptation into *Blade Runner* (1982). A brief comparison here brings out the differing role of time in these two texts. The main reason for the regulation of longevity in Dick's novel as well as in its adaptation is to ascertain that the androids, or replicas as they are called in the film, do not develop emotional and intellectual responses and thereby begin to question or threaten human control. Time is thereby portrayed in Dick as an essential part of becoming human. Making sure that the workers are always nearly out of time in Niccol's *In Time* constitutes a similar strategy of curtailing human traits. Positioning the possession of time as essentially human, the common theme of the worker as machine that both Dick and Niccol address, is sharpened in the contrast between difference in kind in Dick and difference in class in Niccol.

3. Indeed, the similarities between Niccol's film and Ellison's story were enough to warrant a plagiarism suit, which Ellison later abandoned.

FIVE

Vision, Allegory, Control

'The crimes of the postmodern American empire', Michael Rogin argues, are concealed much in the same way as Edgar Allan Poe's famous purloined letter (Rogin 1990, 99). If we have read Poe's short story or maybe one of the many analyses of it, we know that the letter in question remains undiscovered because it is placed in full view. In the postmodern empire, Rogin notes, spectacle and secrecy are not opposites, as one might think, but function together as a form of power that places the political spectacle as more than a form of diversion (Rogin 1990, 100). In the previous chapters, we have begun to discuss this tendency of placing the political spectacle at the forefront. In this final analytical chapter, I primarily address a set of texts that not only does this, but that also places the technologies of this spectacle more directly at its centre. Suzanne Collins's *The Hunger Games* trilogy is not only part of the tendency towards political allegory discussed earlier but also addresses this very spectacle head on. Having discussed spatial and temporal dimensions of the links between allegory, totality, and control in previous chapters, this chapter reads Collins's texts in order to comment on what is arguably one of the most potent forms of power today—that of vision.

Vision sits deeply embedded in the structures of power as well as in the nature of contemporary culture. In fact, one might argue that having traced our discussion of control and cultural critique through configurations of space and time in the previous chapters, this last one on vision takes us to the very heart of the matter. As an initial and hopefully illuminating example we may take a look at one of the more poignant cultural representations of the force of contemporary configurations of vision and politics in recent years. In the British miniseries *Black Mirror* (2011–) created by Charlie Brooker, each episode comments on the developments and deployments of visuality today as well as on their social, cultural, and political implications. Indeed, the title itself points to the reflective surface of the ubiquitous screens that infiltrate and dominate our spatial field in the present. We will return to this series later as well but for now, let us look at a couple of examples. The very first episode of the first season, 'The National Anthem', directly addresses the way in which a culture of viewing screens for pleasure or information is increasingly exchanged for one of watching for watching's sake. Briefly, the story revolves around the kidnapping of a member of the British royal family. The only demand issued by the kidnapper in exchange for the princess's freedom is that the prime minister has 'full unsimulated sexual intercourse with a pig' and that this event is broadcasted on all British television networks at a specified time that same afternoon. The episode depicts the increasingly panicked attempts to get around this demand. But the ultimate irony of the story, it turns out, is not the perversity of this request itself in the face of so many other potentially more political or economic demands. Rather, the irony is that once all other solutions have been abandoned and the required act is performed and aired, the princess has already been freed and stumbles along the streets of London, but there is no one there to notice her since everyone is busy watching the prime minister and the pig on television. The point is underlined further as we learn that the kidnapping has been a piece of performance art engineered by an artist wanting to illustrate exactly how we are so busy watching screens that we fail to notice the more unmediated reality taking place away from the black mirror.

Where the first episode thus comments on the tendency of watching for watching's sake, the second episode, 'Fifteen Million Merits', takes us straight to the core of the crisis in cultural critique as I am addressing it in this book. If the first episode comments on how the seduction of screens makes us oblivious to what might be going on outside the black mirror, this second one suggests that there is no such outside. The episode warns against a near future in which our bodies are completely subject to a virtual and highly controlled life on the screen. In this society, in which the characters spend their lives surrounded by computer screens and largely live through them, it is not possible even to close your eyes to block out unwanted ads or other imagery without punishment. As the protagonist Bing (Daniel Kaluuya) closes his eyes to the screening of his girlfriend's forced debut as a porn star, for example, a piercing noise invades his room, and a loud voice repeats 'Resume watching' until he has no choice but to do so. In other words, the preoccupation with watching screens, which was at least theoretically still optional in 'The National Anthem', has grown here into a systemically engineered obligation in this second episode—'all tiny cells and tiny screens, and bigger cells and bigger screens', as Bing describes the world in which he lives. The impossibility of opting out of the system is further underlined when Bing finally finds a way of airing his critique of the visual control system characterising this society as well as of the talent show that encapsulates the logic of this society. This show, 'Hot Shots', is a poignant parody of the plentiful talent shows existing today—'The X-Factor', 'Idol', and 'Got Talent', to mention a few prominent examples—and that have proliferated across numerous countries. In *Black Mirror*, the perverse power of such shows is underlined, not only by the fact that the performers are made to drink a cup of 'cuppliance' before they go onstage or because the jury has the power to select alternative careers for them, for example in the porn industry. Also, when Bing manages to sneak onstage in the middle of a show without drinking his 'cuppliance' and delivers a vehement and scathing critique of the show as well as the system that supports it, he is applauded and immediately given a show of his own. Thus, his critique can be regularly aired as entertainment. Although the setting is dystopian, this episode illustrates with some force the usurpation of critique and the nature of the culture industry theorised as the crisis in critique in chapter 1. It also constitutes a fictional example of what we will discuss later as the political spectacle as a form of power. Critique is entertainment too as its revolutionary force is undermined by its practically immediate incorporation into the system it aims to question. Outside of the fictional realm, if it is indeed possible to say so in this context, our comment on the blending of critique and entertainment in contemporary culture expressed in *Black Mirror* acquires an additional twist when the speaker voice on the Channel Four trailer for the episode uploaded to YouTube declares that 'Fifteen Million Merits' will be aired 'Sunday, nine thirty at Four, after the X-Factor final'.

VISUAL PREOCCUPATIONS

In the introduction to his tome on the role of vision in twentieth-century French thought, Martin Jay performs a playful and elegant demonstration of the ubiquity of visual metaphors. Filling his first paragraph to the brim with such metaphors, he directly but implicitly makes his point to the *'optique lecteur'* upon whom he counts to see them (Jay 1993, 1). Alongside this 'ocular permeation of language' he also notes the riches of historically and culturally dependent 'visually imbued cultural and social practices' (Jay 1993, 2). Tracing linguistic, scientific, religious, and cultural attitudes towards what René Descartes called the 'noblest' of senses, Jay focuses specifically on a theoretically diverse but specifically French philosophical and theoretical tradition that includes George Bataille, Jean-Paul Sartre, Maurice Merleau-Ponty, Michel Foucault, Louis Althusser, Guy Debord, Jacques Lacan, Luce Irigaray, Roland Barthes, Christian Metz, Jacques Derrida, and Jean-François Lyotard, all of whom, he argues, express some sort of hostility towards the primacy of vision (Jay 1993, 13). This 'antiocularcentric discourse', as he notes, is not a coherent one but constitutes, rather, a 'contradictory texture of statements, associations, and metaphors' (Jay 1993, 16). What many of them have in common, however, is the struggle to negotiate a sense of alienation in relation to vision, be it via a Heideggerian inability to transcend an individual viewpoint, a Lacanian conflicting of selves constituted through the mirror stage, or a feminist critique of the male gaze. Sartre's work, Jay argues, conflates many of the concerns expressed by others, his critique of ocularcentrism blaming it for contributing to the domination of nature, the domination of space over time, and for producing troubling intersubjective relations and misconceived notions of the self. This way, Jay notes, Sartre's interrogations include negative appraisals of vision in its social, psychological, as well as existential dimensions (Jay 1993, 276). Human freedom and human relations are disrupted by the look of the Other that alienates one from one's own body and the dialectics of vision that undermines the possibility of true reciprocality. For Sartre, vision also stands as the fundamental impediment to the idea of totalisation. Seeing the overcoming of alienation as fundamentally linked to the possibility of a normative totalisation based on a full knowledge of reality and linking totalising cognition with totalising action, his realisation of the impossibility of transcending the individual perspective leads to a pessimistic view of totalisation as well as of the liberating power of the visual (Jay 1993, 291). As linked to alienation and totalisation, vision constitutes a key dimension of the political for Sartre and Merleau-Ponty as well as post-Marxist thinkers such as Althusser, Debord, and Foucault. Increasingly, the yearning for a normative totality is displaced by a recognition of vision as performing a less-positive totalising function in modern society. Whether you focus on the spectacle as a scopic regime disciplining its subjects by means of seduction as do Debord and many others involved in the Situationist movement or place the emphasis on the role of visual surveillance as does Foucault, vision comes to be seen as a key player in modern forms of power.

And indeed, one of the most central features of discipline—itself not an apparatus or an institution, as Foucault stresses, but a type of power (Foucault 1995, 215)—is that of vision. 'The exercise of discipline', Foucault notes, 'presupposes a mechanism that coerces by means of observation; an apparatus in which the techniques that make it possible to see induce effects of power, and in which, conversely, the means of coercion make those on whom they are applied clearly visible' (Foucault 1995, 170–71). Tracing a development during the eighteenth century and onward in which vision as power becomes an increasingly important aspect of architectural society planning, Foucault notes how the aim of its constructions is no longer simply to be seen (palaces) or to look out from (fortresses), but to enable internal detailed control that renders visible, and thereby manageable, also the individuals it shelters (Foucault 1995, 172). This 'hierarchized, continuous and functional surveillance' brings with it an integrated and self-sustaining system of disciplinary power that keeps bodies in control by means of optics and mechanics—an 'uninterrupted play of calculated gazes' (Foucault 1995, 176–77). Jeremy Bentham's panopticon—this classic model of surveillance which subjects a particular and enclosed space to a single but centralised gaze—is the architectural figure Foucault adopts to illustrate disciplinary power. With the panopticon, power becomes visible yet unverifiable—the tower itself is visible and constitutes a reminder of the possibility of surveillance, but the certainty of exactly when surveillance is or is not taking place remains unspecified. (A mechanics of which is, incidentally, pertinently allegorised in another of J. G. Ballard's short stories, 'The Watch-Towers', from 1962.) This way, power is automatised and disindividualised—it is not linked to a particular person but to a distribution of bodies and gazes (Foucault 1995, 201–2). If the transition from a disciplinary to a control society means a crisis of institutions, a proliferation of borders, and a redistribution of space by which inside and outside are no longer clearly defined, as I have argued earlier in this book, this necessarily affects—or is part of an effect of—the role of vision as power. The type of surveillance that Foucault identifies as part of eighteenth-century discipline and that functions by means of a specific organisation of space that enables hierarchal and functional lines of vision (of which the panopticon constitutes a prime example) loses in efficiency.

Two key changes in the role of vision can be identified in the period in which discipline increasingly turns into control. First, the redistribution of space and the development in technology that revolutionises where, how, and what we can see and what can be seen has entailed a virtual explosion of the panopticon. Where it is no longer possible to exercise power by means of controlling clearly delineated spaces, power steps down from the tower, fragments, and proliferates into a multitude of smaller, mobile units. The border between the inside and outside becomes blurred as macro- and microscopic vision enable us to see and analyse even the smallest parts of bodies, DNAs, and brains from within. This border is also under question on a larger scale. If it is still constructive to talk about citizens under surveillance as 'inmates', as Foucault does, these are no longer inmates to a panoptical system with a delimited spatial organisation but rather inmates of a world in its entirety. There seems to be no outside to this newer type of multiplied and proliferating surveillance—what Paul Virilio calls 'the democratization of voyeurism on a planetary scale' (Virilio 2002, 109). It is no longer easy to identify a position from which the seeing and controlling is done, and it is even more difficult to determine who is doing the seeing. A 'banalization or popularization of global surveillance', as Virilio puts it, by which viewing, filming, or recording happens anywhere and everywhere, contributes to a new kind of self-sufficiency of control that does not require a tower. Information technologies such as mobile phones and computers enable new forms of control based on the restriction, the gathering, and the manipulation of information. The management and organisation of information in distributed and decentralised networks, Alexander Galloway suggests, is the panopticon adapted to control societies (Galloway 2004, 13).

Thus, a key development in the transition between disciplinary and control society is that the deployment of biopower becomes increasingly dispersed. As Patricia Clough describes it, political power is no longer primarily about the creation, education, and socialisation of individual subjects by means of interpellation into a predetermined system of socialised norms but rather about the continuous modulation of moods and affects, of capacities and potentialities, of data and information (Clough 2003, 360). The production of normalisation and socialisation is no longer primarily a job for the family and other civic institutions but becomes part of a broader investment in what Clough calls 'a market-driven circulation of affect and attention' (Clough 2003, 360). Attention time itself thereby becomes of great value to contemporary capitalist accumulation. 'Attention time' is an important formulation that we will return to later, but we can begin here by noting some of the implications of this developing biopower on vision. In a disciplinary society that relies on creating and maintaining clearly identifiable identities and positions, surveillance is about supervising and safeguarding this process. In a control society, however, what needs to be secured is not so much the disciplining of subjects into fixed identities but, quite differently, a continuous process of manipulation of moods and affects where what needs to be registered is fluctuating data such as preferences, ratings, and statistics (Clough 2003, 260). This means that controlling populations is increasingly about storing, accessing, and manipulating data. The panopticon, as Galloway puts it, has been replaced by the protocol of information networks (Galloway 2004, 13). Instead of being constructed as individuals as part of a mass, Gilles Deleuze suggests, we have become 'dividuals' as part of data and markets (Deleuze 1992, 5). By means of codes, our access to information can be denied or accepted, and also, most importantly, monitored. What needs to be under surveillance, in other words, is attention time itself. We are watched watching.

A central panopticon has not only become an impossibility in the new and largely virtual organisations of space but it has also become superfluous. Surveillance in contemporary control society, which is executed by means of computer software as much as cameras, is increasingly a job performed by the public itself. As allegorised in the film *The Final Cut* (2004) in which small implants are inserted into people's heads to enable a continuous recording of their whole lives—not because they have to but because they feel they want and need to—Western society of the past decades is characterised by an enthusiastic and arguably naïve affirmation of the coding and more or less implicit surveillance enabled by technological and digital developments. Similarly, the third and final episode of the first season of *Black Mirror*, 'The Entire History of You', portrays a memory chip with a recording device implanted behind the ears of the characters. The characters can play back everything they do and see to themselves as well as to others. Needless to say, this creates complications, for example, as jealous partners can demand to see their respective partner's previous experiences. Such fictional accounts of the constant recording that happens between people only push to the extreme a reality where people are already monitoring each other more or less intentionally. Vision remains a highly important political tool in control society, but its focus has changed; at the same time as the panopticon has multiplied and been put in the hands of each and every person, the importance of each and every person watching increases in significance. As Jean Baudrillard notes, watching has become a banality—we watch even when there is nothing to watch. When we are not watching each other's everyday banality by means of, for example, Facebook, we are watching 'reality shows' that, supposedly, enable us to watch other people's banality.

To some extent, of course, this is the same banality that Theodor W. Adorno and Max Horkheimer observe as a decisive factor of the culture industry already in the late 1940s. Incorporating everything within itself and reducing outside truths to entertaining lies for consumption, the culture industry that Adorno and Horkheimer see emerging in the mid-twentieth-century United States provides amusement that demands no effort by its consumers. Culture becomes but a 'prolongation of work'—an efficient way of remolding a desire to rest from the monotony of labour into the monotony of entertainment without thought. 'Entertainment', as they put it quite simply, 'is the prolongation of work under late capitalism' (Adorno and Horkheimer 2002, 107–9). While Adorno and Horkheimer's point about the purposeful banality of the culture industry is still valid, we have noted already that Antonio Negri suggests that Adorno and Horkheimer's groundbreaking critique forwarded in 1940s needs replacing not because it is wrong but because it has become redundant. The exponential proliferation of images and information today by means of all possible channels is evident not only in the endless production of trash culture and the simultaneous construction of an audience for it but also more generally in a 'capitalist production of repetitive images' that obfuscate reality and narrate global fantasies by means of viral immediacy (Negri 2007, 49–50). At this point, Negri argues, indignation is pointless—'history is over'—and to go somewhere new we have to take this perversion of culture not as an object of analysis itself but as a starting point. Instead of looking for a beyond of the culture industry—'the escape routes have been blocked' (Negri 2007, 54)—we must work to locate alternatives within it.

If there is little point, then, in spending time commenting on the banality of what we watch, it seems to have become all the more important to take a closer look at the act of watching itself. As the first episode of *Black Mirror* illustrated above, the importance of the content of the image is often overtrumped by the importance of the fact that we are watching it in the first place. While the act of watching itself was important already in Adorno and Horkheimer's critique as the seduction of the masses was largely about keeping them harnessed to the 'unity of production' (Adorno and Horkheimer 2002, 98), vision, as we have already noted, has become increasingly more complex. The power of visual culture is no longer simply about keeping people securely located in their TV-sofas. Instead, we are increasingly part of a larger and more mobile apparatus of watching. As Virilio notes, the 'tele-presence' that now brings us images of world events in live time and the direct access to programs, news, and more-or-less edited information via live cameras streaming online far exceeds the controlling power of the television of the past fifty years (Virilio 2002, 108–9). The panoptical power of this developed visuality can barely be compared with the visual economy of the television as this information can be employed by anything from marketing specialists to the military forces (Virilio 2002, 109). The panopticon and the culture industry have merged into one. The price we have to pay for tele-presence, Virilio notes, is that we inevitably have to subject ourselves to the same all-encompassing surveillance (Virilio 2002, 110). Importantly, this surveillance is not only about being watched but also about being watched watching. We continually give up information about what we watch and about the kind of information we search for and access. Exploring the internal logic of visuality in control society, a preliminary observation says that we should shift focus from the consumption of trash to the consumption of vision itself.

This brings us, after some detours, to a second key development in the function of vision for control society, and one that is inevitably related to the first. This is the instability between image and reality associated with a Baudrillardian postmodernity. The 'precession of simulacra' that, according to Baudrillard, breaks up the relation between seeing and referent means the end of the panopticon as it forever undermines the link between vision as truth (Baudrillard 1994, 29). Vision becomes a power in and of itself—it is not only a case of control by surveillance but also control by means of occupying the spatial field in its entirety with simulation. Simulacra, in this view, block and undo the possibility of accessing the real or even do away with the real itself. This understanding of postmodernism, as Jay notes, can be seen as the 'apotheosis of the visual, the triumph of the simulacrum over what it purports to represent, a veritable surrender to the phantasmagoric spectacle' (Jay 1993, 543). Vision as power, in this sense, is not necessarily related to the surveillance of people and movement but is rather about purposing the very function of images—of controlling the visual field. As Rogin's work underlines, visual politics is not so much about hiding politically controversial or ethically questionable actions but about presenting them in a format that makes them seemingly acceptable. And as my work in this book attempts to stress, the allegorical format that has grown so pervasive of late plays a role in this development.

BREAD AND CIRCUSES: *THE HUNGER GAMES*

Collins's immensely popular *The Hunger Games* trilogy fits into all the central categories addressed in this book: it is a blatant allegory of contemporary culture and politics, it portrays a society struggling with both totality and totalitarianism, and it addresses questions of discipline and control. It is also a highly mainstream set of texts. While *Black Mirror's* creator Brooker is well-established in British media as a presenter, journalist, and producer and is also an established satirist and critic of contemporary culture, and while his TV series also earned an International Emmy award, its general impact on a wider audience is still quite limited compared to the enormous popular reach of *The Hunger Games* novels.[1] This trilogy, consisting of *The Hunger Games*, *Catching Fire*, and *Mockingjay*, published between 2008 and 2010 for a young adult audience, is a US bestseller equaled only by J. K. Rowling's *Harry Potter* books (1997–2007) and Stephanie Meyer's *Twilight* series (2005–2008). Collins's books offer a dystopian vision of an America in which political control merges with the entertainment industry to horrifying effects. In this dystopian world, an entertainment industry is built around children being forced to kill children. Strikingly, this admittedly science-fictional set-up increasingly comes to resemble our contemporary reality. Indeed, Collins states in an interview that the idea for the books emerged as she was channel surfing and realised she had problems telling a reality show apart from actual war coverage (Collins 2008, 457). Like Brooker's *Black Mirror*, which is described by its creator as being 'about the way we live now—and the way we might be living in 10 minutes' time if we're clumsy' (Brooker 2011, n.p.), Collins's texts provide but a twist on the reality we already live in. My question, in consistency with the earlier chapters, is to what effect the allegorical format is put to use. As in the previous chapter, I will pay attention to the ways in which the political dimensions of control and vision are played out both on the level of content and on the level of form.

In terms of content, Collins's trilogy comes across as a critical commentary on the direction in which cultural, political, and technological developments seem to be taking us. Compared to the analysis of *In Time*, and in which we saw time becoming absorbed into the social and affective realms of society, *The Hunger Games* depicts a drive towards totality based largely on the visual dimensions of control. Collins's fictional country, Panem, is run by a central Capitol, which has twelve districts surrounding it. These districts are divided into efficient labouring areas that supply the Capitol with the various goods it needs—from foods to textiles to coal. There used to be a district thirteen, but after a failed rebellion against the Capitol, twelve of the districts were defeated and the thirteenth supposedly obliterated. As a way of reminding the districts of its power and of what they have to lose should they ever think of instigating another rebellion, Capitol arranges annual 'Hunger Games'. For these games, one boy and one girl between the ages twelve and eighteen from each district are chosen as 'tributes'. The process of selecting is by means of a 'reaping' in which the names of the tributes are drawn. This system is far from equal. The children from the Capitol do not have to participate, and the poorest in the districts repeatedly have to sign up for 'tesserae'. This consists of meager rations of grain and oil to keep them through the year in exchange for their children's names being added multiple times in the drawing. Each year a new enormous arena is constructed for the games, and each year, the tributes are forced to fight and kill each other until there is only one survivor. The Games are filmed in their entirety and from multiple angles, and the whole of Panem can watch them as a twenty-four-hour reality show.

Where Andrew Niccol's film presented a world-system as an overviewable totality monitored by means of time, *The Hunger Games* portrays a similar sense of totality but one in which the visual comes to dominate both the temporal and the spatial dimensions of the political system. The global distribution of power, which, as I discussed in the previous chapter, increasingly separates a Western society based on immaterial labour and consumption from a more linear labour of production in countries outside itself is clearly reflected in Panem's marked distinction between the Capitol and the districts. On the one hand, the division of districts into functional units specialised in different types of production is indicative of a disciplinary system resembling a nineteenth-century industrial society. Panem is constructed almost literally as a panopticon. With the Capitol as a central point of control, the districts surrounding it are under constant surveillance. Apart from the 'Peacekeepers' who patrol the districts, the system relies on hierarchised and continuous surveillance. This keeps the citizens in control by means of optics and mechanics—they are under the constant gaze of the Capitol. Surveillance safeguards economic efficiency. As such, it corresponds to labour under capital which, as Foucault notes through Marx, is a labour necessarily tied to superintendence and in which surveillance thereby becomes a decisive economic factor (Foucault 1995, 175). Employing a Taylorist mode of production building on the specialisation and distribution of labour, the Capitol, as the centre of power, outsources manual labour to the districts while maintaining very high living standards for its own citizens. Not having to bother with dirtier modes of production and manual labour, the citizens of Capitol turn money around by means of consumption. Grand colourful buildings, shiny cars, and wide streets characterise the city's spatial set-up, and high attention levels when it comes fashion and entertainment characterise its inhabitants (*Hunger* 72).

The spectacle of the Hunger Games stands as the pinnacle of this system. To begin with, the 'show' functions as a vehicle for much of the immaterial labour performed in the Capitol. It constitutes a riveting mode of entertainment that keeps its Capitol consumers in the grip of excitement, gossip, and betting. The 'reality' of this show clearly cannot be grasped by citizens who are happily pulled into the affective involvement ascertained by the Games and the marketing industry that surrounds and supports them. But the people of the Capitol contribute to the system not only by investing their interest and affectivity in the Games but also by partaking in the large machinery of service, design, and fashion associated with them. Never exposed to manual labour and mainly feeding off the labour outsourced to the districts, their labour can thus be described as what Michael Hardt calls 'the very pinnacle of the hierarchy of laboring forms', which has developed during the past decades along with the capitalist economy (Hardt 1999, 90). From being associated primarily with care and nurture, affective, or immaterial labour has been adopted by capitalist structures to become value-effective. Maurizio Lazzarato notes two different aspects of immaterial labour that organises work in control society. First, there is the labour associated with the '"informational content" of the commodity', that is, the work which is decreasingly about direct physical labour and increasingly about processing cybernetics and computers. Second, there is the work producing 'the "cultural content" of the commodity', that is, the immaterial labour related to defining and determining cultural, artistic, and consumer standards and norms, shaping tastes and fashions, and public opinion (Lazzarato 1996, 133). Both these aspects are clearly delineated in the Capitol. There are those involved in constructing, editing, and broadcasting the Games as well as those designing new arenas with new challenges to its players, thereby ensuring new topics of conversation, new targets for betting, and new fashions. Promoting a continuous innovation, as Lazzarato notes, immaterial labour relies on continually updating forms and conditions of communication and consumption, a process that will in turn engender new needs and tastes. Indeed, a central point about the commodity produced by means of immaterial labour is that it is under continual growth and transformation and as such, that it keeps producing and reproducing the capital relation (Lazzarato 1996, 138).

The second way in which the Hunger Games constitute the key of the political system of Panem is by controlling the workers in the various districts. The system relies, not only on the Capitol's constant gaze on the workers but also on the workers' own gaze being forcefully locked on the screens displaying the Hunger Games. The Games thus have the twofold effect of maintaining a level of control and consumption in the Capitol while at the same time reminding the citizens of the districts of the logic of this kind of power. 'Taking the kids from our districts, forcing them to kill one another while we watch—this is the Capitol's way of reminding us how totally we are at their mercy. How little chance we would stand of surviving another rebellion. Whatever words they use, the message is clear' (*Hunger* 22). In other words, the relation between vision and power is no longer only a matter of workers being disciplined by means of surveillance. They are also controlled by an 'entertainment industry' that forces them to literally look at their own submission.

The spatial logic of Panem serves as a comment on the spatial distribution of power on a worldwide scale discussed also in previous chapters. The Capitol relies on immaterial labour and control for its internal politics at the same time as it also relies on maintaining the structures of linear production in the parts of the country to which it has outsourced its production. As such, the text recognises a distribution of space that separates a First World dominated by leisure and consumption from a Third World to which its production has been outsourced. This separation also comes with a physical as well as emotional detachment from the realities of production and its concomitant expenditure of lives. Comparing this separation with the similar separations in the texts discussed in the previous chapters helps to further underline the importance of visuality in Collins's works. In Ballard's last set of novels, as I noted in chapter 3, the world of production is made tangible in its absence, as if the world in its entirety consisted of the smooth spaces of the rich West. In Niccol's film, by contrast, and as discussed in chapter 4, the line of production is very clearly portrayed as part of a totality. In both these instances, however, the spaces of material production are hidden away, thus keeping suffering and hardship from the view of those with material wealth. In Collins's books, this separation of the spaces of production from those of consumption is still underlined by means of the spatial set-up of the districts, but here, crucially, the system of control builds on visibility rather than invisibility. While the spaces of material production are separated from the spaces of immaterial production geographically by means of the districts, the 'dirty' side of production is not kept outside the gaze and the awareness of the leisurely world it services. Quite on the contrary, the visual politics of the Hunger Games places this relation in direct focus. Not only are the inhabitants of the Capitol reminded of the districts by means of their annual tributes to the Hunger Games, the various modes of production in them are also underlined by means of the representational logic that underpins it. The tributes to the Games are supposed to be dressed to reflect their district. In line with the creation and maintenance of clearly identifiable identities and positions in Foucault's disciplinary society, each tribute needs to wear something that 'suggests your district's principal industry' (*Hunger* 80).

The power of the entertainment industry that the books depict is not one of television so much as one based on the ever-present 'tele-presence' that Virilio discusses. The arenas for the Hunger Games are enormous but delineated spaces constructed by Gamemakers every year to vary the challenges facing the participants. What does not vary is the ubiquity of cameras. Far from the central tower of the panopticon, the high-tech construction of the arena makes it possible to follow the tributes' every move. What is important here is not only that each step is recorded but that it is assessed. The visual economy of surveillance is designed not so much to ensure economic efficiency in the traditional Marxist sense but as to enable a more distributed affective economy. Even before they enter the arenas, the tributes learn the vital importance of acting for the cameras. The individual tributes are—or are not—sponsored by the people in the Capitol depending on whether they manage to secure their liking, pity, or admiration. Survival thus comes to depend on behaving in a manner that appeals to the people watching the show. The participants quickly learn that acting for the cameras is the same thing as acting to survive. As two of the protagonists, Katniss and Peeta, learn to play the game by acting out a relationship that satisfies the audience's desire for romance, the supposed reality of the show disintegrates. So does the experience of it by its 'actors' who soon lose track of the meaning and reason behind their own actions. For the system in place, however, this loss of meaning is not a loss but a victory: the behaviour of the participants can be modulated in accordance with audience wishes. This system of sponsoring mirrors a world in which the concern about the world politics is largely dependent on the extent to which it is made visible and recognisable. Apart from being subject to political and economic considerations, the possibility of coverage and subsequent 'sponsoring' also tends to rely on the spectacular nature of events and on the presentation of events in ways that make people relate. Should the controlling power of the cameras not be enough to manipulate the participants' behaviour to ensure the best possible entertainment, the power of editing the material leaves the organisers of the Games in full control of what aspects of the Games are made visible. As the second and third books make increasingly clear, the same logic applies also outside the arenas. In short, what the visual event displays is not primarily reality, or even entertainment, but power.

The visual event as power in Collins's books reflects the way 'real-life' footage turns coverage of world wars into spectacular events with a questionable relation to 'reality'. Baudrillard's claims that the Gulf War 'will not take place', may not really be 'taking place', and, ultimately, 'did not take place' comment on the way in which an endless exchange of signs has come to replace the direct intervention into reality. In response to the more recent events of 9/11 and the Abu Ghraib images, he writes that the grotesque images that emerged from the prison in Baghdad turn into parodies of violence and war. They constitute a type of pornography or grotesque reality show that does not illustrate war so much as it demonstrates power that 'no longer knows what to do with itself' (Baudrillard 2006, 86). Such power can find nothing better to do than to exert gratuitous violence and humiliation. *The Hunger Games*, however, points back to a visual economy in which power knows exactly what to do with itself. The visual is not indicative of excess but of the very core of control. If the truth of the images that Baudrillard speaks of lies in 'the excessiveness of a power designating itself as abject and pornographic' (Baudrillard 2006, 87), the truth of Collins's fictional world takes this one step further: the visual does not point to the excessiveness of power so much as it locates itself at the very centre of power. The citizens of Capitol may think they look at the events of the Hunger Games but, and as many of the citizens of the rest of Panem have already realised, they are really looking at power. And as we have seen, their entertainment is not just at the expense of the districts—their entertainment constitutes the basis of the economy and control of the country at large. On the one hand, the preoccupation with the Hunger Games (and indeed, our own preoccupation with *The Hunger Games*) functions the way the entertainment industry has been seen to function ever since Adorno and Horkheimer. It keeps the people of the Capitol in control, busy watching 'reality shows' rather than the world. On the other hand, a crucial intensification of this cultural logic has taken place. Collins's books depict as well as reflect a situation in which the reality show constitutes a 'prolongation of work' as Adorno and Horkheimer put it, in a more radical sense. It cannot be separated from reality as it constitutes the basis for the entire economic and political system.

Proposing, then, that *The Hunger Games* provides an allegory of control society and in particular the centrality of its visual components, should it be seen primarily as an illustration of Baudrillard's two theories outlined above, one pertaining to the role of simulacra and the other one to the complete subsumption of critique into control society? Or are there ways of reading these texts as more or less avertedly providing the means to think of how agency can be recuperated also in a control society? On the level of content, the answer to the last question would be 'yes'. A first thing that the novels make clear is that an earlier mode of resistance that responds to the power structures of disciplinary society no longer suffices. As we noted at the end of the previous chapter, disciplinary power involves a politics of representation that relies on representation and institutions but that also to some extent makes space for resistance by means of a transgression of institutional norms and identities (Clough 2003, 360). While the distribution of labour to the different districts in Collins's books to some extent speaks to a politics of representation insofar as the subjects in the districts are molded into particular social groups and functions, the overreaching system of control relies rather on the manipulation of moods and behaviours by means of affectivity and visual control. As we noted above, two systems to some extent coexist. The earlier and half-failed rebellion to some extent reflects what appears to be an older form of power struggle. Geographical factors are of major importance as one reason for the failure of the rebellion was the barrier of mountains between the Capitol and the rebelling districts as these made the transgressing rebels easy targets for the air forces of the Capitol (*Hunger* 71). Ultimately, nuclear bombs put district thirteen in ruins. As we learn in the later books, however, this district was not obliterated but was capable, thanks to its nuclear power assets, to enter into an agreement with Capitol that it would remain independent but also hidden from the rest of Panem. On the one hand, this speaks to a Cold War tactics of nuclear balance. On the other hand, the agreement of invisibility here—suggesting that the most dangerous threat to the powers of Panem is the very recognition of a force outside itself that it has not managed to quench—points to a politics of visuality more in line with more contemporary control systems. Where the tactics of the Cold War were based on overt and polarised displays of power, the tactics in Panem are to render the very idea of an outside invisible. This is a tactics that the rebels have recognised and learned to use to their own advantage once the second cycle of the revolution begins to gain pace. Because the manipulation of visuality and information are key to power and control in Panem, the rebels increasingly come to work the system by its own means. Like the anti G8 demonstrators in Genoa in 2001 who, as Negri points out, rebelled against the police and its presented version of the events by producing more images themselves (Negri 2007, 49), the rebels in Panem recognise the visual as a key to control and therefore, also, the key to change. If the society depicted in *The Hunger Games* is one clearly in the grips of visual control, it is also through this focus on the visual that the rebellion becomes possible.

Tellingly, when district thirteen prepares for its new revolution it is not by means of atomic bombs but by means of gradually infiltrating and subverting the visual field. A central factor in this is the initial styling of Katniss Everdeen. Like all participants in the Hunger Games, she is subjected to hours in a 'Remake Centre'. Here, she is attributed a certain image, style, and outfit. The districts are rendered visible by means of their outfits, as we saw earlier, and Katniss comes from the coal district. Previous years, tributes from this district have been made to wear 'skimpy outfits and hats with headlamps' (*Hunger* 80). Katniss's stylist, Cinna, however, is a rebel who has infiltrated the Games, and he dresses Katniss in 'what will either be the most sensational or the deadliest costume in the opening ceremonies' (*Hunger* 81). Only wearing black and with synthetic flames attached to her cape and headpiece, Katniss is made out like 'the girl who was on fire' (*Hunger* 82). The outfit is a great success with the Capitol audience, all in line with the Hunger Games as a spectacle and mode of entertainment. But what neither Katniss nor the audience (nor the reader) know at this point is that this is an image that will be gradually built up to become the key symbol of the rebellion against the Capitol. As 'the girl on fire', Katniss acquires a central role as the system itself 'catches fire' through the rebellion growing in the second volume of the series. There are several additional examples of how the rebels in the books use the system against itself in ways that pertain specifically to the central role of the visual. Attention time, as a central factor in the maintenance of control, is employed to gradually undermine and eventually overturn the system. I have noted earlier how the power structures of control society are harder to identify and to resist since they lack clearly identifiable institutions. The manipulation of moods and behaviours constitutes a more flexible way of maintaining a control in tune with market-driven systems than the constitution of subjects into fixed norms. This also makes the control system more efficient and all-encompassing. Collins's books suggest that this flexibility is not only its strength but also its weakness as it remains open to repurposing.

In *The Hunger Games*, the free-floating nature of the meaning of images turns out to be a key weapon not only in critiquing but also in resisting and overturning the powers of the Capitol. The gradual development of this repurposing is poignantly captured in the image of the Mockingjay pin that Katniss has received from a friend before her first Hunger Games and which she wears throughout them. As Katniss's popularity increases in the eyes of the Capitol audience, the Mockingjay begins to appear as a fashion item. At this point, it is but part of the merchandise that comes with the entertainment industry. The Mockingjay represents a manageable level of rebellion quite suitable for the fashion industry. Like the Che Guevara T-shirts sold in the shopping mall, it evokes a titillating but harmless dose of feeling insubordinate. As Katniss escapes 'the Gamemakers, making me their star' and 'President Snow, trying to use me to put out the flames of the rebellion', she finally agrees to become the symbol of the rebels—the Mockingjay (*Mockingjay* 70). Having been made over by her prep team for the various versions of the Hunger Games, she mistakenly thinks that '[a]s a rebel, I thought I'd get to look more like myself'. However, she soon learns, 'it seems a televised rebel has her own standards to live up to'. The importance of her visual appearance is essential: 'With my acid-damaged hair, sunburned skin and ugly scars, the prep team has to make me pretty and *then* damage, burn and scar me in a more attractive way' (*Mockingjay* 71). Made up in this way, Katniss, as the Mockingjay, becomes a key motivator in the revolution.

The importance given to infiltrating the visual field and broadcasting the rebellion points towards a key change in the role of visual culture as its power mechanisms intensify along with control society. The entertainment as a prolongation of work that Adorno and Horkheimer analyse in the 1940s is closely associated with a type of mechanised labour from which the worker thinks s/he is resting when slumping down in front of the TV at night. It is an effortless, schematic, and prescribed mode of leisure that functions in tandem with the mode of production. The sense of television as that which devours the attention and the energy of the worker has continued to shape approaches to the entertainment industry. 'The revolution will not be televised', sang Gil Scott-Heron in the early 1970s, picking up this line from a slogan from the 1960s. 'You will not be able to plug in, turn on and cop out.' Although this aspect of the entertainment industry is certainly still active, the changing nature of labour in the Western world from industrial production to immaterial and affective labour brings with it a shift also in the role of visual culture. Its nature and thereby its role as a political tool has changed quite profoundly. Placing Brooker's and Collins's works next to each other, not to mention historical events such as the Genoa demonstrations and the rebellions associated with the Arab spring, suggests that in line with the logic of control society, the revolution is actually extremely likely to be, if not televised, then screened. As the possibility of stepping outside the televisual field diminishes, the question is no longer whether the revolution will be televised. Rather, the question must be whether the revolution will be transformed into harmless amusement—a development theorised by Baudrillard and projected in Brooker's work as we have seen earlier—or if it will be able to retain its subversive force. Perhaps 'televised' is no longer the best term to describe the continuous televisuality of contemporary society as it suggests a recording of events that somehow happen apart from and independently of the camera. Indeed, the totality of culture industry that Adorno and Horkheimer analyse is such exactly because it has devoured all art and culture within itself—'what is destroyed as truth outside its sphere can be reproduced indefinitely within it as lies' (Adorno and Horkheimer 2002, 107). In the present, the idea of an outside truth is increasingly difficult to uphold. As Negri notes, while television continues to reconstruct dominant truths, the current state of telematics communication also opens for subjectivation. There is space, within this field, for 'the spirit of the multitude' to produce its own images and thus to transform the visual field from within (Negri 2007, 49). The 'monstrosity' of postmodern innovation is exactly the mutation of its own internal limits (Negri 2007, 54). In the light of these changes, the point is not what happens outside the screen but how it is employed. If the once avant-garde strategy of détournement has become part and parcel of mainstream postmodern culture of repurposing, as Bonnett suggests, we can give up on its radical potential, but we can also recognise that its potency is all the stronger since not only the potential objects for repurposing but the very strategy itself is located at the very heart of this cultural logic.

CULTURAL CRITIQUE AND FORM

But while *The Hunger Games* seems to point to revolutionary ideals, the books, as I stated at the very beginning of this study, also constitute central examples of those contemporary texts that press the question of why American mainstream culture so readily seems to present allegories of contemporary forms of capitalism and control. If the level of content suggests a revolutionary approach to society, how are we to relate this to the laying bare of critique, to the empty conspiracy that Baudrillard theorises, and to the political spectacle that Rogin discusses? As I noted in the introductory chapter, resistance, subversion, and critique have typically been the labour of alternative cultural expression, a critique that either by choice or necessity has been performed from the 'outside'. The arena for political commentary has been marked by the avant-garde or the underground or other positions that gain strength exactly by being other than the society they critique. On the level of content, this is also exactly what happens in Collins's books. It is in the most distant and exploited parts of society that the resistance is sparked. On the level of context, on the other hand, the matter becomes more complex. *The Hunger Games* and its reception can hardly be understood in terms of underground or alternative cultural politics. As over twenty-five million copies of the books are sold, and as its adaptations bring in a record audience at the cinemas, and as young adults and adults in the West are offered an exciting story but also a mirror that reflects back on the society in which they live, how are we to interpret the political implications of this phenomenon? Do *The Hunger Games* novels, like *The Matrix* in Baudrillard's reading, participate in the dissemination and refraction of the monopolistic superpower it represents (Baudrillard 2005, 203)? Do they, like *Wall-E* in Mark Fisher's argument, perform 'our anti-capitalism for us, allowing us to consume with impunity' (Fisher 2009, 12)? Do they constitute but another example of the disappearance of critique and the disappearance of the outside in a society in which resistance is built into culture and rendered innocuous? Or can they assist a new imagining of a resistance that emerges from within the system, a means of interrogating the internalisation of control and search for potential resistance? If analysing new techniques of social control is meaningful only insofar as it makes it possible to identify potentialities of contestation within the paradigm itself, as Hardt suggests (Hardt 1995, 41), does *The Hunger Games* emerge as a good example of how the two-faced interiority of contemporary biopolitics can be used against itself? I will suggest, in a moment, that the only way of making this possible is to return to the question of form.

Black Mirror and *The Hunger Games* hardly constitute the first popular works to present dystopian versions of commodified entertainment generally and the game show particularly. When it comes to Collins's work, it needs to be positioned as a part of a current trend of dystopian young fiction. Mary F. Pharr and Leisa A. Clark note a development in the genre of young adult novels with dystopian and/or postapocalyptic thematics from more individual struggles against 'oppression, aliens, or the environment' towards a focus also on social change. Veronica Roth's *Divergent* trilogy and their adaptations into film, for example, depict a postapocalyptic world in which people are controlled by being divided into factions. Pharr and Clark's own examples include James DeVita's *The Silenced* (2007) and Clare B. Dunckle's *The Sky Inside* (2008), both of which in different ways portray the young resisting totalitarian regimes (Pharr and Clark 2012, 8). Most of these new novels, they note, depict resistance against a totalitarian government recognised as such mainly by the young people—adults being either ineffectual or indoctrinated. Pharr and Clark position this development in relation to a post-9/11 context in which less is taken for granted and a sense that the United States is not doing so well, and 'may eventually fall like the Roman Empire' (Pharr and Clark 2012, 9).

Collins's texts have also been situated in relation to works that address politics as entertainment more specifically. Some examples that have appeared as references include Richard Bachman's (pseudonym for Stephen King) novels *The Long Walk* (1979) and *The Running Man* (1982, adapted into film 1987). There are also the similarities to the novel *Battle Royale* by Koushun Takami (1999, adapted into film 2000), which instigated accusations of plagiarism. *The Long Walk* features a walking competition for young boys taking place in a dystopian totalitarian United States where slowing down means getting ticketed and too many tickets means death. This game show is not televised although it is clearly written in response to the entertainment industry. Most chapters of the book, it has been noted, open with epigraphs from a creator or host of real-life classic television game shows such as *Jeopardy!*, *You Bet Your Life*, and *Gong Show*, the quote from the latter stating how '[t]he ultimate game show would be one where the losing contestant was killed' (Wiater, Golden, and Wagner 2006, 426). *The Running Man*, too, is set in a dystopian totalitarian United States, and in this novel television is included as a factor in the game. This time, the game involves a man being hunted by hitmen, making money for every hour he manages to remain alive. The game show is very popular, and its followers can increase the excitement by betting on their favourites and they can also be rewarded for helping locate the runner. *Battle Royale*, which is written as well as set in a Japanese dystopia, features an annual death camp in which teenagers are placed in a closed environment and are forced to kill each other. As in *The Hunger Games*, the purpose is to scare the citizens into obedience. Unlike in *The Hunger Games*, the event itself is not publicly televised. All these works are dystopian, and all of them position the entertainment industry as an important tool of political control.

Although contemporary 'real-life' game shows have not reached their 'ultimate' form of killing off contestants, it seems clear, knowing that the two Bachman novels were published in the late 1970s and early 80s, that they anticipate some of the developments in Reality TV as it appears on our screens today. Without digging too deep into the nature of reality television and the scholarly field it has given rise to, what is of immediate relevance here is the relation between these programs and their sociopolitical context. As a forerunner of Reality TV, it has been argued that *Candid Camera*, which started airing in the United States in 1948, responded to contemporary developments in technology as well as to the Cold War by means of 'simulation-anxiety'. This anxiety was raised by difficulties in distinguishing between the real and the fictional. It also responded to an increasing 'surveillance anxiety' in the shape of the fear of being secretly monitored. By assuaging these anxieties, Bradley D. Clissold argues, *Candid Camera* filled an ideological function as it helped 'perpetuate a "poetics of the real"' and downplay the dangers of surveillance to the point where supposedly private moments become light entertainment even endorsed by the person surveilled (Clissold 2004, 33). The program responded to and functioned as a comic relief of such anxieties but also worked to distract from the real-world political implications. Clissold notes how anxieties provoked by a radio show during the Second World War in which soldiers were recorded without first being alerted to the fact caused *Time* magazine, almost quaintly, looking back, to argue that radio had crossed 'the last threshold of privacy' (quoted in Clissold [2004, 34]). At the same time, however, and as Clissold points out, the fact that the whole country was encouraged by government propaganda to spy on each other for signs of 'un-American activity' positions the radio program as a cultural response to such surveillance politics rather than as its source (Clissold 2004, 34). Tracing the development of modern-day surveillance and culture through the Cold War, Clissold notes how the most classic of political allegories and the mother of 'Big Brother', Orwell's *1984*, was also part of this cultural response to the sense of an all-pervasive surveillance (Clissold 2004, 38). Similarly, Clissold argues, as have many others, that the popularity of Reality TV during the past decades responds to postmodern anxieties about the intensification of hyperreality, simulation, and the sense of losing the grip on the real (Clissold 2004, 49). Because of the way in which such programs, from *Candid Camera* to *Survivor*, are implicated in sociopolitical concerns of surveillance and simulation it is necessary, Clissold summarises, to explore also the ways in which contemporary Reality TV programs share the 'deep-seated ideological alliances' of *Candid Camera* (Clissold 2004, 51).

The Hunger Games, of course, is not a Reality TV show but rather a fictional portrayal of one. We have already analysed in the previous section how this phenomenon is played out in the plot, so now, let us see what to make of the fact that in reading Collins's books, we as readers are placed in the position of reading about watching watching or, as viewers of the adaptations, in the position of watching watching watching. As I suggested earlier in this chapter, the dispersal of biopower that comes as disciplinary society turns into one of control entails a shift from a system of interpellating subjects into predetermined systems to a system based on the continuous modulation of moods, affects, and information. By the same token, attention time shifts from centring on the surveillance of individuals towards being focused on monitoring and manipulating the attention time of these individuals itself. Taking as a basic premise the idea that the books reflect and constitute a part of a sociopolitical development of a cultural politics of vision in line with Clissold's reading of *Candid Camera*, we need to take into consideration the two dimensions of the cultural anxiety they may reflect and the political function they perform. Just as it seems easy to accept Clissold's suggestion that the early days of *Candid Camera* reflected anxieties of surveillance and simulation related to Cold War political and technological developments, it is easy to establish that Collins's books reflect contemporary concerns with the way in which the entertainment industry and the politics of control are merging today. A more complex argument, and one that Clissold skirts, is the one about the political function of these cultural forms of expression. Clissold touches on the idea that *Candid Camera* not only alleviated anxieties but also worked to distract from the more politically informed modes of surveillance going on at the same time. Similarly, I would like to suggest that *The Hunger Games* trilogy has a political function that, while appearing as critique of political control on the level of content, ultimately serves as a part of the contemporary political control systems itself on the level of form.

In terms of *Candid Camera* and the subsequent Reality TV tradition, the tension, insofar as the two sides can be separated, is between a cultural response to current developments and a political dimension of this response as being implicated in, even as it distracts from, these developments. As we saw, Clissold reads the messages conveyed by *Candid Camera* as powerful but implicit. Reading the jingle he identifies a set of ideologically informed messages. Thus, for example, we find that 'surveillance is fun ("Smile!") and fortunate ("your lucky day")' and also 'random democratic selection ("least expect it" and "elected"), open and instant access to celebrity status ("You're a star today")' (Clissold 2004, 43). In other words, and in a fairly unsurprising way, a show of supposedly straightforward entertainment is riddled with ideological motifs. When it comes to *The Hunger Games*, the ambivalence is more complex since the thematic content itself is overtly political. In this case, reading the texts not only as a cultural response but also as part of a politics of control means that the political function is not only on the level of distraction but also directly connected with an explicit political message. Thus,

we are not necessarily more illuminated by drawing out its political content as I did in the first part of this chapter. Instead, we must address
directly the political implications of its form. This includes positioning
the books in relation to the cultural trend of mainstream political allegory
today.

The ambivalence of how to approach the overtly political allegories of
the present becomes evident if we examine politically informed readings
of Collins's trilogy. In a section of an edited collection entirely devoted to
these novels titled 'History, Politics, Economics and Culture', a set of
critics analyses the trilogy from the viewpoint of its contextual commentary. Thus Anthony Pavlik argues, for example, that the books are not so
much 'an allegorical warning about the future as it is a portrayal of the
nature of current times and the way the same scenario is constantly
played out in both domestic and international politics' (Pavlik 2012, 36).
Pavlik also draws connections to American history suggesting that the
thirteen districts of Panem can be linked to the thirteen original states of
the United States and their uprising against Great Britain (Pavlik 2012,
37). Valerie Estelle Frankel analyses how the novels mirror the 'the dystopia of present-day America' by looking closely at the Reality TV theme
and the difficulties of drawing lines between entertainment and reality
(Frankel 2012, 49, 58). Bill Clemente offers a detailed reading of how the
books intricately interweave references to the gladiator games of the Roman Empire with the contemporary American political system. The trilogy, he notes, includes multiple references to Roman names. The very
name of the nation, Panem, means bread, and Clemente finds a direct
thematic connection here through the Roman poet Juvenal who wrote a
satire on '*panem and circenses*, "bread and circuses"', in which he pointed
towards and cautioned against the tendency of the Roman populace to
abdicate their social and political responsibility. 'Only two things really
concern them: bread and the Games' (Juvenal cited in Clemente [2012,
21–22]). These games were, of course, the bloody entertainment of bat-
tling gladiators to which the Hunger Games in Collins's trilogy are often
compared. Along with a whole set of other Roman names and references—the names of the leaders and people in power include Plutarch,
Caesar, Flavious, Octavia—this clearly encourages a reading that situates
the narrative of Collins's books as 'a future repetition of Rome's inglori-
ous past, but one made more brutal and spectacular through technological advances' (Clemente 2012, 22). At the same time, Clemente notes how
the books reflect contemporary structures of US politics (Clemente 2012,
23). Especially, he points to the way in which the presidential elections
have been compared to a show the political purpose of which is not so
much to allow the people to choose a leader but to make them think they
do, the real political power all the while residing on Wall Street. Clemente compares Matt Taibbi's description of the elections as a 'beautifully
choreographed eighteen-month entertainment' with the way the Games

in Collins's books are part of a 'modern global conglomerate, a fully integrated industry, the complexity of which the media coverage of the Games hides' (Clemente 2012, 24).

While many of these readings constitute politically informed takes on the thematic content of the novels, and while many of the scholars, such as Clemente, clearly connect the books to contemporary politics, a dimension that they do not include in this 'fully integrated industry' is the extraliterary position of Collins's books in the contemporary world. Without a recognition of irony, not only as an integral element of allegory in general in de Man's sense, but as an element that texts and films like these seem to curtail, readings remain seduced by the seeming stability of correlations. We need irony here not only to problematise such stability but also to analyse the political implications of its representation. Including irony, we can link Clemente's point about how the entertaining show of politics serves to conceal the 'fully integrated industry' behind it to the way the relationship between totality and vision has been understood as the relationship 'between the totality of the world and our capacity to see it' (Bull 1999, 168). This is not just an attention to context—many—indeed most readings do link the book to contemporary political systems—but also an attention to the function of the format itself as political. If the media coverage of the Hunger Games hides the 'modern global conglomerate' on the level of fiction, then what does *The Hunger Games* trilogy itself and the considerable media coverage of this literary—and cinematic—phenomenon, hide? Quite simply, is it not, too, a political spectacle in a global capitalist world?

As we have seen, the novels depict not only a totalitarian society but a society that clearly also lays claim to a totality configured largely by means of vision. Panem, as we have noted, is a fully integrated system purposefully identifiable as such by all its citizens. The panoptical layout of the nation, the participants in the Hunger Games deliberately made out to represent their respective district, and the ever-present cameras and screens all contribute to a sense of a social and political totality. The way in which the citizens are forced to contribute to and watch the Hunger Games is, as I argue above, not just a distracting mode of entertainment but a powerful way of constantly reminding and making each citizen see the system as a whole. Now, if we take a step back and look at ourselves reading these books, we may begin to ask what system the books themselves are part of. This way, we might ask what kind of insights the novels might yield in terms of linking cultural critique to political totality. The texts clearly render a portrayal of a dystopic totality on the level of content, but the more important lesson they may teach us concerns the way in which the novels formally fit within the totality of a control system that integrates everything within itself.

As discussed in chapter 2, new formalism inquires into the links between form and political practice. As Marjorie Levinson suggests there, we need to pay attention to the way in which discourses and genres affect the representation of the real (Levinson 2007, 561). Collins's *The Hunger Games* trilogy portrays a totality that, the allegorical format underscores, has clear similarities to our present sociohistorical and political context. We need not disparage this function as it may draw the attention of its large young audience towards political issues. At the same time, and especially in a context of multiple mainstream political allegories, we should pay attention to the way in which these allegories, like Rogin's medial coverage of political 'secrets', may hide pressing political concerns in full daylight. The political spectacle, Rogin points out, becomes not simply a diversion from power but a form of power in itself (Rogin 1990, 100). Contemporary film directors, as I noted in the introductory chapter, have responded exactly to the sense of dealing with open cards that they see in the Obama administration. This strategy of 'transparency' thus has resonance in mainstream fiction with political ambitions. But the question remains of the effect of this tendency to keep things in full view. One central way in which the power of politics takes specular form, Rogin notes, is by insistent repetition which creates a normalisation that thereby renders the political material invisible (Rogin 1990, 103). Rogin has in mind the media coverage of wars and other political interventions. We can also employ this observation, however, to see how the portrayals of political totality in the contemporary political allegories analysed here make it more, not less, difficult to see the political 'material' of contemporary control systems.

Allegory, as we saw in chapter 2, emerges as a dominant form of expression in response to a world that has lost its sense of coherent meaning. It constitutes a way, as we have seen via Walter Benjamin, of tying together fragments of a lost whole. Via Fredric Jameson, we have seen how allegory constitutes the means to create meaning and a (vain) sense of overview in and of a postmodern global world that seems to slip through our fingers. The allegorical mode, in other words, is a tool that serves to create a sense of meaning in the face of fragmented totality. The kind of power that Rogin discusses points towards a political configuration of the relationship between totality and vision that relates to but must also be updated in relation to early Marxist theories of the spectacle. The idea of the spectacle as the creation of illusionary meaning and unity, theorised by Adorno and Horkheimer as a distraction from the political reality of everyday life and by Debord in terms of the society of the spectacle, is certainly applicable to the structures of Panem in Collins's books. There is an added dimension, however, in the way in which the spectacle has developed into becoming a strategic locus of playing out the political. In this sense, it no longer constitutes an illusion of unity. It may create an illusion of democracy, as in Taibbi's view of the presidential elections, but by allowing the political to play out all its secrets in full view, the unity is in a sense real. As long as we address Collins's books on the level of content, we are distracted from this fact. As we relate the content to a political context, as we have seen several critics do, we benefit from the possibility of analysing the mechanisms of the political spectacle on the level of representation. Thus, for example, Gretchen Koenig takes up Rogin's argument about the political spectacle addressed here in her analysis of the visual politics of the books' fictional President Snow (Koenig 2012, 42). Even as she thus pays attention to the same political strategies, the focus on content delimits the reach of the political implications. This way, the formal mode fills the classic function of political allegory to point back to the material it allegorises. This is a reassuring strategy that creates exactly the sense of political overview that Jameson discusses. As I have tried to analyse in this chapter, however, it is not enough to analyse the politics of vision as they are represented in the novels. To see the totality that these allegories ironically come to hide, we need to take another step back and analyse the politics of the politics of vision of which they are part. The irony here emerges with the way that the allegorical mode comes to hide rather than illuminate this fact, as if its dual levels are unable to stretch to include these added levels of simulacrum. The allegorical format does position us as politically aware 'seers' of a political totality. This way it does the job that Jameson ascribes it. At the same time, however, reading these allegories without irony means failing to account for the fact that we are also positioned in a similar position to the citizens of Panem, buying into the spectacle even as we watch it.

NOTE

1. That being said, one of the episodes of *Black Mirror*, 'The Entire History of You', has been optioned by Robert Downing Jr. after winning what the *Independent* calls a 'bidding war' with George Clooney for the rights to remake the episode. This again points towards the hunger for these kinds of topics in mainstream culture and the absorption of them into the entertainment industry. According to the *Independent*, Downing Jr. is planning to remake it into an American sci-fi thriller (Jones 2013, n.p).

SIX

Conclusion

In my preface, I referred to Paul de Man's explication, in his preface to *Allegories of Reading*, of how his plan to write a historical study turned into a theory of reading. De Man found himself unable to refer directly to the historical moment he wished to address as he ran into 'local difficulties of interpretation'. These difficulties forced his study in the direction of modes of reading and interpretation themselves. As I noted then (while indicating numerous differences between de Man's work and mine), I too found myself struggling with such 'local difficulties of interpretation'. These really were local difficulties as they can be directly related to the cultural and political context that I aimed to address. De Man found it necessary to look into problems of his age. For the present project, my problem was how to approach a material the form of which seemed to preempt and thereby possibly prevent critique. Thus, I wanted to explore the role of cultural critique in control society and found that the control mechanisms that I wanted to explore were repeatedly staged in contemporary culture itself. This is, of course, a phenomenon worthy of attention all of its own. But at the same time, the allegorical format in which these mechanisms were presented also prescribed a mode of reading that seemed to add nothing. Worse than that, I found that 'adding nothing' was in fact less harmless than it sounds. In effect, the allegorical format subtracts constituent elements of a reading that amounts to participating in a political spectacle. This spectacle, as I noted through Michael Rogin, functions precisely by placing its secrets in full view.

Regardless of how we understand allegory, it is about both subtracting and adding something. The different conceptions of allegory evoked in this book—centrally de Man's, Walter Benjamin's, and Fredric Jameson's—all in different ways centre on what allegory as a tool can bring to our understandings of the world as a whole. As a concept, de Man suggests, it most fundamentally adds the recognition that any reading of a text brings with it differential interpretations. What it adds therefore, beyond this recognition itself, is, for de Man, a resistance to totalising conceptions of literature and history. As a tool, allegory may add, in a Benjaminian framework, a sense of continuity to a fragmented present and the possibility of a critical response to a totality in ruins. In the face of the insight that unity is an unattainable goal, allegory helps creating fictions of coherency. Jameson shows also how allegorical interpretation is situated in relation to a 'particular interpretative master code' and therefore adds insight into the political unconscious of its particular historical context. And in a more straightforward 'contrapuntal' mode, political allegory illustrates its point by adding a layer of representation onto another more or less hidden message. Classical allegories such as George Orwell's *1984* function this way as do more modern examples such as the famous baseball game that frames Don DeLillo's *Underworld* (1997). This novel ties its eight hundred or so pages together by making the search for a baseball a central trope for the search for a very American cultural meaning that keeps slipping through its fingers but that also continues to inspire — 'He speaks in your voice, American, and there's a shine in his eye that's halfway hopeful' (*Underworld* 11).

But what exactly does a reading and theorising of contemporary allegory add? Via Jeffrey T. Nealon, Bruno Latour, Antonio Negri, and Jean Baudrillard, I noted earlier in this book how it has become increasingly difficult to mobilise theory as well as culture as the means to interrogate political structures that seem largely coextensive with the logic of much postmodern theorising and modes of expression. Having spent a bit of time analysing some of these entanglements in this book, I would like to stress that like Nealon, and like Jameson as he reads him, the aim has not been to attempt a moral claim on the relation between cultural and economic production. Just as the goal could not possibly be some outside to capitalism, some pure culture, or some unadulterated critique, the idea of arguing for or against forms of cultural expression themselves seems pointless. As Nealon notes, the fact that cultural production 'shares a "logic"' with neoliberal economic production' is in itself axiomatic. Therefore, and if we want to 'add something', the collapsing 'of cultural production into the logic of economic production' must be not a conclusion but a starting point (Nealon 2012, 176).

And indeed, the observation about the logic of contemporary cultural and economic production and more specifically what has come to be called control society was where this book began. The forms of power that Michel Foucault begins to trace in his lecture series on biopolitics in the late 1970s, as Nealon notes, saturate everyday reality today. This saturation and its mutations lands us in what Gilles Deleuze calls 'control society' and what Michael Hardt and Negri, following the same route, describe as 'an intensification and generalisation of the normalising apparatuses of disciplinarity that internally animate our common and daily practices' (Hardt and Negri 2000, 23). As Nealon notes, where our economic present takes off from *The Birth of Biopolitics* (1979), any analysis must take off also from the same basic premise about power—it is not about trying to determine whether it is good or bad but about recognising its dangers. Therefore, our project, like Foucault's, must be descriptive rather than prescriptive—'how we respond to it are largely dependent on our analysis of how it works, what effect it produces, and how it might produce effects otherwise' (Nealon 2012, 182). What we might add, in other words, may not be 'the kind of vanguard resistance to totalisation that you used to be able to count on from any concluding paragraph of virtually any essay in the era of big theory' but a diagnostics and cartography of the present cultural logic and its processes and mutations (Nealon 2012, 182). In a very limited sense—I make no claims to having found the 'new weapons' to deal with the continuous modulations of control society (Deleuze 1992, 4), to having identified a new terrain for the critique of culture (Negri 2007, 50), or to having contributed to 'a new theoretical and methodological toolbox for responding to post-postmodern culture' (Nealon 2012, xii)—this book constitutes an attempt to add to these responses to contemporary figurations of biopower an analysis of their relation to allegory as a particular and currently pervasive cultural form.

THE FATE OF ALLEGORY IN CONTROL SOCIETY

So what do theories of allegory bring to a cultural material seemingly set on commenting on the capitalist logic of our contemporaneity and to our observations about a critique in crisis? In the first of the analytical chapters, I presented J. G. Ballard's oeuvre as a gradual coming into allegory. Although we cannot ask Ballard's work to carry the burden of representability all on its own and although it is not associated generically to the mainstream trend also analysed here, reading the emergence of allegory traceable in his work alongside theories of control society served to underline a development from the 1960s to the present when it comes to politics as well as the politics of form. This emergence, I argued, is aligned with an intensification of control and an ensuing sense of a new form of totality during these decades. Where the early Ballard worked to resist modes of representation that encourage an illusion of continuity, his formal employments, like the building gradually coming into being, seem to reflect the societies he depicts—as if contemporary sociopolitical developments demand an allegorical mode of knowledge. More than that, I suggested in that chapter, the allegorical mode of knowledge at play here promotes a sense of unity that is politically decisive as it works to subsume rather than bring out tensions and elements of resistance.

While Ballard's work to some extent allows for the irony that questions such unity and coherence, the texts and films analysed in the subsequent chapters seem rather to expulse such uncertainties. As such, Ballard's work foregrounds the politicisation of allegory as a form during the past decades.

This is not to say that the transitions between disciplinary and control society can be temporally determined to this period alone. Indeed, and as I noted in chapter 1, Foucault locates the emergence of disciplinary society to the seventeenth and eighteenth centuries. However, the high-speed intensification of biopolitics enabled by technological, digital, and scientific developments during the past few decades makes this period of particular interest when it comes to the dissolution of the power of what constituted central players in disciplinary society—institutions, States, identities. The 'coming of age' of capitalism in a post-1960s context is frequently analysed in terms of its all-absorbing function. As Sheldon S. Wolin puts it, a new corporate logic does not merely exert political influence but incorporates and transforms the political (Wolin 2004, 588). As analysed by Jameson and Nealon, the sociopolitical development between the 1960s and the present has a particular relation to cultural production and cultural critique. The 'cultural rebellion narratives of the '60s', as Nealon puts it, which typically centred on liberation from social repression, can be pronounced officially dead as the official sponsor of the Rolling Stones' 2005 tour was a now defunct mortgage company (Nealon 2012, 21). Nealon's book *Post-Postmodernism or the Cultural Logic of Just-in-Time Capitalism* (2012) situates itself in the orbit of Jameson's seminal book with a similar title while highlighting and redeploying certain of its strands as it sees 'some further structuring mutations in the relations among cultural production and economic production' in the years following this study. Capitalism has intensified rather radically since the 1970s and '80s that saw the beginning of Jameson's work on postmodernism. This, Nealon's book argues, requires an updated theoretical and methodological toolbox capable of responding to the 'just-in-time Capitalism' of 'post-postmodern culture' (Nealon 2012, x–xii). Nealon is careful to stress that his aim is not to overcome or displace Jameson's work but rather to intensify its reading of the present and the near past of the 1980s to respond to the intensifications of capitalism since then (Nealon 2012, 8). Following on Jameson's method of periodisation in his essay 'Periodizing the 60s' (1984) in which he positions this period as one based on a set of 'of transversally linked revolutionary historical developments' beginning in the mid-1950s and ending in the mid-1970s, Nealon suggests that the period following upon this, defined as a period of 'a loose cultural, economic, and political affinity' reaching from the beginning of the 1980s until the fall of 2001, has now evolved into yet another period, one which we may just be in the position to start describing (Nealon 2012, 8–12). Nealon sees the task of periodising this present as a collective project of constructing a vocabulary that will enable us to discuss its post-Fordist, globalised, heavily market-economy-based 'new economies' and 'their complex relation to cultural production in the present moment' (Nealon 2012, 15).

I have had no ambition here to perform a comprehensive periodising or to construct workable vocabularies, but it does seem worthwhile to consider the analysis performed in this book in relation to the demise of cultural rebellion and its relation to control during these decades. An example of the fate of the 1960s cultural rebellion more directly related to the literary and cinematic context addressed in the present book can be seen in the numerous adaptations of Philip K. Dick stories in recent years. These stories—'Adjustment Team' (1954), 'The Golden Man' (1954), 'The Minority Report' (1956), *A Scanner Darkly* (1977) to mention a few—have become popular targets for adaptation during the past decade resulting in *The Adjustment Bureau* (2011), *Next* (2007), *Minority Report* (2002), and *A Scanner Darkly* (2006), respectively. (There are also earlier adaptations, most famously *Do Androids Dream of Electric Sheep* (1968) into *Blade Runner* (1982) and 'We Can Remember It for You Wholesale' (1966) into *Total Recall* (1990), the latter which was filmed again in 2012.)[1] Two main observations can be made here, the first of which is the way a particular genre of 1950s and '60s dystopian science fiction seems to have become suitable material for dealing with anxieties and concerns centring around surveillance and control in the present. The second observation concerns the way this material has also become part of mainstream entertainment. Dick, as Jameson notes, is a 'supreme embodiment of 1960s countercultural themes'. His work addresses the drugs and schizophrenia of this culture and abundantly exemplifies the theoretical critique of the society of the spectacle and commodity reification á la Guy Debord (Jameson 2007, 347). In their recent adaptations, however, the dystopian societies portrayed in the Dick stories appear rather as entertaining high-tech allegories of millennial control systems. Especially when put in connection with the general trend of mainstream cultural critique analysed in this book, it seems clear that the manipulations of life in these adaptations have crossed over not just from written fiction to cinema, and not just from the 1950s and '60s to the 2000s, but also, crucially, from a counterculture context troubled by the political forces of representation and spectacle to a mainstream form of entertainment relying exactly on such forces. As such, they fit at least partly into the tendency towards political allegory as analysed in this book and most certainly into the tendency towards a generalised mainstreaming of what was once part of counterculture features.

The countercultural writer most explicitly associated with control is, as we have noted earlier, William S. Burroughs. The 'new monster' that Deleuze sees depicted in Burroughs's work is the control emerging alongside the revolutionary movements and the counterculture of this period as it responds to the increasing depletion of coherent values and political fervour associated with the postmodern. Burroughs's work may best be described as 'amodern', in Timothy S. Murphy's terms, to indicate a distancing and an alternative to a dialectics of modernism and post-modernism. Like Latour's 'nonmodernism' and Negri's 'anti-modernity', Murphy's 'amodernism' wants to opt out of this dialectics. The 'amodern' is intended to recognise that the means and ends of the modernist project might have failed without accepting that all critical strategies must there-fore fail. Murphy's purpose is to trace, through the work of Burroughs, 'an alternative trajectory through the literature and history of the contem-porary period, a trajectory that participates in the production of new cultural values to replace those that (post) modernism has bankrupted'. Burroughs's work, Murphy argues, is emblematic of the amodern be-cause it is committed to social transformation 'in the face of the postmod-ern evacuation of the political sphere' (Murphy 1997, 2). Positioning Ralph Ellison as a starting point, Murphy includes a heterogeneous set of names in the 'amodern' including Joseph Heller, Thomas Pynchon, Toni Morrison, Robert Coover, and Kathy Acker, all of whom, in very different ways, can be read as aiming, like Ellison, to develop a 'plan of living' in the face of the diffusion of meaning characterising (post) modern times (Murphy 1997, 3). In other words, where Burroughs is positioned as a literary forerunner of writing on control society, his work is also charac-terised by resistance. As Murphy suggests, there is a development in his writing from a sense of inescapable control in the earlier texts to a sense of revolutionary hope in the later. From the *Nova* trilogy published dur-ing the first and mid parts of the 1960s and onward, Burroughs, as Mur-phy puts it, works on 'systematic and sophisticated attempts to evade the dialectic, which continually returns in unexpected forms to reinscribe Burroughs's revolutionary enterprise within despotic capital and lan-guage'. His cut-up method is crucial in this enterprise as it provides the means to escape his earlier cynicism and commit to the idea of social change (Murphy 1997, 5). Especially his last novels, *Cities of the Red Night*, *The Place of Dead Roads*, and *The Western Lands*, all published during the beginning and mid-1980s, add to the deconstructive task the affirmative possibility of organising society by other means than by social and lin-guistic control (Murphy 1997, 5).

In his experimental approach to form, Ballard too seems to search for strategies of expression that problematise the control mechanisms of rep-resentation. At one point, these experiments included cut-up techniques as seen, centrally, in *The Atrocity Exhibition* (1970), but here, I have fo-cused especially on how his engagement with allegory functions to nego-tiate control mechanisms in a post-Burroughsian context. Looking at his oeuvre on an overarching level, Ballard's experimental strategies, as I tried to show in chapter 3, highlight some of the tensions between countercultural resistance and control mechanisms that characterise the post-1960s period. And although his oeuvre seems to increasingly give in to an allegorisation that strengthens rather than questions control, his work can also be see to inherit to some extent Burroughs's 'amodern' hope for critical strategies in the midst of their seeming exhaustion.[2] If nothing else, his work helps illuminate how political configurations of space, time, and vision increasingly conform to the idea of a control system where everything is accounted for. De Man's interrogation of rhetoric, as I noted in the preface, caused him to question historicism and other totalising models claiming to grasp a unity of meaning. While this reminds us to be careful in making generalised claims also about the contemporary context of interest here, Ballard's work helps us see how the allegorical model we have taken to task does come across as a totalising model. In its mainstream instantiations it functions alongside a control society intent on incorporating everything including the critique of its own logic. Like the Situationist tactics employed in Ballard's later novels discussed in chapter 3, the critique emerging from the texts and films analysed in chapters 4 and 5 appears much like Penrose's 'organized rattisages' in *Super-Cannes*, that is, like manageable doses of 'willed madness' intended not to disrupt but to maintain the functionalism of an efficient control society. Overall, the tendency towards mainstreaming cultural critique speaks to a continuity based on the very lack of alternatives. When read from this perspective, the totality that seems so alien to a postmodern fragmented world remerges as all the stronger in a world where everything is hooked up to the same basic economic principles and cultural logic.

But while Ballard's work invites us to consider the function of allegory in relation to control, the popular works discussed invite us to read them allegorically in a much less critical fashion. If the allegorical brings out the tensions between inside and outside in the very specific cultural sense of reality and representation, my readings in chapters 4 and 5 suggest that we arrive at a dead end the moment we continue pursuing what these films mean allegorically. Maybe the analogous nature of allegory relies on particular ontological presuppositions that get us as far as Baudrillardian disillusionment but not any further? As long as we discuss what texts of this kind mean then maybe we cannot get out of the problem of the conspiracy of art that Baudrillard poses. But what if we look at what they do? The Spinozan question of what a body does rather than what it means has been famously picked up by Deleuze and Félix Guattari and, via them, by many coming after. It seems particularly potent in this context. The question applies across the board and not the least to literature: 'It is absolutely useless to look for a theme in a writer if one hasn't asked exactly what its importance is in the work—that is, *how it functions* (and not what its "sense" is)' (Deleuze and Guattari 1986, 45). So how do contemporary mainstream allegories function?

WHAT CONTEMPORARY ALLEGORIES DO

Far from using allegory as a weapon against censorship—although the idea of 'smuggler's cinema' that James DeMonaco evoked and that, as I noted in the introduction, works to slip less easily digestible aspects into genre films may want to position it as such—the contemporary mainstream allegories analysed here flaunt their political theme. As such, they function at best as what Ismail Xavier notes as the critiqued form of calculated and didactic allegories and at worst as placating political impulses in the mode of conspiracy that Baudrillard proposes. Regardless of how we choose to interpret them, it seems that the interpretation of them in accordance with their more-or-less prescribed allegorical format makes it difficult for us to locate ways of considering this kind of political critique as anything but a mirage—a sexy, fast, and elegant hallucination of political change. But is it only if we read them allegorically that we remain within the mirage? It is an important question upon which depends not only our conception of these particular films but also of the 'allegorical turn', which, as I have noted throughout this book, finds continuous nurture in the convolutions of contemporary control society. Are there ways of mobilising other modes of reading the allegorical that correspond less to Baudrillard's mirage and more to the internal critique that Negri calls for?

I have already begun to try to answer this question in the chapters of this book. But in order to begin to understand the function of form in relation to contemporary politics more generally and to end this book with a preliminary theory of allegory in the present, I want to take a moment to look more closely at what the texts analysed in this book do in the light of allegory's underlying presumptions about immanence and transcendence. Explicating his understanding of the notion of historical allegory, Richard Halpern underlines the crucial role of the allegorical in the reading of historical texts. The allegorical, he notes, constitutes a way of negotiating historical differences. As such, it deserves careful consideration because while it may elucidate elements of history in the light of contemporary concerns and vice versa, it may also gloss over the historical. The very point of addressing historical allegory, however, is to provide a mode of reading that is aware of rather than falls victim to its own anachronisticity (Halpern 1997, 4). 'Historical allegory', he argues, 'must hobble its own analogising impulse by granting the material it studies some unassimilable residue or opacity with respect to the present' (Halpern 1997, 8). The allegorical impulse studied in the present book is, as we have seen, fundamentally concerned with the present rather than history but importantly, it fails to grant its material the 'unassimilable residue' of this present. There are many dimensions of this residue and it would be impossible to try to account for them here, but one that is particularly relevant because it pertains to the central question of form is the 'residue' of the relation between reality and representation.

Arguably, the loss of transcendent meaning that characterised the collapse of the allegorical in modernist writing is no longer a major preoccupation in cultural and critical theory. Here, the analogical tension exists rather in the relation between fictional representation and reality. Still, the creation of a fictional portrayal of characters, actions, and events to be read allegorically rests on an understanding of signification that fundamentally relies on the separation between reality and representation. Reaching back to Plato's allegory of the cave, the sense of the shadows, or representation dominating the perception of everyone but the philosophers who have exclusive access to reality, we see how the allegorical stands at the very heart of the matter. Significantly, and as we saw in chapter 2, Plato's allegory constitutes the foundation for a conception of the relation between reality and representation that has dominated Western aesthetics throughout most of its history. Allegory is thus positioned at the very core of the way in which the shadows of representation constitute the veil that prevents us from accessing reality. And perhaps the outside cannot be more clearly illustrated than this—the essence that exists beyond the appearance that determines our conception of life. Allegory functions to illustrate relations existing outside themselves by means of conveying their conditions by other means. This way, allegory becomes a copy intended not to detract from but, quite on the contrary, put light on the model it comments on. As such, at least in its most classical sense these allegories may be said to rely on what Deleuze calls 'the world as icon' (Deleuze 2004, 299). This is a conception of aesthetics that sees an iconic or model world from which copies and representations can be made, that is, a conception that takes its starting point in identity. As we saw earlier through Northrop Frye, classic definitions of allegory rely on a sense of an explicit relation between the text and reality and also between the text and some external ideas or precepts. When we read texts as allegories we tacitly agree on a relation that corresponds to the first conception of aesthetics.

Through Deleuze, however, we can mobilise a contrasting model that relies rather on difference as a starting point. Starting from difference, identity and similitude become but possible side effects. According to this conception, the world is not icon but simulacra from which modes of individuation emerge. Centrally, the latter starting point renders all ambition to compare model and copy or essence and appearance pointless. Such hierarchies disappear as there is no privileged viewpoint that determines and dominates the others. This conception rises from Deleuze's philosophy of immanence, which necessarily rejects analogy as the equivocal parallelism associated with representation. In his Bergsonian conception of univocity, being is expressed in the same way in all instances which stands in direct opposition to theories of the analogy of being as well as representation as somehow separate on an ontological level. From a Deleuzian perspective, a theory of representation based on analogy divides expression into lines of the model or truth and lines of the copy or the false. Such a theory undermines the power of expression itself and fails to see it as a force inseparable from reality. If Baudrillard sees the simulacrum as that which has lost touch with reality, Deleuze sees no such connection to be lost. The simulacrum points rather to the 'triumph of the false pretender'—the ultimate proof that the division between model and copy is without constructive force. From the world as simulacra, expression emerges as a differential force that can, and tends to be, contained in boxes of identity by means of representation. In itself, however, expression does not make these distinctions but acts directly on and in the world. It is here, in the sense of expression acting directly on the world that cultural critique reemerges as a possibility.

The reemergence of allegory in postmodernity that Jameson points to stands in a curious relation with a political system that, if we are to agree with Deleuze, has abandoned the analogical. While Deleuze's philosophy is grounded on an ontology of immanence that is in itself ahistorical, he also sees the transition between disciplinary and control society itself as a shift between a politics relying on the analogical to one relying on the differential. As we saw in chapter 1, Deleuze describes the disciplinary society that Foucault theorises as based on enforced analogical relations. Power is exercised by means of distinct spaces of enclosure such as family, school, army, factory, prison, and so on which function as analogical spaces gravitating towards the same end. The whole system is analogical—while all spaces carry their own internal logic, they are ultimately molded to serve the same model (Deleuze 1992, 4). The control society that Deleuze theorises as emerging after and partly supplanting the disciplinary model does not build on this kind of analogous structure. As production is outsourced to the Third World and the capitalist system in the West stops centring around production and starts centring around the product, the analogical spaces of enclosure such as the family, the school, and the factory that the earlier system relied on turn into transformable codes. They become modulations that rely less on an analogous system and more on open circuits and markets and exchange rates that are in continuous fluctuation (Deleuze 1992, 6). Unlike the more continuous enclosures of discipline, control is about modulation 'like a self-deforming cast that will continuously change from one moment to the other, or like a sieve whose mesh will transmute from point to point' (Deleuze 1992, 4).

On the one hand, one might expect the cultural capital of allegory to dwindle alongside the analogous system of disciplinary society. A system of correspondences and parallel lines could accommodate a type of cultural critique built on a 'contrapuntal technique' that builds on making a fictional space run parallel to and comment on a real-world happening around it and thereby make the fictional space yet another line in the analogous structure. The dissolution of such permanent 'casts' into open circuits and fluctuating rates, however, not only reshapes the spaces of discipline such as the school, the army, and the factory, and not only the spaces of fiction either, but also the relation between them. And indeed, as Jameson notes, the time of reading allegory according to stable relations of equivalence has passed as allegory today tends to reflect the discontinuity and heterogeneity of equivalences themselves. If Frye's classical theory of allegory argues that it tends to 'smooth out and reconcile an originally metaphorical structure by making it conform to a consistent conceptual norm' and create a unity of representation (Frye 1981, 223), Jameson, as we have seen, notes how more traditional conceptions of allegory that rely on a notion of direct equivalences miss out on the fact that equivalences are themselves changing and transforming over time. Indeed, he argues that the interest in allegory in contemporary literary theory is related specifically to the profoundly discontinuous spirit of allegory today. It has become, rather 'a matter of breaks and heterogeneities, of the multiple polysemia of the dream rather than the homogeneous representation of the symbol' (Jameson 1986, 73). The dispersal of 'one-to-one' equivalences can be related to a transition from a pre-postmodern world that had fewer quarrels with the relation between reality and representation. Whether this is an actual shift or a conceptual one matters less here. What is more important is the way in which this can be related to perceptions of an outside to which representation can create an analogous line. If Orwell's *Animal Farm*, as a classic example of political allegory, could be constructed around a more-or-less stable table of equivalences this was also because it was still possible to let the fictional text look to an outside—both of fiction and of the current political system. As such, it was possible to construct the text as bearing a particular relationship to external precepts and systems. As the political system becomes not only all-encompassing but also based on continuous modulation, however, the possibility for allegory to remain stable decreases. Analogy, as Deleuze suggests, disappears as a governing model.

If analogy is disappearing as the central model of political organisation in control society, the contemporary preoccupation with allegory as a method of representation and interpretation becomes all the more intriguing. Today, our motives are decidedly different from the Romanticist rejection of allegory as conveying but the 'empty echoes which the fancy arbitrarily associates with apparitions of matter' (Coleridge cited in Culler [1976, 263]). Today, the allegorical needs interrogation not because it fails to capture the relation between expression and the natural but because it fails to capture the relation between expression and action. As I noted in chapter 4, many of the mainstream allegories I discuss in this book rely exactly on the idea of stable references. While corresponding to the trend of allegory in postmodernity that Jameson discusses, they also diverge from it in what can only be perceived as an anachronistic insistence on stable referentiality. By means of their neat allegorical form, they encourage a direct and transparent understanding of politics and society and thereby curtail and modulate the political message. If our contemporaneity is characterised by the 'indistinctness between screen and life' where we 'are on both sides at once' (Baudrillard 2005, 197), representations and interpretations of texts as analogous allegory apply a model of how the world works that does not correspond to its actual entanglements. Being on 'both sides at once' necessarily jumbles the analogous relation. We could refer to Jameson's more complex conception of allegory, but in the case of the works discussed here, the allegorical structure is actually not very complex at all. Indeed, it seems important to note that in contrast to a context of an aesthetic as well as political shift from the analogous to the differential, the films and novels in question here seem to rely exactly on the straightforward equivalences we are supposedly moving away from. Indeed, their very 'politicality' lies in the way they with more or less explicit intentionality illustrate the society in which they are produced.

Jameson suggests that interrogating the allegorical transposition makes it possible to uncover the metaphysical and ideological underpinnings of any given interpretive practice (Jameson 1981, 44–45). What the texts analysed in this book reveal is our need to interrogate the allegorical transposition itself as a metaphysical and ideological foundation for cultural critique. Perhaps our possibility of critique lies in understanding representation as mirroring differently. The analogy on which the allegorical relies crumbles when the text is not so much a parallel line to the real world as intermingled with it. Looking beyond the direct equivalences that our texts blatantly put on display, the potential of these texts can be found rather on a meta-level. Here, the point is less the allegorisation of control society by means of content and more the way in which such texts function as an active part of this same society on the level of form. On the one hand, this can take us to Baudrillard's concern, which, as we have noted, is about the impossibility of stepping outside control society and the ensuing demise of cultural critique. But such an abandonment of hope continues to rely on a mourning for the outside. On the other hand, and as I hope I have begun to show in this book, an understanding of expression that does away with the analogous relations on which allegory fundamentally relies opens up ways of conceiving cultural expression less as an empty representation of what is and more as a way of acting out the political directly. This is where the attention to form called for by new formalist writers becomes very useful. A formalist strategy focused on analysing the political function of form potentially opens a gap—if not for locating an efficient cultural critique, then at least for addressing works that seem to preempt their own reading.

It seems hard to find a way of employing Deleuze's Burroughsian suggestion, as noted in the introduction, that we might be able to elude control by creating 'vacuoles of noncommunication' and 'circuit breakers' on this smooth and seemingly seamless material. A more applicable strategy in the face of this particular material is irony, which would seem as a crucial tool to at least begin to make space for critique in the face of these preemptive texts and films. Irony, as we have seen through de Man, reveals a temporality of 'distance and difference' that disallows totality (de Man 2013, 528). The kind of totality emerging with control society and that I have mapped through space, time, and vision is one that relies less on an ideology of a unitary political system comprising institutions and individuals and more on the total integration of fragments and 'dividuals'. As I suggested in chapter 1, Wolin's concept of 'inverted totalitarianism' alerts us to the totalising tendencies of contemporary control society at the same time as it underlines how these are not founded on an ideological preconceived political system so much as they constitute a result of the ways in which the intensification of biopolitics has entailed that all dimensions of society and its inhabitants are plugged into the political system directly. The reading of the contemporary allegorical trend in this book suggests that allegory itself is integrated in this context as it shifts from constituting an element of critique, as it does for Benjamin, to becoming an element of control. This allegorical mode, as I suggested in chapter 5, works to hide the political in full view. As my reading of *The Hunger Games* trilogy and the scholarly reception of these same texts underlined, the allegory encourages a reading of the political contents while distracting from the political function of the format itself. But if allegory as a critical tool is undermined by control mechanisms, irony as a 'critical act' in the Benjaminian sense as that which, de Man notes, ironises or destroys the form by demystification, may still be recuperated (de Man 1996, 182). The critical potential of irony as an inevitable interruption of the allegorical is located, not in the narratives themselves that seem more than unwilling to acknowledge it, but in the way in which the seductive continuity of the logic they represent is simultaneously in and out of sync with the logic of control society. As I have argued throughout, the societies and revolutions portrayed repeatedly rely on a logic of identities and institutions characteristic of a disciplinary society on the wane. At the same time, this very disjunction is perfectly in line with a society that builds on moderating and modulating the more free-floating affects and impulses upon which it relies. Where the allegorical smooths over this disjunction, irony brings it into focus.

Addressing the link between allegory and cultural critique in contemporary culture, I have attempted to approach the 'local difficulties of interpretation' as well as the crisis in critique by trying to resist the thematic abstraction of sexy, revolutionary content and by paying attention to what this cultural material does. Much as it tries to tell us otherwise, this material is not a representation of the political; it is the political. Ceci une pipe. Commercial and mainstream as they are—these works do not portray the political reality of control society—they constitute the political reality of control society itself. Political allegory, Jameson suggests, may expose a 'master fantasy about the interaction of collective subjects' (Jameson 1981, 68). I believe this is what these works do—not on the level of content but on the level of form. Of relevance is not primarily the relations represented in the texts themselves but the way in which these texts, by virtue of their allegorical nature, expose or even insist upon a continued reliance on an outside that no longer exists. This is the master fantasy we need to take to task. In order to do so, we need to see the irony in the fact that we are dealing with a political spectacle about a political spectacle. And in the way we are watched watching watching. Importantly, and as I have tried to show in this book, this is not simply a matter of acknowledging the ironic dimensions of contemporary political allegory but also of recognising the political effects of their apparent absence. As such, our most important interpretative task lies not in working out what contemporary mainstream allegories mean but in recognising the political implications of how they come to act on and in the world.

NOTES

1. *The Truman Show* from 1998 is not officially an adaptation of Dick's novel *Time Out of Joint* (1959) but is based on the same premises.

2. Indeed, Ballard insisted on an expressed optimism and a conviction that the human imagination can transcend almost everything (Ballard and Self 2006, 35–36).

Bibliography

Adorno, Theodor W. 1984. "The Idea of Natural History." Translated by R. Hullot-Kentor. *Telos* 60:111–24.
———. 1977. "The Actuality of Philosophy." Translated by Benjamin Snow. *Telos* 31:120–33.
Adorno, Theodor W., and Max Horkheimer. 2002. *Dialectic of Enlightenment: Philosophical Fragments*. Edited by G. S. Noerr. Translated by E. Jephcott. Stanford, CA: Stanford University Press.
Agamben, Giorgio. 1993. *Infancy and History: The Destruction of Experience*. Translated by Liz Heron. London: Verso.
Ahmad, Aijaz. 1987. "Jameson's Rhetoric of Otherness and the 'National Allegory.'" *Social Text* 17:3–25.
"Allegory." Oxford Dictionaries. http://www.oxforddictionaries.com/definition/english/allegory.
Arato, Andrew. 1985. "Esthetic Theory and Cultural Criticism, Introduction by Andrew Arato." *The Essential Frankfurt School Reader*. Edited by Andrew Arato and Eike Gebhardt. New York: Continuum.
Aristotle. 1920. *Aristotle's Poetics*. Translated by Benjamin Jowett. Oxford: Oxford University Press.
Ballard, J. G. 2009. "Chronopolis." *The Complete Stories of J. G. Ballard*. New York and London: Norton.
———. 2009. *The Complete Short Stories of J. G. Ballard*. New York: Norton.
———. 2008 [1973]. *Crash*. London: Harper Perennial.
——— 2008 [1975]. *The Drought*. London: Harper Perennial.
———. 2006 [1964]. *High Rise*. London: Harper Perennial.
———. 2006. *Kingdom Come*. London: Harper Perennial.
———. 2004. *Millennium People*. London: Harper Perennial.
———. 2000. *Super-Cannes*. London: Harper Perennial.
———. 1996. *Cocaine Nights*. London: Fourth Estate.
———. 1978 [1966]. *The Crystal World*. Frogmore: Triad/Panther Books.
———. 1974. *Concrete Island*. London: Fourth Estate.
———. 1970. *The Atrocity Exhibition*. London: Jonathan Cape.
———. 1962. *The Drowned World*. London: Fourth Estate.
Ballard, J. G., and W. Self. 2006. "Ballard." In Will Self, *Junk Mail*. London: Bloomsbury.
Baudrillard, Jean. 2006. "War Porn." Translated by Paul A. Taylor. *Journal of Visual Culture* 5 (1): 86–88.
———. 2005. *The Conspiracy of Art: Manifestos, Interviews, Essays*. Edited by Sylvère Lotringer. Translated by Ames Hodges. New York: Semiotext(e).
———. 2001. "Consumer Society." In *Jean Baudrillard: Selected Writings*. Edited by Mark Poster. Stanford, CA: Stanford University Press.
———. 1994. *Simulacra and Simulation*. Translated by S. F. Glaser. Ann Arbor: University of Michigan Press.
Baudrillard, Jean, and Arthur B. Evans. 1991. "Ballard's 'Crash' ('Crash de Ballard')." *Science Fiction Studies* 18 (3): 313–20.
Baxter, Jeanette. 2012. "Encountering the Holocaust in J. G. Ballard's Post-War Science Fictions." *Textual Practice* 26(3): 379–98.

———. 2009. *J. G. Ballard's Surrealist Imagination: Spectacular Authorship.* Burlington, VT: Ashgate Publishing Company.

Beckman, Frida. 2013. "Chronopolitics: Space, Time, and Revolution in the Later Novels of J. G. Ballard." *Symploke* 21 (1–2): 271–89.

Benardello, Karen. 2011. "Exclusive Interview with J. C. Chandor on Margin Call." *We Got This Covered.* http://wegotthiscovered.com/movies/interview-jc-chandor-margin-call/.

Benjamin, Walter. 2003. *The Origin of German Tragic Drama.* Translated by John Osbourne. London: Verso.

———. 1999. *The Arcades Project.* Translated by H. Eiland and K. McLaughlin. Cambridge, MA: Harvard University Press.

———. 1978. "Surrealism, the Last Snapshot of the European Intelligensia." In *Reflections: Aphorisms, Essays and Autobiographical Writings,* Peter Demetz, translated by Edmund Jephcott. New York: Harcourt Brace, Jovanovich.

Best, Stephen, and Sharon Marcus. 2009. "Surface Reading: An Introduction." *Representations* 108 (1): 1–21.

Black Mirror. 2011–. Created by Charlie Brooker. *Zeppotron* and *Channel Four.*

Blomkamp, Neill. 2013. *Elysium.* Tristar Pictures, Media Rights Capital, QED International.

Bonnett, Alastair. 1999. "Situationist Strategies and Mutant Technologies." *Angelaki: Journal of the Theoretical Humanities* 4 (2): 25–32.

Bradshaw, Peter. 2012. "*Killing Them Softly*—Review." *Guardian.* September 20. http://www.theguardian.com/film/2012/sep/20/killing-them-softly-review.

Breton, André. 1972. *Manifestoes of Surrealism.* Translated by Richard Seaver and Helen R. Lane. Ann Arbor: University of Michigan Press.

Brooker, Charlie. 2011. "The Dark Side of our Gadget Addiction." *Guardian.* December 1. http://www.theguardian.com/technology/2011/dec/01/charlie-brooker-dark-side-gadget-addiction-black-mirror.

Brooks, Xan, and Henry Barnes. 2013. "Elysium Director Neill Blomkamp: 'It's About the Third World Trying to Get into the First' Video Interview." *Guardian.* August 21. http://www.theguardian.com/film/video/2013/aug/21/elysium-director-neill-blomkamp.

Brown, Bill. 2010. "Introduction: Textual Materialism." *PMLA* 125 (1): 24–28.

Bull, Malcolm. 1999. *Seeing Things Hidden: Apocalypse, Vision, and Totality.* London: Verso.

Butterfield, Bradley. 1999. "Ethical Value and Negative Aesthetics: Reconsidering the Baudrillard-Ballard Connection." *PMLA* 114 (1): 64–77.

Captain America: The Winter Soldier. 2014. Directed by Anthony and Joe Russo, Marvel Entertainment.

Casarino, Cesare. 2003. "Time Matters: Marx, Negri, Agamben, and the Corporeal." *Strategies* 16 (2): 187–206.

Cevasco, Maria Elisa. 2012. "Imagining a Space That Is Outside: An Interview with Fredric Jameson." *Minnesota Review* 78:83–94.

Clemente, Bill. 2012. "Panem in America: Crisis, Economics, and a Call for Political Engagement." *Of Bread and Blood and The Hunger Games: Critical Essays on the Suzanne Collins Trilogy.* Edited by Mary F. Pharr and Leisa A. Clark. Jefferson, NC: McFarland.

Clissold, Bradley D. 2004. "*Candid Camera* and the Origins of Reality TV: Contextualising a Historical Precedent." *Understanding Reality Television.* Edited by Su Holmes and Deborah Jermyn. London: Routledge.

Clough, Patricia. 2003. "Affect and Control: Rethinking the Body 'Beyond Sex and Gender.'" *Feminist Theory* 4 (359): 359–64.

Cohen, Tom, Barbara Cohen, J. Hillis Miller, and Andrzej Warminski, eds. 2001. *Material Events: Paul de Man and the Afterlife of Theory.* Minneapolis: University of Minnesota Press.

Cohen, Tom, J. Hillis Miller, and Barbara Cohen. 2001. "A 'Materiality without Matter.'" In *Material Events: Paul de Man and the Afterlife of Theory*. Edited by Tom Cohen, Barbara Cohen, J. Hillis Miller, and Andrzej Warminski. Minneapolis: University of Minnesota Press.

Collins, Suzanne. 2010. *The Hunger Games: Mockingjay*. New York: Scholastic Inc.

———. 2009. *The Hunger Games: Catching Fire*. New York: Scholastic Inc.

———. 2008. *The Hunger Games*. New York: Scholastic Inc.

———. 2008. "Getting to Know Suzanne Collins." *The Hunger Games*. New York: Scholastic Inc.

Colombino, Laura. 2006. "Negotiations with the System: J. G. Ballard and Geoff Ryman Writing London'd Architecture." *Textual Practice* 20 (4): 615–35.

Copeland, Rita, and Peter T. Struck. 2012. *The Cambridge Companion to Allegory*. Cambridge: Cambridge University Press.

Cowan, Bainard. 1981. "Walter Benjamin's Theory of Allegory." *New German Critique* 22:109–22.

Crary, Jonathan. 1986. "J. G. Ballard and the Promiscuity of Forms." *Zone* ½:159–65.

Culler, Jonathan. 1976. "Literary History, Allegory, and Semiology." *New Literary History* 7 (2): 259–70.

Debord, Guy. 2006. "Toward a Situationist International." *Situationist International Anthology*. Edited by K. Knabb. Berkeley, CA: Bureau of Public Secrets.

———. 1994. *Society of the Spectacle*. Translated by D. Nicholson-Smith. Cambridge, MA, and London: MIT Press.

Deleuze, Gilles. 2004. *The Logic of Sense*. Translated by Mark Lester and Charles Stivale. London: Continuum.

———. 1995. *Negotiations*. Translated by Martin Joughin. New York: Columbia University Press.

———. 1992. "Postscript on the Societies of Control." *October* 59:3–7.

Deleuze, Gilles, and Félix Guattari. 1986. *Kafka: Toward a Minor Literature*. Translated by Dana Polan. Minneapolis and London: University of Minnesota Press.

DeLillo, Don. 2003. *Cosmopolis*. New York: Picador.

———. 1997. *Underworld*. New York: Picador.

De Man, Paul. 2013. *Blindness and Insight: Essays in the Rhetoric of Contemporary Criticism*. London: Routledge.

———. 1996. *Aesthetic Ideology*. Edited by Andrzej Warminski. Minneapolis and London: University of Minnesota Press.

———. 1979. *Allegories of Reading: Figural Language in Rousseau, Nietzsche, Rilke, and Proust*. New Haven, CT: Yale University Press.

Derrida, Jacques. 1989. *Memoires for Paul de Man*. Revised edition. Translated by Cecile Lindsay, Jonathan Culler, Eduardo Cadava, Peggy Kamuf, and Avital Ronell. New York: Columbia University Press.

Donato, Matt. 2014. "Exclusive Interview with Director James DeMonaco on The Purge: Anarchy." *We Got This Covered*. http://wegotthiscovered.com/movies/exclusive-interview-director-james-demonaco-purge-anarchy/#!bFxKXL.

Elysium. 2013. Directed by Neill Blomkamp. TriStar Pictures.

Equilibrium. 2002. Directed by Kurt Wimmer. *Dimension Films* et al.

Esposito, Roberto. 2008. "Totalitarianism or Biopolitics? Concerning a Philosophical Interpretation of the Twentieth Century." *Critical Inquiry* 34 (4): 633–44.

Fisher, Mark. 2009. *Capitalist Realism: Is There No Alternative?* Winchester, UK: O Books.

Fletcher, Angus. 2010. "Allegory without Ideas." *Thinking Allegory Otherwise*. Edited by Brenda Machosky. Stanford, CA: Stanford University Press.

———. 1964. *Allegory: The Theory of a Symbolic Mode*. Ithaca and London: Cornell University Press.

Foster, Roger. 2007. *Adorno: The Recovery of Experience*. Albany: State University of New York Press.

Foucault, Michel. 2008. *The Birth of Biopolitics: Lecture at the Collège de France, 1978–79*. Edited by Michel Senellart. Translated by Graham Burchell. Hampshire, UK: Palgrave Macmillan.

———. 2003. *Society Must Be Defended: Lectures at the Collège de France, 1975–76*. Edited by Mauro Bertani and Alessandro Fontana. Translated by David Macey. New York: Picador.

———. 1995. *Discipline and Punish: The Birth of the Prison*. Translated by A. Sheridan. London: Vintage.

———. 1990. *The Will to Knowledge: The History of Sexuality*, vol. 1. Translated by Robert Hurley. London: Penguin.

Frankel, Valerie Estelle. 2012. "Reflection in a Plastic Mirror." *Of Bread and Blood and The Hunger Games: Critical Essays on the Suzanne Collins Trilogy*. Edited by Mary F. Pharr and Leisa A. Clark. Jefferson, NC: McFarland.

Frye, Northrop. 1981. "Literary History." *New Literary History* 12 (2): 219–25.

———. 1957. *Anatomy of Criticism: Four Essays*. Princeton, NJ: Princeton University Press.

Galloway, Alexander. 2004. *Protocol: How Control Exists after Decentralization*. Cambridge, MA, and London: MIT Press.

Gasiorek, Andrzej. 2005. *J. G. Ballard*. Manchester: Manchester University Press.

Genosko, Gary. 1999. *McLuhan and Baudrillard: The Masters of Implosion*. London: Routledge.

Guillory, John. 1993. *Cultural Capital: The Problem of Literary Canon Formation*. Chicago: University of Chicago Press.

Haas, Elizabeth, Terry Christensen, and Peter J. Haas. 2015. *Projecting Politics: Political Messages in American Film*. Second edition. London and New York: Routledge.

Habermas, Jürgen. 1979. "Consciousness-Raising or Redemptive Criticism—The Contemporaneity of Walter Benjamin." *New German Critique* 17:30–59.

Halliwell, Stephen. 2002. *The Aesthetics of Mimesis: Ancient Texts and Modern Problems*. Princeton, NJ: Princeton University Press.

Halpern, Richard. 1997. *Shakespeare Among the Moderns*. New York: Cornell University Press.

Hansen, Jim. 2004. "Formalism and its Malcontents: Benjamin and de Man on the Function of Allegory." *New Literary History* 35 (4): 663–83.

Hardt, Michael. 1999. "Affective Labor." *boundary 2* 26 (2): 89–100.

———. 1998. "The Global Society of Control." *Discourse* 20 (3): 139–52.

———. 1995. "The Withering of Civil Society." *Social Text* 45 (14): 27–44.

Hardt, Michael, and Antonio Negri. 2009. *Commonwealth*. Cambridge, MA, and London: Harvard University Press.

———. 2000. *Empire*. Cambridge, MA, and London: Harvard University Press.

Hardt, Michael, and Paulo Virno, eds. 1996. *Radical Thought in Italy: A Potential Politics*. Minneapolis: University of Minnesota Press.

Harvey, David. 1990. *The Condition of Postmodernity: An Enquiry into the Origins of Cultural Change*. Cambridge: Blackwell.

Higgins, George V. 1974. *Cogan's Trade*. New York: Vintage.

Homeland. 2011–. Creators Alex Gansa and Howard Gordon. Teakwood Lane Productions et al.

House of Cards. 2013–. Developed by Bruce Willimon. Media Rights Capital et al.

Hughes, David. 2013. "Dreamwatch Interview: Achieving Equilibrium." *Equilibrium Fansite*. http://www.equilibriumfans.com/kwinterviewdwtext.htm.

In Time. 2011. Directed by Andrew Niccol. Regency Enterprises.

Jameson, Fredric. 2007. *Archaeologies of the Future: The Desire Called Utopia and Other Science Fictions*. London: Verso.

———. 2003. "The End of Temporality." *Critical Inquiry* 29 (4): 695–718.

———. 1992. *The Geopolitical Aesthetic: Cinema and Space in the World System*. Bloomington: Indiana University Press.

————. 1991. *Postmodernism, or, The Cultural Logic of Late Capitalism.* Durham, NC: Duke University Press.

————. 1987. "A Brief Response." *Social Text* 17:26–27.

————. 1986. "Third-World Literature in the Era of Multinational Capitalism." *Social Text* 15:65–88.

————. 1981. *The Political Unconscious: Narrative as a Socially Symbolic Act.* London and New York: Routledge.

————. 1977. "Class and Allegory in Contemporary Mass Culture: Dog Day Afternoon as a Political Film." *College English* 38 (8): 843–59.

————. 1971. *Marxism and Form: Twentieth-Century Dialectical Theories of Literature.* Princeton, NJ: Princeton University Press.

Jay, Martin. 1993. *Downcast Eyes: The Denigration of Vision in Twentieth-Century French Thought.* Berkeley: University of California Press.

————. 1984. *Marxism and Totality: The Adventures of a Concept from Lukács to Habermas.* Berkeley: University of California Press.

Johnson, Gary. 2012. *The Vitality of Allegory: Figural Narrative in Modern and Contemporary Fiction.* Columbus: Ohio State University Press.

Jones, Alice. 2013. "Robert Downing Jr. Beats George Clooney in Black Mirror Film Rights Showdown." *Independent.* February 14. http://www.independent.co.uk/arts-entertainment/films/news/robert-downey-jr-beats-george-clooney-in-black-mirror-film-rights-showdown-8495025.html.

Joselit, David. 2003. "An Allegory of Criticism." *October* 103:3–13.

Kellner, Douglas. 1991 [1964]. "Introduction to the Second Edition." In Herbert Marcuse, *One-Dimensional Man: Studies in the Ideology of Advanced Industrial Society.* London: Routledge.

Killing Them Softly. 2012. Directed by Andrew Dominik. *Plan B Entertainment* et al.

Knabb, Ken. 2006. *Situationist International Anthology.* Berkeley, CA: Bureau of Public Secrets.

Koenig, Gretchen. 2012. "Communal Spectacle: Reshaping History and Memory through Violence." *Of Bread and Blood and The Hunger Games: Critical Essays on the Suzanne Collins Trilogy.* Edited by Mary F. Pharr and Leisa A. Clark. Jefferson, NC: McFarland.

Lambie, Ryan. 2014. "James DeMonaco Interview: The Purge, Anarchy, Genre Filmmaking and More." *Den of Geek.* July 21. http://www.denofgeek.com/movies/james-demonaco/31299/james-demonaco-interview-the-purge-anarchy-genre-filmmaking-and-more.

Latour, Bruno. 2004. "Why Has Critique Run out of Steam? From Matters of Fact to Matters of Concern." *Critical Inquiry* 30 (2): 225–48.

Lazzarato, Maurizio. 1996. "Immaterial Labor." *Radical Thought in Italy: A Potential Politics.* Edited by Michael Hardt and Paul Virno. Minneapolis: University of Minnesota Press.

Lefebvre, Henri. 2002. *Critique of Everyday Life: 2: Foundations for a Sociology of Everyday Life.* Translated by J. Moore. London: Verso.

————. 1991. *The Production of Space.* Translated by D. Nicholson-Smith. Oxford: Blackwell.

————. 1987. "The Everyday and Everydayness." *Yale French Studies* 73:7–11.

Lentricchia, Frank. 1983. *Criticism and Social Change.* Chicago and London: University of Chicago Press.

Levinson, Marjorie. 2007. "What is New Formalism?" *PMLA* 122 (2): 558–69.

Lotringer, Sylvère. 2005. "The Piracy of Art." In Jean Baudrillard, *The Conspiracy of Art: Manifestos, Interviews, Essays.* Edited by Sylvère Lotringer. Translated by Ames Hodges. New York and Los Angeles: Semiotext(e).

Lukács, György. 2005. "The Ideology of Modernism." *The Novel: An Anthology of Criticism and Theory 1900–2000.* Edited by Dorothy J. Hale. Malden, MA: Blackwell.

Mackay, Robin, and Armen Avanessian. 2014. "Introduction." *#Accelerate: The Accelerationist Reader*. Edited by Robin Mackay and Armen Avanessian. Falmouth, UK: Urbanomic.

Marcuse, Herbert. 1993. "Some Remarks on Aragon: Art and Politics in the Totalitarian Era." *Theory, Culture and Society* 10(2):181–95.

———. 1991 [1964]. *One-Dimensional Man: Studies in the Ideology of Advanced Industrial Society*. London: Routledge.

Margin Call. 2011. Directed by J. C. Chandor. *Before the Door Pictures* et al.

McDonough, Thomas F. 1997. "Rereading Debord, Rereading the Situationists." *October* 79:3–14.

McLuhan, Marshall. 1964. *Understanding Media: The Extensions of Man*. New York: McGraw-Hill.

McQuillan, Graeme Macdonald, Robin Purves, and Stephen Thomson. 1999. "The Joy of Theory." In *Post-Theory: New Directions in Criticism*. Edited by McQuillan, Graeme MacDonald, Robin Purves, and Stephen Thomson. Edinburgh: Edinburgh University Press.

Mitchell, W. J. T. 2003. "The Commitment to Form: Or, Still Crazy after All These Years." *PMLA* 118 (2): 321–25.

Moore, Nathan. 2007. "Nova Law: William S. Burroughs and the Logic of Control." *Law and Literature* 19 (3): 435–70.

Murphy, Timothy S. 1997. *Wising Up the Marks: The Amodern William Burroughs*. Berkeley: University of California Press.

Nealon, Jeffrey T. 2012. *Post-Postmodernism: Or, The Cultural Logic of Just-in-Time Capitalism*. Stanford, CA: Stanford University Press.

Negri, Antonio. 2014. "Reflections on the Manifesto." *#Accelerate: The Accelerationist Reader*. Edited by Robin Mackay and Armen Avanessian. Falmouth, UK: Urbanomic.

———. 2007. "Art and Culture in the Age of Empire and the Time of the Multitudes." Translated by Max Henninger. *SubStance* 36 (1): 48–55.

———. 2005. *Time for Revolution*. Translated by Matteo Mandarini. London: Continuum.

———. 2004. *Negri on Negri: In Conversation with Anne Dufourmantelle*. Translated by M. B. Debevoise. New York: Routledge.

Newmark, Kevin. 2012. *Irony on Occasion: From Schlegel and Kierkegaard to Derrida and de Man*. New York: Fordham University Press.

Noys, Benjamin. 2010. *The Persistence of the Negative*. Edinburgh: Edinburgh University Press.

———. 2007. "Crimes of the Near Future: Baudrillard/Ballard." *Ballardian*. http://www.ballardian.com/crimes-of-the-near-future-baudrillard-ballard.

Owens, Craig. 1980. "The Allegorical Impulse: Toward a Theory of Postmodernism." *October* 12:67–86.

Palumbo-Liu, David. 2008. "The Occupation of Form: (Re)theorizing Literary History." *American Literary History* 20 (4): 814–35.

Pavlik, Anthony. 2012. "Absolute Power Games." *Of Bread and Blood and The Hunger Games: Critical Essays on the Suzanne Collins Trilogy*. Edited by Mary F. Pharr and Leisa A. Clark. Jefferson, NC: McFarland.

Pharr, Mary F., and Leisa A. Clark. 2012. "Introduction." *Of Bread and Blood and The Hunger Games: Critical Essays on the Suzanne Collins Trilogy*. Edited by Mary F. Pharr and Leisa A. Clark. Jefferson, NC: McFarland.

Pizer, John. 1993. "Jameson's Adorno, or, the Persistence of the Utopian." *New German Critique* 58:127–51.

Plant, Sadie. 1992. *The Most Radical Gesture: The Situationist International in a Postmodern Age*. London: Routledge.

Robots. 2005. Directed by Chris Wedge and Carlos Saldanha. *Twentieth Century Fox Animation* et al.

Rogin, Michael. 1990. "'Make My Day!' Spectacle as Amnesia in Imperial Politics." *Representations* 29:99–123.

Ross, Kristin. 1997. "Lefebvre on the Situationists." *October* 79:69–83.

Roth, Veronica. 2013. *Allegiant*. New York: HarperCollins.

———. 2012. *Insurgent*. New York: HarperCollins.

———. 2011. *Divergent*. New York: HarperCollins.

Shear, Michael D. 2014. "The Rise of the Drone Master: Pop Culture Recasts Obama." *New York Times*. April 29. http://www.nytimes.com/2014/04/30/us/politics/pop-culture-puts-spin-on-grim-realities-of-obama-presidency.html?_r=0.

Spivak, Gayatri Chakravorty. 1999. *Critique of Postcolonial Reason*. Cambridge, MA: Harvard University Press.

Steinberg, Michael P. 1996. *Walter Benjamin and the Demands of History*. New York: Cornell University Press.

Szeman, Imre. 2001. "Who's Afraid of National Allegory? Jameson, Literary Criticism, Globalization." *The South Atlantic Quarterly* 100 (3): 803–27.

Tambling, Jeremy. 2010. *Allegory*. London and New York: Routledge.

Taylor, Jonathan S. 2002. "The Subjectivity of the Near Future: Geographical Imaginings in the work of J. G. Ballard." In *Lost in Space: Geographies of Science Fiction*. Edited by Rob Kitchin and James Kneale. London: Continuum.

The Final Cut. 2004. Directed by Omar Naim. *Lions Gate Entertainment* et al.

The Purge: Anarchy. 2014. Directed by James DeMonaco. *5150 Action* et al.

The Purge. 2013. Directed by James DeMonaco. Universal Pictures et al.

Trebitsch, Michel. 2002. "Preface." Translated by Gregory Elliott. In *Critique of Everyday Life 2: Foundations for a Sociology of Everyday life*. Translated by John Moore. London: Verso.

Virilio, Paul. 2002. "The Visual Crash," *CTRL [Space]: Rhetorics of Surveillance from Bentham to Big Brother*. Edited by Thomas Y. Levin, Ursula Frohne, and Peter Weibel. Translated by S. Clift. Cambridge, MA: MIT Press.

———. 1999. *Polar Inertia*. London: Sage.

Wagar, W. Warren. 1991. "J. G. Ballard and the Transvaluation of Utopia." *Science Fiction Studies* 18 (1): 53–70.

Walder, Dennis. 2011. *Postcolonial Nostalgias: Writing, Representation and Memory*. London: Taylor and Francis.

Wall-E. 2008. Directed by Andrew Stanton. *Walt Disney Pictures* et al.

Weber, Samuel. 2008. *Benjamin's—Abilities*. Cambridge, MA, and London: Harvard University Press.

Werner, Andrea. 2013. "'Margin Call': Using Film to Explore Behavioural Aspects of the Financial Crisis." *Journal of Business Ethics* 122:643–54.

Wiater, Stanley, Christopher Golden, and Hank Wagner. 2006. *The Complete Stephen King Universe: A Guide to the Worlds of Stephen King*. New York: St. Martin's Griffin.

Williams, Alex, and Nick Srnicek. 2014. "Accelerate: Manifesto for an Accelerationist Politics," *#Accelerate: The Accelerationist Reader*. Edited by Robin Mackay and Armen Avanessian. Falmouth, UK: Urbanomic.

Wolfe, Cary. 2008. "The Idea of Observation at Key West, or, Systems Theory, Poetry, and Form Beyond Formalism." *New Literary History* 39 (2): 259–76.

Wolfson, Susan J. 2000. "Reading for Form." *Modern Language Quarterly* 61 (1): 1–16.

Wolin, Sheldon S. 2010. *Democracy Incorporated: Managed Democracy and the Specter of Inverted Totalitarianism*. Princeton, NJ: Princeton University Press.

———. 2004. *Politics and Vision: Continuity and Innovation in Western Political Thought*. Expanded edition. Princeton, NJ, and Oxford: Princeton University Press.

Wolosky, Shira. 2010. "Relational Aesthetics and Feminist Poetics." *New Literary History* 41 (3): 571–91.

Wright, Benjamin. 2012. "Cannes: 'Killing Them Softly' Helmer Andrew Dominik Talks Music as Film: 'Jesse James' Was My Leonard Cohen Song, 'Killing Them Softly' Is a Pop Tune." *Indiwire*. May 23. http://blogs.indiewire.com/theplaylist/

cannes-killing-them-softly-helmer-andrew-dominik-talks-music-as-film-jesses-james-was-my-leonard-cohen-song-killing-them-softly-is-a-pop-tune-20120523.

Xavier, Ismail. 2004. "Historical Allegory." *A Companion to Film Theory*. Edited by Toby Miller and Robert Stam. Malden, UK: Blackwell.

Zeitchik, Steven. 2012. "Cannes 2012: Brad Pitt's *Killing Them Softly*: Anti-Capitalist Screed?" *Los Angeles Times*. May 22. http://latimesblogs.latimes.com/movies/2012/05/brad-pitt-killing-them-softly-cogans-trade-movie-cannes-review.html.

Žižek, Slavoj. 2001. *Did Someone Say Totalitarianism? Five Interventions in the (Mis)Use of a Notion*. New York: Verso.

Index